RC

D0850494

WITHDRAWN

THE CULT OF THE COURT

THE
CULT
OF THE
COURT

John Brigham

TEMPLE UNIVERSITY PRESS
PHILADELPHIA

Temple University Press, Philadelphia 19122
Copyright © 1987 by Temple University. All rights reserved
Published 1987
Printed in the United States of America

The paper used in this publication meets the minimum requirements of
American National Standard for Information Sciences—Permanence of Paper
for Printed Library Materials, ANSI Z39.48–1984

Library of Congress Cataloging-in-Publication Data

Brigham, John, 1945–
  The cult of the court.

  Bibliography: p.
  Includes index.
  1. United States.   Supreme Court.   I. Title.
KF8742.B73   1987   347.73'26   86-30179
ISBN 0-87722-486-2 (alk. paper) 347.30735

PREFACE

THIS BOOK does not try to put a "human face" on the Court. That has been done often lately (Woodward and Armstrong, 1979) and it has often been done well. The temptation is that when done well, as in the case of Anthony Lewis's *Gideon's Trumpet* (1964), the books do seem to endure. Nevertheless, the "non" human story of the institution and the law is the subject here, presented, perhaps, through its human faces.

The sources are the ones called "secondary." This is because the book is about interpretation, and the dusty facts of historiographic lore tell no tales if they are not handled. There is some material gotten first-hand, as opposed to from the library, the newsstand, and the bookstore. This has often meant from the Supreme Court. Materials from "the Court" are handled carefully so as not to seem as if the author is partici-pating in an authorized activity or creating his own institution. The mea-sure of the book's contribution will be in the originality of the reading. If this seems like a secondary book, whatever its sources, then I will have failed.

Although the work that follows purports to be original, there are some recent books I wish to identify with even if they do not identify with each other. Lief Carter's *Contemporary Constitutional Lawmaking* (1985) brings interpretation and contemporary jurisprudence into the arena of political science; so do I. Sotirios Barber, in *On What the Constitution Means* (1984), gives a powerful reading of the Constitution that does not rest on the Supreme Court. I try to do that too.

Finally, because excellent books of a more comprehensive and de-tailed sort exist (Baum, 1984; Hodder-Wiliams, 1980; Wasby, 1984), the focus of this one is quite narrow. The institutional approach to the

v

Supreme Court self-consciously advances the proposition that "It is a Court we are looking at." And the treatment suggests that this approach can be generalized to other institutions, but the purpose is to illuminate a transformation in institutional reality, the emergence of a "cult" of the Supreme Court.

My debts on this project have accumulated over the years. They begin with my mentor in constitutional studies, C. Herman Pritchett, who set an example that should keep me motivated well past "retirement." Another student of Pritchett's, Walter Murphy, has also been a teacher and an example. Sheldon Goldman, Kenneth Dolbeare, Stuart Scheingold, Phyllis Farley Rippey, Joe Martin, and Timothy O'Neill have provided support and criticism that I appreciate. In my department, Vera Smith and Donna Dove skillfully helped to prepare the manuscript. In Amherst, seminar meetings on legal process and legal ideology with Austin, Susan, Sally, Barbara, Ron, Brink, and Adelaide provide fellowship and inspiration in very generous proportions. Christine and Peter give that and, more, they indulge the spirit from which the work draws. Thank you all.

JOHN BRIGHAM
Amherst, Massachusetts

CONTENTS

THE CULT OF THE COURT

INTRODUCTION

INSTITUTIONS LIKE the Supreme Court amount to ways of acting. In America, the steps to the "marble temple" behind the Capitol Building are the ultimate symbols of having gone "all the way," and when robed men (and a woman) give opinions from the Temple, those opinions have authority sufficient to reprieve the convicted and compel that the rejected be accepted. Because institutions give action authority, they require more reflective scholarly attention than they have been given. We need to think about how institutional authority works. Such attention would place the Supreme Court in a conception of government linking the institution to a larger system of authority. This is an investigation of the Court as it is constituted in American public life, and the emphasis is on the institution's place in the American polity.

Like Justice Potter Stewart's response in another context, we have trouble when we try to define an institution, but we know one when we see it, or hear about it. We know the Court, or most of us do, so when it serves as background for a picture of a robed person we know something of the place that person has. We know the Court is awesome and we are encouraged to be in awe when we take it in. We know the justices when they are in place, but very few people know them away from the place, and then if knowing them is about judging, they are still known in reference to the Court. All people are not equal in this knowledge. While lots of Americans would recognize the Court if they were shown a picture of the building and told it is in Washington, D.C., few would be able to distinguish the building from the New York State Library in Albany.[1] And although the words of opinions are available in most libraries, only a small percentage of the population knows how to make sense of them. This inquiry proceeds from that knowledge, rather than a new framework.

3

Thus, instead of taking a model from some realm of social science, such as organization or systems theory, the analysis offered here draws on perceptions of the institution. These come from journalists, scholars, lawyers, and citizens. Judicial commentary and commentary on the justices in all its forms, from opinions to personality profiles, is a special source for the treatment. These materials are increasingly available (O'Brien, 1985). In half a dozen years, *The New York Times Magazine* published feature articles on "The Supreme Court: A Decade of Constitutional Revision," November 11, 1979; "A Candid Talk with Justice Blackmun," February 20, 1983; "The Partisan: A Talk with Justice Rehnquist," March 3, 1985; "A Life on the Court: A Conversation with Justice Brennan," October 5, 1986. This access to information is part of the modern institution and must be handled with care. Pursuing the "cult" of the Court guarantees some resistance to the pull of authorized material or official opinion from the bench. In addition, the effort to portray the cult around the institution provides a framework for interpreting a variety of Court-related materials. Cases, history, and commentary on the institution are a key to the possibilities around which institutional politics is conducted.

While this is not an insider's view of the Supreme Court, the views of insiders can provide insight. I had occasion to talk with an intern at the Court about the value of access. The issue arose as to what might be gained from being on the inside and, conversely, what one risked losing. In a spirited defense of the insider perspective, this intern claimed that the advantage in getting behind the scenes was that one could never teach constitutional law with a "straight face" again. This insider argued that the reality of Chief Justice wearing his slippers inside the Court demystified the Constitution. As a political scientist who began the academic study of law and politics in the 1970s, I was introduced to legal realism as established fact and, of course, I appreciate its insight. I was taught that decisions made by men and women have human qualities. The most extraordinary thing about many insiders and lawyers generally is that they present the Supreme Court through the perspective of realism as if it was a new discovery. The political view of judging has become the orthodoxy and the authoritative foundation of law has shifted.

The story of this institution is more than a synthesis of personality traits and individual interests. Consequently, my interest in idiosyncratic behavior taking place behind the bronze doors of the Supreme Court is limited. The book is not about politics at the surface (or behind the scenes). It is not simply about interests either. I do teach constitutional law, and I teach it with a straight face. A new orthodoxy—political skepticism—is an institutional reality. What interests me is how from the inside, and to an increasing extent on the outside of the institution, political explanations have become a nearly sufficient basis for the authority of the Supreme Court. At the bicentennial of our constitutional polity, the surprise is not that the Court is political, but that those who work with the institution, like the Congress, and those who observe it closely, like journalists, accept this aspect of the institution as an adequate basis for its preeminant place as an authority on the Constitution.

Since the height of Supreme Court activism in the 1960s there has been enthusiastic debate about the role of this Court and the lower judiciary in American politics. This debate reached a new height in the mid 1970s with the conservative appointments to the Supreme Court by a series of Republican presidents. Often dealing with the capacity or competence of the courts in general and the Supreme Court in particular to decide controversial questions, the debate was intensely policy oriented. It was a normative debate, as policy debates often are, with support for divergent political perspectives and policy choices often only thinly veiled. There were partisans marshaling evidence both against intervention (Horowitz, 1977) and for intervention (Cavanaugh and Sarat, 1980) and the interests were reflected in jurisprudential commentary (McDowell, 1982; Ely, 1980). These debates and their jurisprudential manifestations are a source for the following inquiry into what the Supreme Court has come to be. What the policy commentary takes for granted as it assesses competence, the existence of courts as they are conventionally known, and the form of jurisprudential discourse as it evaluates judicial authority, a dichotomy between law and politics, these become the focus in this investigation.

The challenge is to provide insight into the Supreme Court through a perspective that transcends investigative journalism and resists excessive indentification with the institution. Attention to the Court has ranged from muckraking exposé, like *The Brethren,* to fawning iconography, like Fred Friendly's *The Constitution: That Delicate Balance.* The authors of *The Brethren,* Bob Woodward and Scott Armstrong had money and investigative experience that produced a vivid picture behind the scenes that upset many. Yet, they merely intensified a view of judges as political actors that has been around for some time. Friendly, a self-described "salesman for the Constitution" developed his book from material produced for television. It no doubt settles some nerves jarred by *The Brethren* in its engaging but sanitized portrayal of what the Supreme Court does. Both contribute to the cult surrounding the institution and both depend on it.

The modern Court functions through a dynamic between politics and law, human interest and institutional practice. The Court stands apart from individual instances of action. We expect more than the play of interests even as we are fascinated by them. That is why *The Brethren* received so much attention. There is politics on the Court and there is a politics in the way we know the institution. The second kind is newer, but it is hard to show. We can begin to see this kind of politics in the new debate over the Supreme Court and the Constitution. Attorney General Edwin Meese stimulated the debate in a series of speeches from 1985 to 1986. First with the idea that the doctrine of incorporation applying the Bill of Rights to the states should be repealed, then with the view that the Supreme Court itself had set up the independent regulatory agencies, and finally with the observation that the Supreme Court was not the last word on the Constitution, Meese produced a lively examination of the Court's role in the American political system. He was promptly condemned much as the authors of *The Brethren* were condemned, and by some of the same people. In the present inquiry we try to show how the understandings Meese challenged came to be so ingrained and their association with the institution today is depicted through the ideological underpinnings of institutional authority. Here, we eschew inside information for informative insight. In this approach, there is less interest in what very few know and more in what is known and taken for granted by many. The expectations we learn as we learn what something like a Supreme Court is gives meaning to behavior and sets limits on action.

Others have described the meaning of an institution as existing in the "possible forms of conduct" (Rawls, 1971) or, more economically, "practices" (Flathman, 1976; Bourdieu, 1977) that we associate with it. We draw on those views and show how an institution is revealed through evolving traditions of possible action and in terms of the practices that constitute them. This work develops from studies of language and ideology in the law. My work in those areas[2] led me to a need to show that ideas and symbols matter. They determine the things we can do in a society because, as "practices" they are real. Chief Justice John Marshall, for instance, did not give us the practice of judicial review in *Marbury* v. *Madison* (1803). He started things off by presenting a possibility. The practice of judicial review is a much more recent development in interpretation that links the Court and the Constitution. The linkage as it manifests itself is presently less dependent on Marshall's claims to authority and far more a function of the modern Court's location in the governing apparatus. The operation of such possibilities and practices is discussed in the first chapter. This chapter presents a framework for studying the Supreme Court. It looks at the Court as an institution in which practices account for institutional life such as the Supreme Court's ability to transcend the changing personalities that have taken a seat behind the bench. In fact, those practices give meaning to various benches that have served the Court. Ultimately, practices show how the Court has come to be the last word on the Constitution.

The second chapter explores the relationship of this institution to the government's authority in the United States. By its identification with a written document the Supreme Court was able to situate its claim to special competence in delineating the range of constitutional, that is, acceptable, political action. The legal profession and academic lawyers brought this claim to fruition in the last years of the nineteenth century. From the "Higher Law" background of American constitutional law, with law's "artificial reason" as the basis for a claim of special competence by the legal profession, the American state system has been moving to a hierarchical form of authority. Hierarchy as an institutional form emphasizes the Supreme Court's place at the pinnacle of the legal system, rather than the traditional claim of a special judicial competence in the elucidating legal texts. As Supreme Court Justice Robert Jackson noted in 1953, the Court is "not final because we are infallible, but we are infallible only because we are final" (*Brown* v. *Allen*). Although it is often quoted, Jackson's observation is rarely examined for what it says about the institution. Jackson may have meant it as a kind of demystification but it has a deeper meaning today. Using analytic tools appropriate to interpreting the possibilities governed by the Supreme Court we consider the ideological understandings that have emerged to support institutional authority of this kind. We note that a shift in those understandings has taken place. This shift is evident in how we see the justices, the workplace, and the Court's business.

The third chapter tracks the "cult of the judge" as a transformation of the cult of the robe. Perception of the judge is thus linked to how the institution is seen and reflects the ideologies of authority on which the institution relies. As "high priests," justices of the Supreme Court have contributed to the "institutional charisma" that helped elevate the Supreme Court to its special position in American politics. Jurists like Marshall and Story, constructed a legal edifice from political reality; Harlan and Holmes, stood for the future; Douglas and Warren, had an "idea of progress" that solidified the structure. The modern Court depends on law and politics as characteristics of the judge. The cult is evident in the appointment of justices to the Supreme Court and is examined in the evaluation of selected justices from John Jay to Antonin Scalia. While law seems to lose out to political considerations in determining who is appointed and in evaluating success or failure on the bench, the practices, though changing, are not so one sided as some commentary would lead us to believe.

Unlike the "President's House" or the Capitol, a home for the Supreme Court was constructed only recently. Having wandered homeless if not aimless for 150 years, the institution achieved a "worthy" setting and a physical expression of its power in 1936. The setting is examined in the fourth chapter beginning with the calculations, architectural and political, that allowed it to be built. Its foundations are the professional, political, and public expectations that delineate the institution. Other national institutions refine the range of political action through control over appointment, jurisdiction, and revenue. The present shrine symbolizes the cult of the Court. Within the building, conventions further reflect the nature of the institution. The analysis in the chapter is divided into three kinds of support—institutional, legal, and policy—to reflect the diverse contributions made by the staff. The generalist from public information officer to administrative assistant are treated as "institutional support." The clerk, the reporter, and some other staff members are discussed in terms of their contribution to the institution's legal work. Finally, individual law clerks and the attorneys for parties before the Court are linked to the formulation of policy at the institution. In this way, we get greater complexity than the familiar picture of a marble temple holding an appellate bench.

Chapter 5 looks at the business of the Court, the flow of litigation and its influence on the institution. Since the Court's place in the policy process is only partially revealed by the highly publicized cases in which it hears oral arguments, we draw from the model Felix Frankfurter and James Landis (1928) employed to assess changes in the Court's undertakings. The nature of its work has varied as has the quantity. From a few early admiralty cases to the constitutional disputes of the twentieth century, the Court has risen to a position of eminence in the present system. Controversy surrounding access to the Court, the allegedly expanding caseload, and discretion over jurisdiction are some facets of a changing institutional environment revealed in the work done by the Supreme Court. The picture contrasts with the historical frame offered by Robert McCloskey (1960) and differs from most recent work (Baum, 1985; O'Brien, 1985) on the institution in the extent that institutional practices are investigated.

Chapter 6 describes institutional action, particularly the decision and the opinions announced by the justices. Special attention is given to rejoining law and politics. The treatment integrates doctrinal matters with institutional life and action, including past ways judicial action has been interpreted. The language and symbol systems of the law influence the initial consideration of cases, while institutional practices transform interests into law. These practices include the Court's nine month term, since it determines what can be decided and when; the process of sifting through petitions for review; consideration of the merits in oral argument; and the way a decision is reached. The bargaining that produces Court opinions is seen through conceptions of the legal tradition and the institution that are derived from the study of language. Here, the institutional model as possible forms of action gives new meaning to the decision and shows how the "procedures determine what the law is."

Authority and policy, in Chapter 7, are linked in the highest court in America. The policy and the outcomes reached by the Court are related to the dominant belief system of the culture within which it operates. This chapter reformulates the "impact" question. Policy is discussed from three perspectives: as rules for the judicial bureaucracy, as a focus for public discourse, and as a graven channel for political action. Attention to the symbolic dimension of judge-made policy brings treatment of the Court full circle, back to law and the sources for judicial action. Here, traditional concerns such as compliance and impact reveal the institutional nature of authority and policy. Thus "constitutive practices" rather than rules or norms are the institution's product and its contribution.

The last chapter evaluates institutional independence and the Court's policy contribution, past and future. Two polarities, one between law and politics, and the other between institution and doctrine, provide the foundation. From these perspectives we can interpret the traditional terms in which evaluation has been conducted. Practices linking interpretation to the institution such as "strict construction," activism and restraint, and "principled" decisions are taken up here. We go beyond the "legalist paradox." The Court's insulation from public opinion and its control by a profession, originally grounded authority in legal symbols. Now legal authority has shifted to place. This allows the way we see the institution, the cult of the Court, to structure constitutional discourse in an age of realism.

1

THE INSTITUTION

FOR THE productive life of more than one academic generation, or at least twenty years, social research on courts and law has been grounded in political jurisprudence (Shapiro, 1964). Whether the subject has been judicial interpretation, doctrinal developments, or policy impact, the epistemological frame gave priority to interests, and intellectual fascination examined the exercise of power under stress. Culminating, as journalism, in *The Brethren* (Woodward and Armstrong, 1979), this research was diverse. It included, among other things, the game theoretic models of Walter Murphy (1964), the attitude studies of Glendon Schubert (1965; 1974), and the impact work of Kenneth Dolbeare (1967). Research spanned the spectrum of experience from a criminal suspect to the Supreme Court and back to the suspect again. During this period, social scientists reconstituted the reality of courts and the legal environment according to a political perspective.

The dominant view emerged from legal realism in law schools and became implanted through the work of behavioralists in political science departments. The nature of judging was made definitively political in the bloc analysis pioneered by C. Herman Pritchett (1948). Confidence in the rigor of the new methods and their compelling certainty led to developments far beyond Professor Pritchett's work. Since the mid-1970s, that work has taken stock of its contribution, and contemporary examples reveal some sensitivity to the collective quality of institutional behaviors (Tate and Handberg, 1986). Yet the research and the method remains political in the "realist" sense, because its insight is drawn from disagreement and the "storms" of political controversy (O'Brien, 1986). The conventional wisdom became the view that the judge can do whatever he

11

wants and that only in some unenlightened prior age did people believe the law really mattered. We heard that the justices decide as they wish and write the opinion as a rationalization. The result was that social science research on appellate courts described politics, not law.

The political approach is also evident in the focus on struggle central to the "disputes" paradigm. With its source in the correlative disciplines of anthropology and sociology, a focus on disputes has turned social research away from appellate courts and the traditional doctrinal material of law. By offering a culturally transcendent framework, the disputes industry bridged disciplines and placed law in society (Abel, 1974). Its success was greatest in the hallways and the corridors where the disputes could be observed. But these hallways had their limits (Cain and Kulcsar, 1981/82). Elements of political reality in court are so widespread today that they have lost their critical edge. Both politics and disputes have broadened our knowledge of the bench and increased familiarity with courthouse corridors, judicial chambers, and law offices.[1] Yet for some time the lack of serious attention to the legal terrain and the diversion of interest from the traditional subjects—law and legal thought—has been a problem. This inquiry proposes leaving the preoccupation with disagreement and struggle to move toward a study of social practices, especially as they provide insight into the cult surrounding the Supreme Court.

To advance public law research it has become important to pay more explicit attention to the paths that have been shared. We have seen initiatives in the area of doctrine (Harris, 1982; O'Neill, 1981) and in the institutional studies where attention to symbolic phenomena has traditionally been rarer (Harrington, 1985; Provine, 1980). More generally, in political science scholars have been turning away from the politics of interests and behavior to shared practices in legislatures (Ethridge, 1985), in international political economy (Goldstein, 1986), and public opinion (Bennett, 1980). Some have even described a "new institutionalism" (March and Olsen, 1984). The turn from more traditional political inquiry and necessarily from dissents and disputes in the material that follows is a natural one for public law scholarship that never totally lost its connection to the stuff of tradition. That stuff, law and courts, doctrine and rhetoric, is brought back to the fold of social research through explicit attention to social practices.

"BEYOND" POLITICS

It has seemed as if a culturally specific frame, one necessarily incapable of universal application, was required to understand legal material. From apprenticeships to modern law schools, legal education has been immersed in the richness of time and place. It has drawn heavily from cultural artifacts. We see it in the cases of the common law and the stories that reconstitute courtroom reality in modern drama. Politics and disputes provided the more abstract frame demanded by the scientific style, but they tended to exclude unique social institutions from rigorous scientific investigation. By definition, those aspects of legal or cultural practice idiosyncratic to a particular setting, such as the community where research like William Muir's study of attitude change took place (1967), resisted generalization. In the name of science, countless towns lost their identity and innumerable cases had their distinguishing features removed. Yet there is, around law and courts, a universal conception that might facilitate penetration of the particularities and sociosyncratic nature of individual systems of law and courts. The common element is that legal doctrine and legal institutions, law and office, are comprised of social practices, the same aspects of social life from which conflict stems and to which it must appeal. Practices are the mirror image of conflict and, like conflict, they allow cross-cultural comparison, generalization, and theory-building. In contrast to politics, with its emphasis on interests and disagreement, practices are the things about which there is agreement and they can be the basis for a rigorous investigation of culture and social institutions.

Appellate courts in general and the Supreme Court in particular are associated with symbols and rules; however, they have not been thought to confine the action. Here, nevertheless, the institution demands attention. In the context of social science research on law, the perceived opposition of the lawgivers of the high courts to the more pervasive context of disputes, called "upper court myth," has limited the interest in investigations of the appellate courts. Yet at the very least these courts are characterized by legal phenomena and are part of social life. There is law around the Supreme Court of the United States, although perhaps not as much as we once took for granted. Consequently, this discussion focuses on that court, an institution that demonstrates the manner in which conventions, as possible forms of conduct, contribute to the construction of social reality.

A position associated with the tradition of political jurisprudence, but offering a way out, provides a framework for the discussion that follows. Martin Shapiro's description of courts (1981) suggests an institutional link between disputes and practices in the resolution of conflict. Building from the triadic structure of dispute resolution, Shapiro describes the legal phenomena of law and office as maintaining authority over a dispute. Legal doctrine and legal institution are the terrain for disputing in a culture that relies on these institutions. They are not the only terrain and not always the dominant terrain, but when a dispute is evident in our culture, law and the offices of a court may well structure how the dispute develops. Shapiro's contribution thus incorporates judicial office and law into the processes abstracted by researchers as conflict resolution and traditionally seen in terms of politics or disputes. Law and office, the sociological abstraction, provide a route back to traditional concerns of social research on law, the shared beliefs about which people dispute and that form the basis for dispute resolution. But coming from a social research paradigm by way of a spokesman for political jurisprudence, authoritative institutions serve as the conceptual background for the description of the Supreme Court that follows. Authority will thus be grounded in institutional settings that are themselves constituted by belief.

The implications of going "beyond" politics in this investigation also means that there will be far less attention to cases than is the tradition in political scholarship. Like individual political choices, cases will be illustrative. *Marbury* v. *Madison* and *U.S.* v. *Nixon* are integral to the shifting ideologies of authority discussed in the next chapter. *Brown* v. *The Board of Education,* because there has been so much written about it, and *Gideon* v. *Wainwright,* because what has been written was so significant, help elaborate the story of the institutional setting. *Regents of the University of California* v. *Bakke* is one of my favorite cases for showing how doctrinal material developed in the institution transforms practices into action. And, of course, *Roe* v. *Wade* is the modern case most often associated with Court capacity. As with other instances of choice, the focus will be on the whole, the tradition in terms of which cases are seen, rather than outcomes. The cases share an institutional construction with statutes, like the Judges Bill of 1925, with commentary like the *Federalist Papers* or *The Brethren,* with personality, like John Marshall's for instance, and with place, like the building that has so recently been put up for the Supreme Court. Just as the message of discourse analysis is that law is more than the decisions (Brigham, 1978), the point in this perspective is that the institution is more than its cases.

SOCIAL RESEARCH ON INSTITUTIONS

One quality of a social institution is that we take it for granted. Institutions like the Supreme Court as a whole or some part of it, like the majority opinion, are ways of doing things that provide the background for policy or law. Disputes take place with reference to them and politics is in, around, and about them. Before any cases are decided, we want to know how they will come out and once they are decided the attention shifts only marginally to the impact or implications of a decision. Ordinary or conventional understanding of institutions such as these presents a challenge simply because the understanding is ordinary. We tend not to want to talk about what we know. We might debate the actions of a Supreme Court or the wit of a particular president. But we find it harder to investigate the fact that there is a President or that the justices of the Supreme Court go to a particular building to work. These conventions, though historically contingent, constitute limits on action. They are politically significant not because they determine outcomes but because they determine what cases are about.

The Challenge of Convention

The ways of knowing institutions actually indicate what they are made of. One kind of association is with their physical manifestations. In law, the bench, the robes, and the marbled walls signal that something is going on, and that the activity is important. We know that these "things" are not just physical, but we treat the physical presence as the institution. And although it is no secret that the Court had makeshift quarters until only fifty years ago, we lose track of that fact. After Chief Justice William Howard Taft acquired a new building for the Supreme Court in the 1930s, his successor referred to the black robed justices in their new home as "Beetles in the Temple of Karnak." The new building was a little more than many of the justices believed appropriate for the Court. The institution evident in the pictures we have of it has changed dramatically since ratification of the Constitution established the legal foundations for the American Republic.

Institutions, if they are to be taken on their own terms as meaningful social phenomena, also present a challenge to social scientists because they have a range of significations and a variety of uses. Sometimes an institution is quite animated as when a voice on the other end of the telephone says, "Supreme Court, may I help you?" An institution is often represented by the people who work in it (see Vining, 1986: 110–132). A justice may speak for "the Court" or the Chief may lend his name to the institution, as in the Marshall, the Taney, the Warren, or the Burger Court. On occasion it is a president such as Nixon or Roosevelt who lends his name to the institution, but this indicates a tension and it is usually for a shorter period of time. These names suggest a human quality and reflect a political view of the institution. As applied to the Supreme Court, they are more common today than they were in the past.

An institution is also very unlike mortals in its capacity to endure. Like other cultural phenomena, institutions are able to transcend changes in membership. This is the quality that gives them their "Naturalness" and it is a characteristic of institutions that suggested to Aristotle the analogy of rivers and fountains that have a "constant identity" even as the flow changes the composition of the thing (Barker, 1962: 99). An institution is identifiable across time in ways that rivers are, but people are not. The Supreme Court is said to have decided *Brown* v. *The Board of Education* (1954) and *Board of Regents* v. *Bakke* (1978). Here, the institution mediated policy shifts in the meaning and relevant context for interpreting another "continuous" institution, the Constitution of the United States.

In English, the idea of an "institution" has evolved from an action, the giving of form or order to a thing.[2] It was once simply something that could be done, and apparently little more. By the time the American Republic was founded, the word referred to "an established organization for the promotion of some object." We now speak of a university as an institution, sometimes a bank or corporation, and certainly political establishments such as the Supreme Court. But the concept of an institution has evolved to the point that we have lost track of what it means for an institution to give form or order to our politics. This study reverses the etymological process to capture the fact that institutions are constituted in possible forms of action, that the process of giving form exists even if we don't see it. We must see that we give form to or constitute institutions like the Supreme Court in order to understand the form we are giving to it.

Portrayal of an institution requires a leap from the common sense concreteness, evident in buildings and artifacts like robes and purple curtains, to the shared perceptions that tell us what these things mean. New Dealers saw "nine old men." Their efforts to transform the institution were met by "Lions under the Throne," as portrayed by Charles Curtis in his contribution to the massive literature on the institution stimulated by the "Court packing" fight (Curtis, 1947). The Warren Court was a trumpet or at least responded to the calls of convicts like Clarence Earl Gideon. *The Brethren,* as a title, is a paradoxical allusion to collegiality and institutional tradition while the book plays on discordant personalities and disregard of institutional conventions. Such characterizations are not simply the rhetorical flourish of humanistic commentary; they reflect a public perception. Although traditionally outside more rigorous investigation, there is considerable social meaning in these descriptions. The challenge is to take Learned Hand's picture of the Court as "a piece of tapestry" (1947: xi), examining the threads and what they comprise.

The relative disinterest of social scientists in what it means to be all these things has been due, in part, to professional effort to create a distinct language on the scientific model. That project found interests (politics) and conflicts (disputing) to be appropriate foundations. Students of the Supreme Court and the Constitution have generally been more resistant to the drift away from the formal institutions of social life than most social scientists. Although this has often meant an insensitivity to the enterprise of social research, it has sometimes led to self-consciousness about the objects and methods of study. Judicial behavioralists, in their prime from the early 1950s until the late 1960s, charted judicial attitudes in their research and taught case law in their classrooms. While the frame has been political, discourse and teaching about Court and Constitution has been largely doctrinal. These institutional materials are present to a degree unimaginable to students of voting behavior. Official discourses have remained in the picture even while their significance was being undercut. This has made it difficult for public law to produce a model of their subject susceptible to rigorous investigation.

In the present context, the challenge to providing a sociological account of convention is to be met by looking at the ordinary or folk ways of knowing.[3] Law and office become institutions when there is agreement, expressed or implied, that they exist and must be taken into account. Thus, institution is something that is there in society. It may be as internally complex as "the Pentagon" or "the Catholic Church" or as simple as a squad of soldiers or a person in prayer. There are political, social, and all manner of institutions sharing a capacity to order social life because people act as if they exist, as if they matter. They are isolates of human experience and they can be isolated for social inquiry into the context of authority in social life to which they contribute (Goodrich, 1984). The result is a framework for studying legal institutions as constitutive of social life (Klare, 1979). Appropriately, the slice of that life investigated here, the Supreme Court and the Constitution of the United States, involves institutions about which we know a great deal and whose practices have authoritative significance.

The Study of Institutions

The dominant social science approaches to institutions have treated them as constraints on human action, as settled forms within which politics and social life take place. For Max Weber, political institutions are characterized by written laws and people trained in their administration (Weber, 1958: 16–17). These processes legitimize and routinize more spontaneous social forms. Weber grounded the concept in the late Roman period with its transition from the charismatic basis of religious authority to the "legal-technical legitimation" of the medieval bishops (1954: 168); the Catholic Church was his model (1954: 252). In the scholarly as well as the more ordinary sense, the shared property of institutions was their autonomy from the will of their membership.[4]

The giveness of institutions made them the focus of the "institutional" school of economists in the early twentieth century.[5] The approach joined anthropology, with its cultural frame, to history and law, as practiced by John R. Commons. Anthropological work on institutions has treated them as "the real isolate of culture" (Malinowski, 1944: 154). The relationship here is to an idea given materiality or embodiment in a social milieu. In the study of politics, Arthur F. Bentley, although more often identified with group theory, emphasized the centrality of language and social meaning to placing action in a context, which he called a process. Institutions gave the context a "natural" form because of how they were perceived (1908: 297).

E. E. Schattschneider (1960), like Bentley, was interested in institutions and how they became permanent. In studying political parties, Schattschneider wanted to show that they had become essential to the American system. He argued that parties should not be seen as temporary or amorphous while institutions like the Supreme Court are treated as if they are "simply there, or more than that, anchors for the politics that we have come to share." For Schattschneider, parties had become institutions. Like the Court, he observed, they "anchor" the system and he used the permanency of the Supreme Court to call attention to newer and more marginal institutions. His message might now be reversed: institutions are not "simply there"; they are organic and very much the products of social life. We do well to look into concreteness as a social myth that surrounds our institutions. We, at least, would benefit from seeing how much the Court has those mutable qualities that used to be associated exclusively with such ephemeral institutions as political parties.

Because it has been common to work around "political institutions" during the last generation, critical investigation has been rare. The more common approach has been to employ a framework to lay over or examine the institution. Occasionally, these approaches capture essentials of institutional life, as in the view that courts are organizations or work groups (Jacob, 1983). The most important exogenous category views the Supreme Court as part of something larger, like a "system" (Goldman, 1985). Although there is obvious attention here to the relationship between the institutional settings and the social science frame, this has not been the main purpose. The problem with these treatments is that the social scientific categories and concerns become the object of the scholarship.

While most traditional political research has viewed institutions as if they were inevitable, the best research on institutions has been stimulated by interest in change and transformation such as the developmental perspective from comparative politics that Nelson Polsby drew on to study

Congress (Polsby, 1968). Similarly, an institutional perspective developed by Philip Selznick (1957) as a basis for an investigation of leadership distinguished institutions from organizations by grounding the former in "social needs and pressures" (1957: 5). As an example, he drew from the American Constitution, which he considered an institution to the extent that "social and cultural conditions (class structure, traditional patterns of loyalty, and the like) affect its viability" (1957: 6). Stability was investigated because, for Selznick, it rested on "a secure source of support, an easy channel of communication" (1957: 7). An institution, in formulations like these that consider stability, is a social construction that has become "infused with value" and prized "beyond its technical role." Thus, a seemingly natural quality develops that can be seen in valuations or expectations.

There is a body of scholarship, drawn on in the present inquiry, that is particularly susceptible to the positive valuation of our most powerful institutions. For the Supreme Court, its center is the Supreme Court Historical Society. The characteristics of this work are a rich description of the artifacts and events that make up the history of the Court. The *Yearbook* of the society ran a series in the late 1970s titled "My Father the Chief Justice" where children of the Chief would recall personal details of his life and life around the Court. The 1976 edition was written by Elizabeth Hughes Gossett. In 1978, the author was Lauson H. Stone. These efforts reflect the perils and the glories of detail. It has its place and is an essential part of institutional study but the goal is detail that places the institution in a culture.

Such work is characteristic of Maxwell Bloomfield's treatment in "The Supreme Court in American Popular Culture" (1981). Also part of a tradition associated with the Supreme Court Historical Society, Bloomfield describes early American perceptions of the Court as reflecting Chief Justice John Marshall's comment in *Osborne* v. *Bank of the United States* (1824): "Judicial power, as contradistinguished from the power of the laws, has no existence." Even well into the nineteenth century, political novels like Henry Adams's *Democracy*, published in 1880, and John William De Forest's *Honest John Vane*, published in 1875, ignore the Court in describing the Washington scene (1981: 4). It is not until the Court becomes the bastion of conservatism and source for the legal foundations of industrial capitalism that it becomes the object of attention in American popular culture. Here historical and cultural commentary portray the modern institution coming to be.

Some scholarship on the Supreme Court has addressed the relationship between convention and institution (Schmidhauser, 1960),[6] but in the main, social scientists leave the givenness of the institution unexplored.

Traditional treatments do little more than describe the conventions, rein-
forcing the perception that the institution is simply there. When Stephen
Wasby discusses judicial review (1984: 59–64), he loses his critical in-
stinct, turning to Justice Cardozo for authority. The consequence is a
pronouncement that "judicial review has become fully established"
(1984: 64).[7] Larry Baum on judicial review indicated that John Marshall
asserted the power in 1803, that it survived the contest over slavery fifty
years later, and that it has been employed on the average once every two
years. We see historical moments in the institutional life of judicial review, but not enough about how the institution has changed with that
monumental development. We are not given a basis in social research for
understanding the grounds on which institutional power rests, and neither
Baum nor Wasby provides a framework for putting together the idea, the
normative considerations, or the politics in an institutional frame.

Social research on institutions must account for two aspects. First,
that they are often quite real. They may be constructed of concrete or
marble, for instance. Conversely, that they are anything but "simply
there." In their subjective dimensions, they are like doctrine. The work
that follows builds on this aspect of law and office. In making institutions
problematic in an effort to understand the convergence of Supreme Court
and Constitution, the analysis of practices relies on common perceptions
and conventional understandings. Practices capture the cultural significance of representations without losing track of the social relations that
maintain our culture. Thus, we take as the subject matter *practices* that
get their meaning from experience and their significance as enduring aspects of social life.

PRACTICES AND THE SUPREME COURT

By locating the Supreme Court in society we see it as existing in
practices. Practices give meaning to the steps that lead to the Supreme
Court. They make the steps in Washington the significant ones and not the
ones in Philadelphia, where the Court once sat. They give meaning to a
signature or a name when it's appended to what we call an "opinion."
Applied to the Court, this approach captures institutional transformations
associated with policy, like the authority of the Court to rule against
Richard Nixon in 1974 and interpretive communities like the legal profession and the attentive publics who know the place.

This section begins by distinguishing action based on practices from
another framework, the behavioral. This distinction is followed by discussion of different kinds of practices and their relationship to institutions.

We conclude with an examination of the necessary connection between ideas and social life as that connection is evident in law and the interpretive communities that determine its meaning authoritatively.

Action and Behavior

Understanding an institution requires us to be aware that there is a dynamic between what is believed to be possible and action in accord with the possibilities. Institutions are not simply robes and marble, nor are they contained in codes or documents. Meaningful action makes institutions. John Rawls, who is better known, of course, for his ideas about justice, had some helpful things to say about institutions. He viewed an institution as "an abstract object" realized "in . . . thought and conduct" (1971: 11). Drawing on Rawls, we can see an institution composed of various ways of doing things. These we call practices and the ones that belong together make institutions. Practices account for action and by convention or through interpretation we know the appropriate institutional meaning to give to action. Some actions rely on physical spaces for their meaning, like the steps of the Court that give meaning to a lawyer and client ascending or a newscaster reporting. Other ordinary actions, like signing a name, gain special significance from the practices that associate a judicial signature with an opinion.

Practices may be distinguished from the particular actions, like votes and signatures, where we see them in action. A vote is an intentional action, "the vote" a democratic institution. In the Supreme Court, the meaning of each vote comes from the practices in that setting. Practices are "institutional facts" (Taylor, 1971: 8), their meaning is dependent on the setting. Practices provide insight into the nature of this type of knowledge. In the *Bakke* case, Justice Powell's holding that an aspiring white person should be admitted to medical school is steeped in the traditions of constitutional discourse. Powell's contribution, which opened the doors to Alan Bakke and allowed race to be taken into account in admissions decisions, is a consequence of its institutional status as a holding of the Court. Nobody joined him entirely but the opinion captured the Court. Its status for the country has not been assessed.

In some respects, the institutional approach is similar to that professed by early behavioralists. Practices, like behavior, depend on shifting from words to something more "real" and the perspective holds out the promise of insight beyond ordinary discourse. Yet the institutional approach differs from positive frameworks like behavioralism. As opposed to a focus on maneuvers abstracted from action, like attitudes, an institutional investigation relies on the actual parameters within which action takes place, the "intersubjective" dimensions of the legal environment that some behavioralists all but lost track of in their focus on dissent, disagreement, and divergence from the norm.

Institutional practices are even evident where political jurisprudence is the framework or politics the focus, as in *The Brethren*. This treatment relies on expectations and institutional practice to tell its story. Justices of the Supreme Court are selected and evaluated with reference to an institutional understanding about what a justice should be. Warren Burger pursuing an appointment, with all the manipulations it revealed, made an interesting account because it went against institutional passivity, a practice traditionally distinguishing law from politics. Similarly, the influence-peddling described in *The Brethren* would not have been worth mentioning had the book been about most other institutions in Washington. However political the process has come to be, there are still distinctive institutional expectations. Another approach to the political dimensions of the Supreme Court and the Constitution is work by Professor S. Sidney Ulmer (1986) on the sectional impact of judicial review. Ulmer seeks to explain the authority of the Constitution in various parts of the country. He expects to find significance in "legally irrelevant demographic, cultural, or other non-case factors" (1986: 1). Building on unpublished work by Robert Horn, Ulmer takes decisions of the Supreme Court as indicators of "Constitutional Rectitude or Turpitude" (1986: 5). With data drawn from 1903–1980, Ulmer found evidence of continued support for the Supreme Court in the Northeast and resistance in the South/Midwest on civil liberties questions and interpreted these results as indicators of constitutional authority. The assumption on which his findings are presented is that to resist the Supreme Court on constitutional matters is to resist the Constitution. This is the sort of assumption that a study of institutional practices tries to understand.

Kinds of Practices

The previous discussion presents practices as something like the atomic element in institutional analysis, but it doesn't distinguish among them. There are various kinds of practices in an institutional setting, like wearing robes and meeting in secret. Each has a different institutional significance that can be distinguished as strategies and maxims, conventions, and constitutive or "institutional" practices depending on the relationship that a practice has to the institution.

On one extreme, there are *strategies and maxims* adopted by those who operate within the institution. These suggest how one might best "take advantage of the institution for particular purposes" (Rawls, 1971: 56). A strategy would not be essential to the very nature of the institution.

For example, issuing opinions on various days or circulating drafts of opinions are strategies that are part of the political life in the Supreme Court but they do not determine the nature of the institution (Murphy, 1964). Whether the Court issues most of its opinions on Monday matters a great deal to those who cover the institution, and that day may have some media significance, but we do not think of the Court's depending on that practice for its existence. Similarly, at one time the promulgation of an opinion for the Court by the Chief Justice was a strategy, used by John Marshall to assert his authority over the institution. There was a good deal of variation in this practice over a relatively short period.

Over time, however, the opinion supported by the majority of the justices came, as a matter of *convention,* to be understood as the Court's opinion. With this status in the life of the institution, conventions are not simply ways to get something done. The majority opinion, for instance, is more than an opportunity for influencing the institution; it has become an expectation that gives meaning to individual opinions. Practices of this sort are the terrain on which political strategies are played out. Now, with dissents common again, the institution may be returning to the practice of seriatim opinions. But with a long tradition of opinion by the majority, individual holdings are seen in terms of the majority. Conventions are ways of doing things that we associate with the institution more completely than strategic choices. Conventions, however, do not determine what an institution is.

Practices that take us beyond the conventions within and become indicative or "constitutive" of the institution we call *institutional practices.* Without them the institution would not exist or at least not be the body we know it to be. Certainly the link between the Court and the legal profession, evident in the practice of appointing lawyers to the bench, appears to have become constitutive. Indeed, the role of the legal profession in relation to the Court may be the single most important determinant in its history. From this foundation, we will trace another practice that appears to have become constitutive, the authority to interpret the constitution.

Distinguishing among the various kinds of practices is difficult. This is especially true and particularly important when it comes to distinguishing between conventions and constitutive practices. The extent to which a practice constitutes the Court will be a matter of interpretation. For instance, the assertion of judicial review by John Marshall in *Marbury* v. *Madison* (1803) reiterated a possibility that had been mentioned by others, most notably Hamilton in *Federalist 78* and *81,* but it was certainly not conventional wisdom or an undisputed understanding, much less constitutive of the institution at that time.[8] Marshall articulated the possibility for the Supreme Court, introducing it into the institutional setting. The basis for such a claim was in Blackstone's *Commentaries, The Federalist Papers,* and in the fact of a written constitution (Corwin, 1928), but the practice of judicial review was not conventionally understood as something the Supreme Court did until the late nineteenth century. The key to distinguishing is whether a practice is taken as a given, a fact, or whether some way of proceeding is open for discussion.

In the struggle over authority to interpret the Constitution precipitated by the split between the majority on the Court and the political majority held by the New Deal, the authority of the Court over the Constitution became a matter of debate. The publication in 1938 of Edward Corwin's *Court Over Constitution* is a benchmark indicating the shift from the then "outmoded" doctrine of formal or static constitutionalism to the living constitutionalism of political jurisprudence or legal realism. Corwin's treatment begins by discussing the claim that the Court has the power to declare acts of Congress not consistent with the Constitution to be void. It also begins with a Court out of step with the times, an institution claiming to have no politics but merely proceeding mechanically. The book was published after the shift of 1937.

Remembered as a turn away from the bad old politics of laissez-faire constitutionalism, this shift should also be remembered as a turn away from the myth of mechanical jurisprudence to a new myth of political jurisprudence. From this early statement we see the emergence of a new myth of judicial power. This is the myth that begins contemporary treatments. It is a view of the Supreme Court that treats even the failure of Roosevelt's plan to pack the Court as due to the "switch in time that saved nine" or the political savvy of at least Justice Owen Roberts (O'Brien, 1986: 68). With a judicial review grounded in political jurisprudence as constitutive of the Supreme Court, the consequence is not only a political court but a political constitution. Marshall's suggestion that justices draw authority from the Constitution has been turned on its head. Now it is conventional to know the Constitution through the Supreme Court.

Social Foundations

Practices are socially constructed ways of acting (Winch, 1958; Flathman, 1976). They are evident in folkways from praying to litigating and they exist because actors in a social setting take them into account. It does not matter whether they are formally stipulated. Conversely, a text, a theory, a law on the books is not a practice without more. When two states present a dispute to the Supreme Court, this is understood within the Court's "original jurisdiction." In original jurisdiction cases, the justices will appoint a "master" to hear evidence as a matter of institutional practice. This is a normal Court procedure, an expected form of action. Presidential appointment of justices and oral argument are Supreme Court practices, and judicial review over acts by Congress and the President also have become institutional practices.

When we say that institutions are bodies of practices existing in a society, we mean there are communities who understand the practices and operate according to them. An institution like the Supreme Court is constituted by the communities familiar with it. This means knowledgeable groups or even entire societies where they are accepted. Traditionally these groups know something others don't. We say of a text, in the case of law, or a court, in the case of office, that its social foundation is the group or community that can interpret the text or understand the court. Legal doctrine has been seen for some time as an ideological activity, but its social foundations have been ignored while courts have been so completely understood in terms of action that their ideological qualities have been missed. The special sociological contribution of an investigation into the practices making up an institution comes from identifying the ways of operating and the social relations behind them that give the elements of law and office their significance. The social base makes practices a foundation for a legitimate science of society (Husserl, 1965: 189).

This interest in law's social foundations originates in traditions of literary criticism, which are heavily indebted to language philosophy and hermeneutics. The practices of these disciplines have been introduced into the legal community from a number of quarters, but nowhere more provocatively than by Owen Fiss in an article entitled "Objectivity and Interpretation" (1982). This article portrays the interpretive work of the appellate judge as "neither a wholly discretionary nor a wholly mechanical activity" (1982: 739), but as an interactive process that takes place within an "interpretive community" (1982: 746).[9] The notion of such communities brings in the reality of a professional life. These are the social relations that underlie and maintain legal activity.

The community in law is very well defined, in comparison with other communities, such as those of literary criticism, and consequently it acts as a constraint upon individual lawyers and judges. But its participants are a large group engaged in a variety of tasks, and their place in the community is less clear than the official theories of law would have us believe. Law professors like the late Robert Cover are participants in the legal community and they approach its universes of meanings in a different fashion than the social scientist. He exhorted his colleagues to tell tales, spin yarns, and create a legal order grounded in new practices. This is his job. We expect that the great law teacher will send his students out to break through the paradigms or, to appropriate an epistemological issue, to intentionally confuse "is" and "ought."[10] Cover's call is "to stop circumscribing the nomos . . . to invite new worlds." This is more difficult for those of us who operate outside the great law schools or do not have access to the appellate bench. The community of law professors makes their yarns particularly important. Thus, when we say here that there are social foundations to law and office, we mean that the nomos is not completely up for grabs.

The failure to recognize the boundaries of interpretive communities surrounding the Supreme Court and the Constitution is dramatically evident in a treatment by Lief Carter in his book *Contemporary Constitutional Lawmaking* (1985). Carter offers a view of constitutional interpretation he calls "aesthetic," by which he suggests that the way a justice looks at the Constitution is like the way a concertgoer looks at a performance or a gallery visitor views a work of art, at least according to contemporary conventions. This is offered as a helpful corrective to those who see law as rules and its significance and signification in orders backed by threats. Or as Carter puts it, "*stare decisis,* consistency with canons of legal reasoning, discovery of the intent of those who adopt legal rules, judicial self-restraint, and so forth" (1985: 1). While poetic license in a work such as Carter's must be freely given, it is excessive to say "The Supreme Court has never paid much attention" to the above. But Carter says just that and jeopardizes the insight he provides about interpretation, for he correctly cautions us about the limited bearing the stuff of the law has for the practice of interpretation, especially appellate interpretation in constitutional law. But there is nothing very new here. This is legal realism brought into fashion.

For Carter, "group life depends on maintaining conversations more than it depends on proofs of ultimate truth" (1985: xvii). And while his work has in it some of the sensitivity to institutional practice, the shared ways of doing things we associate with constitutional discourse, like talk about the First Amendment in the context of censorship, the interpretive perspective as he lays it out is set against truth. This move is certainly consistent with the way interpretivists like Fiss have been taken, if not entirely how they present themselves. In deconstructing the confidence of the uncritical in the law field, interpretive practitioners, like the realists with whom they ally themselves, elevate other standards such as attitude and community norms over the traditional legal forms.

Thus interpretation in this formulation is largely a matter of individual choice. As with the interpretivists in law school, the work plays down the sociological dimensions of community. It misses the communities that give some people greater access than others and the institutional structures that do the same thing like those that distinguish the access of a Yale law professor (or new LL.B. from that institution) to the discourse on the appellate bench from that of a local practitioner. Settings like Yale, and of course others in the "higher circles," have a special place, and their aesthetic assumes a priority status in comparison with contributions from the hundreds of other institutions and locales where people have something to say about the Constitution. The Supreme Court, at the apex of this configuration of American legal authority, is subject to the way the authority is organized. The aesthetic perspective, while it restates an important epistemological conception, is very naive sociology.

The present inquiry is motivated by interest in social relations or group life as well as interpretation, because these elements of society enforce the dictates of sensible communication. One of the interesting things about the often discussed case of *INS* v. *Chada* (1983), in which the Supreme Court declared the "legislative veto," a practice by which Congress has exercised ongoing supervision of executive and agency activity, unconstitutional, was that the Court's decision on the Constitution had relatively little effect on congressional practice as it continued to rely on veto provisions in its legislation (Fisher, 1985). Neither the text nor the constitutional logic ultimately determines the social meaning of the fundamental law; it is the practices of those who constitute the state (Goodrich, 1986: 19).

LINKING CONSTITUTION AND COURT

Understanding policy in terms of an institution requires a synthesis. This is the elimination of the distinctions between substance and process or law and office. The approach outlined above mends the split out of theoretical necessity with an eye to the policy sciences as a more practical consideration. The seemingly disparate elements of an institution are both practices. Certain bodies of doctrine, most notably constitutional law and judicial review, are intimately connected with the institutional life of the Supreme Court. Some people know a decision, like the decision on sodomy in 1986, for instance, as a decision of the Court only. This is often true no matter how hard the Court tries to ground its decision in the Constitution. In much the same way, an institutional memory structures the possible doctrinal grounds in any case presented to the Court. In a trivial sense this is pretty obvious. The Court knows its constitutional law, and how it decides cases influences the way questions are framed in constitutional cases. The meanings of *both* the Constitution and the Court are captured by a framework based on a shared phenomenon, institutional practices.

The divergent perspectives in the study of law and legal institutions either excessively reify legal institutions so that investigation of their subjective foundations is difficult or dismiss the work of courts as "simply" liberal legalism, leaving the impression that law is totally subjective. The interpretive perspective avoids either extreme by incorporating both aspects of institutional policy, its givenness and its attractiveness. Working from convention itself, the material that follows looks first at the institutional properties of legal policy and then turns attention to the policy dimensions of the institution. This attempt to synthesize the active alternatives in the field of appellate inquiry into the Constitution will be carried through the entire book to the point of offering a complete study in this vein.

The Court as Legal Practice

Those who have been attentive to control of what Max Weber called "the material means of political power" (1958: 47), the institutions linked directly to the governing apparatus, have been enamored of traditional forms. Current practitioners include John Hart Ely (1980) and Michael Perry (1982). A good example was Alexander Bickel's critique of the progressive orientation of the Warren Court, which he characterized in terms of an "idea of progress" evident in judicial receptivity to the claims of the distressed. Too often these scholars operate at a surface level, content to chronicle institutional achievements or criticize policy outcomes. Consequently they do not penetrate into the relation between institutional practice and the development of policy.

The concept of an institution, like the institution in social life, integrates justices, clerks, and other personnel with the process of deciding and producing opinions. Similarly, the building as symbol and workplace, and the traditions that define what makes doctrinal sense are part of the institution. Practices in each of these areas compliment one another as actions that are part of the institution. From the most mundane change in the work process to matters of jurisdiction and public life, the institution is far more animated than it appears at any given time. In courts, some practices are widely known; others are known only to professionals or the internal staff.[11] For example, after the Watergate events, Court watchers speculated that the news leak of the conference decision on the Mitchell-Stans appeal was a reaction to the Chief Justice's attempt to change the decision. One who knows an institution knows "what the rules demand of him and of others." The web of meaning that gives an institution its appearance of permanence stems from the fact that an individual not only knows the rules, but he also knows that "others know this and that they know that he knows this, and so on" (Rawls, 1971: 55–56).

The interpretive commentary on the Constitution, which is the Supreme Court's best-known work, is itself a "public institution" (Dworkin, 1982: 535) that cannot be understood independently from the Court. Judicial opinion is received as messages from the Court. The institution, as office or process, affects how the pronouncements are taken much as interaction "within" the institution contributes to the product itself. Although it changes, the Constitution is, as Karl Llewellyn noted, "an institution," not a matter of words or rules, but "a set of ways of living and doing" (1934: 17). Changes in the Supreme Court and the ideological basis motivating it at any given time alter how we look at the Constitution. Thus, when the "Four Horsemen" of the 1930s stood against New Deal legislation, the Constitution was referred to by the conservative jurists in static terms and the justices described themselves as operating in mechanical fashion (Belz, 1978).[12]

The attack mounted against using the Constitution to preserve the status quo became the basis for understanding the judicial activity after a group of justices willing to support New Deal policy had been put in place. As the Roosevelt Court broke out of this cocoon, the justices and the public developed a new basis for action, a "Living Constitution," with its doctrinal correlate the "double standard" of constitutional review. The new view of the Constitution became a practice rooted in political interest but surviving under the mantle of institutional reality. The attack on the "Four Horsemen" mentioned above reconstructed institutional power for the justices appointed by President Roosevelt. The political attack on economic due process reached into the scholarly community and subjected the formalism and neutrality of constitutional law to a thorough demystification (Lerner, 1937).

This perspective on institutions, particularly the contribution to understanding institutions as practices, denies the conventional academic presumption that everything is relative and the consequent aesthetic stance (Carter, 1985). Though historically contingent and culturally defined, when an institution is operative in a given culture, when it has a place in the constitution of the social world, it is no longer simply something about which one has a choice. In fact, it is "there." Debates over the Constitution and the fundamental law have contributed to what we understand the Supreme Court to be. Both Court and Constitution are social institutions that have the capacity to constrain human action. In this sense they have the concreteness we sometimes fail to acknowledge in ideas.

Whether action associated with the Supreme Court involves the First Amendment, the code of secrecy behind the bench, or the perception that the institution is the "end of the line," it unfolds from a range of possibilities and opportunities. The consequence is a basis for interpreting the Court's appropriation of authority over the Constitution.

Law and Doctrine as Institutional Practices

Approaches to legal doctrine that have sought to transcend legal formalism have emphasized the contingent character of law (Unger, 1983). This has been associated with efforts at demystification that sometimes degenerate into "trashing," an activity in which the scholar denies all the normative claims in legal doctrine as simply myth. These developments are associated with the movement for Critical Legal Studies (Kairys, 1982) and their appropriation by political scientists has already been discussed (Carter, 1985). They have, with some exceptions (Klare, 1979), stood against studies of the institutional reality of law.[13] But legal doctrine operates as more than myth when it is constituted as a practice by the communities that use it.

Research showing a new concern with the "public phenomenon" of political institutions has emerged from interest in legitimacy. One such effort suggested a move from a "psychologically-based conception of political order" to one more sensitive to institutions, and suggested that the effectiveness of a legitimate institution in securing obedience to its decisions is a function of its "having made them through appropriate institutional procedures" (Grafstein, 1981: 58). This authority of institutions is essential to understanding legitimacy and linking it to the way political action is channeled by institutions. The authority has two dimensions. One is associated with the expectations that derive from legitimate institutional capacities. The other is the constitutive authority that leaves the impression of natural truth. Although they reflect the two approaches indicated above, their pitfalls can be avoided by a synthesis based on institutional practices.

It is through institutions that established ways of proceeding, and ultimately state power, are maintained. In order that the Court be able to perform this function, it must appear neutral. Doctrine emanating from an institution that represents "the rule of law" insulates the state from "the immediate political conflicts of the day and the shifting substantive goals of . . . political actors" (Balbus, 1973: 4–5). Institutions divert political conflicts into settings where "the conditions necessary for meaningful political communication . . . are present" (Bennett, 1980: 817). When individuals ignore either the "formal rationality" residing in Supreme Court opinions or accepted procedures, they jeopardize institutional authority. This power, as Gustavus Myers said some time ago, is "neither . . . accidental, capricious or aimless" but rather represents "the definite expression at a particular time of a definite purpose to conserve ideas or conditions" (1925: 13).

As an analytic tool, legitimacy refers to the capacity of an institution to confine political behavior to "institutionally relevant choices" (Grafstein, 1981: 67). The Supreme Court has been struggling since the New Deal battles to establish its legitimacy and the primary orientation has been toward "process based" justifications (Tribe, 1978) for institutional action. In practice, the Court's place in the process has become the key to its authority. With the Supreme Court, a loss is the end of the line. This was evident in the "obedience" of Richard Nixon when he was ordered to turn over the Watergate tapes and the University of California when it was ordered to admit Allen Bakke to its medical school in Davis.

Institutional authority stems from the place of the institution among the available channels of the political action. The 1973 abortion decision, *Roe* v. *Wade,* had a dramatic impact on various groups. It turned the attention of proabortion groups from grass roots political action, since it amounted to a total victory with relatively little local effort. The effect on those who opposed abortion was to make formerly comfortable adherents of the status quo into the opposition. Here the dramatic decision served as an invigorating tool for movements in the Catholic Church and it made the Pro-Life Movement into a national political force. Abortion is an old issue in support of this point. Sodomy looks like a new one. However, the burden in continuing to struggle is greatest where a group has seen the Court as a last resort. When struggles begin with the intent of thwarting or turning back a Supreme Court decision, the psychological impact of disappointment appears to be less.

The antecedents of a focus on institutional practices are anthropological and view the justices as operating with the limited tools of any craftsmen or "*bricoleur.*" The contribution made by justices through the Court has been to elevate ideas to the level of conventional understanding so that they serve as opportunity and constraint (Garvey, 1971). My approach has been to move away from formalisms to a perspective on legal doctrine that sees it as a linguistic system (Brigham, 1978). This work has been associated with the study of language and law in order to turn attention from rules to systems of belief that are beyond conscious choice. When this effort is successful the "authority" of the institution need not be in evidence and the authority adheres in the belief that something is true. The authority of the institution over the Constitution comes from the practice of judicial review. We have come to speak of the Constitution as "what the justices say it is" and we look for "it" in their opinions. Their words are no longer authoritative gloss on the thing itself; they have become the thing itself.

The "double standard," a distinction in constitutional discourse between the economy and politics for the purpose of attention by the Supreme Court (McCloskey, 1962; Porter, 1977), is the epitome of doctrine
as institutional practice. After the New Deal struggle brought down the
temple that the turn-of-the-century lawyers had built, their "living constitution" required a doctrinal response with deep institutional roots
(Brigham, 1986). This was the "double standard" of constitutional review. By using two standards for review, the justices were to give certain
constitutional rights closer scrutiny than others. The attack on the judiciary that peaked in the 1930s had become associated with a much older
distinction between political and economic life that is rooted in nineteenth-century conceptions of liberalism. On this foundation, the doctrinal distinction became a boundary for judicial action under the new freedom of a "living constitution." Thus, the political attack on economic due
process reached into the scholarly community and subjected the formalism and neutrality of constitutional law to a thorough demystification
(Lerner, 1937).[14]

Once, at the dawn of the behavioral revolution, law studies were
thought to be lagging in the discipline of political science. Many raced to
catch up, but few left the craft of doctrinal analysis and interpretation
completely. Now, those who have worked through the sociological movement in legal studies and turned to ideological investigations are way out
front. We have incorporated in our discipline a familiarity with the rich
cultural materials that are essential to interpretive social research. Behavioral research on law was once considered very "modern." Now, work
that moves from this epistemological frame to incorporate traditional
symbolism must be considered "postmodern." This is an attractive identification that can legitimately be claimed by interpretive work in social
science, having taken stock of the promises held out for science and
passed through a formative period. Thus, we are ready to go beyond the
sterile description of institutional settings and define a new political and
economic social science.

A threat against which we will continually struggle is the prevailing
liberal skepticism about the possibility of authoritative texts. There are
two sources from which we will draw inspiration and insight. One is the
monograph *Reading the Law* by Peter Goodrich (1986) and its dramatic
concluding assessment of the condition in which law is to be found in the
modern age. Goodrich draws attention to "the inter-related social experi-
ences of powerlessness, irrationality and loss of faith" as "closely connected to critical debates in legal studies" (1986: 212) that manifest themselves in the belief that there is nothing more to the legal craft than

low-level skills and sophistic technique. But we share with Goodrich the belief that "It is simple obfuscation to propose that the claim that texts are inherently ambiguous or polysemous is the equivalent of saying that 'anything goes' " (1986: 218).

Another recent volume provides encouragement for those whose primary interest is the Constitution and who are trapped by doctrinal convention into an exclusive focus on the Supreme Court. While the treatment is more normative than semiotic, Sotirios Barber provides an extended analysis *On What the Constitution Means* from a perspective that is not simply about the word of the Supreme Court (1984: 5). Barber is writing a brief for a community on the defensive, one that would constitute itself around the Constitution rather than around the Supreme Court. In this sense he too is reaching back for principles to take us beyond the hierarchies and skepticism of modernity. While his ideal state of affairs may or may not come to pass, its aspiration points up the limited practice of contemporary professional authority.

Judicial authority is grounded in communities of interpretation that share doctrinal and institutional practices and it is to these communities that we will turn in trying to understand the shifting nature of that authority. The Court got its first real home and began asserting the power of judicial review after the bar had successfully become a national profession. That is has authority in this area is taken for granted while it is not hard to show that the Court has more of this authority now than it did at the beginning of its life. The challenge is to understand the complex intersubjectivity through which Court and Constitution became one. As this inquiry progresses we will show that the crucial element in the Supreme Court's capacity for interpretation is where the justices sit in the hierarchy of courts. The materials of law have more significance than some have been given to believe, as just noted, but there has also been a shift in institutional practice from "judgment to will." The Court in the modern American state operates from a new basis for its authority.

2

IDEOLOGIES OF AUTHORITY

THE CONSTITUTION as Higher Law and a maturing bar carried the Supreme Court to its authoritative position in American government. In America, the document engendered a claim by the legal community of superiority in interpretation, particularly the interpretation of texts dealing with fundamental rights and institutional relations. Articulated by Chief Justice Marshall in *Marbury* v. *Madison* (1803), legal supremacy did not become a reality until the twentieth century with the evolution of ideological and organizational support for judicial claims over politics. By then, an expert class had consolidated its authority over national policy, drawing on the Court and Constitution. Thus, the authority to interpret rests on practices linking the justices and the text.

Early in this century, Edward S. Corwin showed the American Constitution being elevated to the status of religion and institutionalized in the "artificial reason" of the legal profession. Corwin characterized the Supreme Court's extraordinary institutional growth by tracing the forms of judicial authority antecedent to law as professional mystery. He defined a "Higher Law" constitution as the basis for judicial authority in America and established a link between modern practice and the Western ideological heritage. Higher law and the special reason of the legal profession offered credible interpretations for the rise of the modern Court. More contemporary political jurisprudence draws on process-based justifications and institutional position, as a foundation for judicial supremacy.

Institutional authority derives from shared understandings of how things are to be done. These understandings or ways the world is known will be treated as "ideologies of authority." This chapter describes how the claim of judicial authority over the Constitution came to be accepted as doctrine in America. We pay explicit attention to the relationship between the Supreme Court and the Constitution as a particular manifestation of this institutional arrangement. In the end, the analysis treats constitutional authority in terms of various communities, including some that find constitutional authority in sources other than the Supreme Court.

HIGHER LAW

Modern portrayal of judicial authority over the Constitution begins with the document as a "Higher Law." The tradition draws on ideas in Western thought about the limits of temporal government. In America, the Higher Law is grafted on to mundane, or at least terrestrial, stock. Ideas associated with the Founding generation did not flourish until well into the nineteenth century. Following the Civil War they came to constitute our politics by incorporation into institutions like the Supreme Court. Judicial supremacy, the uniquely American political form, is now taken for granted and as a result its antecedents and distinctive relationship to the Constitution have received little attention until recently. Articulated by Chief Justice Marshall in *Marbury* v. *Madison* (1803), judicial supremacy did not become a reality until the twentieth century with the evolution of ideological and organizational support for judicial claims over politics. By then, an expert class had consolidated its authority in the profession of the law through the Court and Constitution.

Classical Revival

From 1928 to 1938, Edward S. Corwin, a constitutional scholar at Princeton University, concentrated his work on showing how the American Constitution became elevated beyond the secular sphere to a cultural position on the order of a civil religion. The Constitution became "Higher" owing to its institutionalization in the "artificial reason" of the legal profession. The idea began with Fortesque, who had written of the law's professional mysteries. Corwin developed this phenomenon with reference to the Supreme Court's extraordinary institutional growth. By depicting the antecedent forms of judicial authority, he interpreted the link between contemporary practice and our ideological heritage.[1] Corwin's work was a major contribution to discussion of the Constitution as Higher Law and its relationship to authority in America.

The classical antecedents of the Higher Law idea that came to characterize the Constitution were said to include the Greek idea of law as discovery, the appeal to custom as a source of higher principles, and the juxtaposition of civil law against the law of nature (Corwin, 1928: 59). The Roman achievement was more practical. It has been described as administration through set rules and regulations for governing strangers (Wolin, 1960: 27). Justinian codified this tradition at the end of the Empire and the code was discussed by commentators like Corwin as a source of Higher Law in the Middle Ages. The Church made its appeal against the "sinfulness" of mankind and as a limitation on rulers. While the Greek conception was said to have conferred its chief benefits by "entering into the more deliberate acts of human authority," Higher Law in the Middle Ages operated, according to Corwin, by checking and limiting authority "from without" (1928: 38). The texts of the Roman Law, the scriptures, and the ecclesiastical tradition were all linked to a picture of law above politics. A religious basis for law had been secured by tracing the appeal to law back through the Middle Ages to classical antiquity.

While there is plenty of evidence that Classicism was an inspiration in the Federal Period as the fledgling American culture sought to identify its own creation, constitutional government, with earlier understandings of how men should rule, Corwin's treatise on the Higher Law is far more influenced by the late-nineteenth-century scholarship coming out of Victorian England than intellectual life in the Federal Period. There is Adams and Carlyle, Bagehot and Wilson, Gierke, McIlwain, and Bryce in support of the contention that the classics and the conception of a "Higher" authority matters. It was the late nineteenth century that gave life to the view that the text was a check on human action and that the legal profession would be the key to interpretation.

Artificial Reason. Higher Law found its institutional base in the associations of men whose shared traditions gave them a livelihood and insinuated them into the forums of the government. In England, law administered in the ordinary courts and incorporating indigenous custom depended on professional mystery, the "science of bench and bar" (Corwin, 1928: 37). This professional discourse became the basis for the Higher Law. Originally represented simply by custom, reasonableness in the affairs of state would be characterized as the "right reason" possessed by those men learned in the law. The inns of court enabled men of position to complete their education in preparation for public life (Blackstone, 1859: viii). Thus, the set of social relations that emerged in the guilds and that would develop into professions became the institutional foundation for the common law. They would be characterized by a distinctive body of thought developed and maintained then as today through reading, observing, and arguing (Prest, 1972: 151). The tradition grew independent of ordinary folk to include principles and maxims such as no one should be twice punished for the same offense, and by comparison with the natural reason, the professional mysteries were indeed "artificial."

"Reason," in this sense, included principles of law like the above or that a statute have proscriptive force. Liberalism in the "classic Lockeian sense" (Hartz, 1955) is studded with legal forms.[2] The state is presumed to be autonomous, a neutral referee and servant of the community, and its authority is constituted by reason wielded by individuals trained in the law who are expected to satisfy their interests and desires within stipulated limits. This is the American idea of right. American government was founded on social relations that would come to be constituted by a rhetorical tradition that dissolved natural law into the natural rights of "life, liberty, and estate." Because rights were so central, law became the basis for political action and certain institutional developments followed. Through this sort of reason an ambiguous document came to be the key to American politics, the basis for a claim of special expertness central to judicial power.

The Charter. Constitutional power derived from professional mysteries depended on a referent for authority, a text. The Magna Carta, both in the English experience and as elaborated by Sir Edward Coke for America, provide the historical foundation for political authority. Coke's views were published in 1606, when he helped to write the Virginia Charter. This instrument became the model for royal charters in America. The great charter's significance in England grew as the classes it served widened and as it became identified with the common law. Coke might have been stretching the historical record a bit when he declared in 1628 that "Magna Carta is such a fellow, that he will have no 'Sovereign'," but widespread acceptance of this view became a "potent weapon" (Roche, 1961: 4). The document had been incorporated into the common law and this afforded an institutional setting for asserting the Charter as a basis for parliamentary sovereignty.

In addition to the English experience, Montesquieu's emphasis on institutions in his *Spirit of the Laws* was transformed into American confidence that political practices would provide the basis for stable government (Arendt, 1963: 186–187). His influence on the Founding generation was in the commitment to certain means, like the separation of powers, and the idea that these arrangements would become essential to the stability of the state. The idea that legislating, administering, and judging comprised the core elements of political life was a conventional understanding drawn on by the Founders. From these elements they proposed institutional arrangements that would ultimately come to have the enduring qualities associated here with institutional practices. Montesquieu's place in the first rank of political theorists is assured in America as long as groups in the society continue to identify institutions with that stability.

The Magna Carta as part of the common law and the more pragmatic political thinking of Montesquieu give institutional credibility to the "Higher Law" tradition linked by modern students of the Supreme Court to Western Classicism. Hannah Arendt saw this in her treatment of "the Founding" in *On Revolution* (1963). She was neither an ideologist for the law nor was she writing when Corwin wrote, but in addressing the theoretical problem presenting itself through the struggles of emerging nations after the Second World War—that of institutionalizing the revolution—Arendt too considered the classical antecedents of elevating a secular text to a place of authority akin to religion. Ultimately, however, the roots may be more economic and narrowly traditional than classical.

The Constitution

The men who put together the American Republic, for all their focus on the instruments of government, said very little about the status of the Constitution other than that it should be "the Supreme Law of the Land." Subsequent claims for judicial authority were based on the artificial reason that separated those learned in the law from the sovereign, whether king or citizen. Prior to the ratification of the Constitution, this idea was best expressed by John Adams, who drew on Coke in his defense of legal sovereignty over the writs of assistance. Corwin saw Adams's reliance on Dr. Bonham's case as a vehicle that brought the idea of judicial review to the "very threshold of the first American Constitution" (1928: 770). This would be the Commonwealth of Massachusetts, where courts were understood in "separation of powers" terms. The role suggested by the early constitution makers (Hurst, 1960: 226) would increase the importance of courts as the nation matured.

The significance of the Constitution would expand with the republic and come to be explained as our distinctive legacy. James Willard Hurst traced the development to colonial experience with "trading company charters, proprietary grants or royal charters" (1960: 200–201) and a reliance on written agreement rooted in the English heritage. The ideas of contract and right emerged together in the context of a new rationalism and were described by Max Weber as growing out of the economic system based on "the adjustment of economic means to the attainment of profits" since capitalism required rational structures of law and administration (Weber, 1968). At least the economic order seems to have thrived under these structures. The colonial leaders were drawn to the constitutional system as a basis for the new government as a matter of secular faith with the status of reason. The success with the Constitution put "beyond question that henceforth legitimate governments in the United States must rest on written constitutions" (Hurst, 1960: 200).

Contested violently until and during the Civil War, the document became a subject of reverence in the late nineteenth century. In this period, its stature made it an apt vehicle for transforming the judiciary into the oracle of constitutional government. Because of the American experience with charters, compacts as Higher Law had social significance. Experience enabled them to be treated as possible forms of action and this experience was the basis for successful institutionalization of "court over constitution." In this development, the document would assume those Higher Law qualities that the judiciary claimed the authority to pronounce. From a strategy associated with John Marshall to conventional understanding, the document has become identified with the institution to such an extent that it is hard to understand either Court or Constitution independent of each other.

More Than a Recipe. In *On Revolution* (1963), Hannah Arendt wrote about the process of establishing political order in late-eighteenth-century America. Reflecting the romance in the late 1950s and early 1960s that intellectuals had for the transformation of chaos into order, Arendt's work gives life to a sometimes underdetermined picture of the Founding. "The Constitution," as Corwin reminds us, was "only a project" as it came from the convention (1938: 40). Initially, in fact the Constitution would be examined by the conventions that were to be called in the states. This gave commentary during the ratification process a special status. As an early gloss on the constitutional text, *The Federalist Papers* helped explain the new invention and gave it cultural significance. Such was the confidence in the American project that contemporaries reported that with regard to the French constitution introduced not long after ratification, Americans viewed the French with contempt, "as if a constitution was a pudding to be made by a recipe" (McIlwain, 1940: 1). The argument goes that very shortly the American blueprint had become the structure itself. From Thomas Paine, the contribution of the American Constitution was "to liberty, what a grammar is to language. . . . A constitution is not the act of a government, but of a people constituting a government."

Although Paine's formulation is laced with period rhetoric and political enthusiasm and may not have been descriptively accurate in the late eighteenth century, Americans have had greater success in perpetuating their constitutional frame than the French. Indeed, this picture has colored the American perception of the Constitution, and it seems that the American blueprint had a prescriptive framework almost from the beginning. This, of course, is a reconstruction. It is revisionist history of the sort so central to governing institutions. In everyday usage we refer to the document of 1787 and the amendments as the Constitution. Yet this is only the "formal" constitution, the American recipe. In an institutional sense, the Constitution is the body of rules "in accordance with which a government is organized and operates'' (Corwin, 1938: 87).[3] In America, this process took 200 years to get to its present state, and there is no evidence that the developments have been arrested.

The contractual aspect of the American experience was the social foundation on which a law written by politicians became transformed into a symbolic text (Hurst, 1960). American political practice drew from trading company charters, and like many of those charters, once drawn up, the act of constituting shifted into the background. This was a development more recent theorists have linked to the Hobbesian premises that systems of power must depend on strength to withstand contemporary interests if they are to endure (Scheingold, 1974: 24). Fear of the French experience and belief in the superiority of American practice are part of that belief system. Ultimately, transformation of the Constitution into an anchor for a legal elite was enhanced by the existence of the text as a written expression with legal authority.

A Text? The contrast between the new conception of a ''conscious formulation by a people of its fundamental law'' and ''the older traditional view in which the word was applied only to the substantive principles to be deduced from a nation's actual institutions and their development'' (McIlwain, 1940: 3) is a dynamic framework for studying the ideologies of authority attached to the Constitution. In America, the Constitution incorporated both these meanings. The fundamental law had natural and deliberate qualities. This dual meaning resides in the act of constituting as well as what is constituted. It leads on the one hand to a focus on the thought of the Founders and on the other to the Court as oracle.

The focus on ''Founding'' discourse, at the margins until 1980, came to the forefront of constitutional debate in the Reagan administration, particularly Ronald Reagan's second term with the appointment of Edwin Meese as Attorney General and William Rehnquist as Chief Justice. The roots of this orientation are in the late nineteenth century, when the elevation of the first generation of American statesmen to an apostolic position coincided with construction of the federal Constitution as a barrier to state action. This was characteristic of the work by James Bradley Thayer and it was not without its critics. George Sydney Fisher noted the tendency after the Civil War to treat the Constitution ''as invented by the convention which framed it'' (1897: 3). This was a mistake, according to Fisher, because the practices that went into the Constitution had already become part of the fabric of American life.

The Founders as source are part of the ''doctrine of the text'' on which the Supreme Court has based its authority, but students of the Founding since 1937 have more often held up the work of those who wrote the constitution and argued for ratification as against the Court than in support of that institution. William Winslow Crosskey's work (1953) attacked the notion that the Founders had included the power of judicial review in the Constitution, and he proceeded to offer his own interpretation of the major issues in constitutional law as an antidote to the prevailing liberalism of the high bench as it had been reconstituted by Franklin Roosevelt. Crosskey would be less central to present debates had he not been a key figure in the "Chicago School" of constitutional conservatism. This group, following the tradition of textual exegesis associated with Leo Strauss and applied to the constitution by Herbert Storing and Walter Berns, has produced interpretations of the debates at the constitutional convention and the *Federalist Papers* challenging Supreme Court authority.

John Agresto's *The Supreme Court and Constitutional Democracy* (1984) looks to the authors of the Constitution to support his argument that interpretation of the text was never intended to be solely a judicial prerogative. Paul Murphy placed the work in the tradition of Alexander Bickel, Phillip Kurland, and Felix Frankfurter, "thoughtful men who were convinced that the modern Supreme Court's moral idealism was thoroughly misguided" (1986: 207). Murphy is critical of Agresto as a historian but Agresto's use of history is more like the use of precedent by the Supreme Court than it is like academic history. Agresto presents a brief for the excesses of the modern Court on the basis of the text, its authors, and a selection of subsequent interpretors other than the Supreme Court. Christopher Wolfe's discussion of modern judicial review distinguishes this practice from what he sees as the Founding tradition in terms of the contemporary tendency to stray from the text and produce policy decisions. Wolfe draws on Hamilton's treatment of judicial review to emphasize that this author of the *Federalist* at least distinguished between judicial intervention in policy questions and a reading by the Supreme Court holding a particular statute manifestly outside the parameters of the Constitution (1986: 77). Wolfe's conclusion epitomizes the appeal to a "Founding" as an aspect of contemporary constitutional debate. He calls it "an invitation to us to reexamine our foundations, to renew our acquaintance with the political philosophy of the men who established the Constitution (1986: 356).

The dual meaning of a constitution as tradition and conscious formulation accorded the justices, as experts, a special place in setting the boundaries of politics. That the locus of political authority, which had resided in legislatures or monarchs since the Roman Empire, should shift to lawyers and the judiciary was not inevitable, but the fact of a constitutional text helped. In contract form, the text, as symbol of stability and common agreement, established the basis for judicial review. We know the Founding myths as constituting agreement on the parameters of political action, while actualizing possibilities has become associated with judicial decisions. The remaining part of this drama associates artificial reason with the Supreme Court's place in the American polity and links the Federalist vision to the modern institution. Since institutions are a product of interests operating on possibilities, they become viable where action in accordance with them is expected. Their continuity depends on the expectations.[4] The Higher Law and the institutional base are the ideologies of authority behind judicial supremacy.

JUDICIAL SUPREMACY

The source of political authority in America is the Constitution. The Supreme Court, like the other institutions of the federal government, draws authority from this configuration of beliefs about how politics should be conducted. Here, we turn to the ideological links that have been the basis for the claim to judicial supremacy. In his extraordinary work, *Court over Constitution: A Study of Judicial Review as an Instrument of Popular Government* (1938), written, like so much seminal legal scholarship, around the time of Roosevelt's struggle with the Court over New Deal legislation, Edward Corwin viewed the competing theories of judicial review as either "juristic" or "political." Those theories provide a framework for examining the historic sources and lines of argument. The political conception, he argues "regards the Constitution as an instrument of popular government and hence stresses the role of opinion in its interpretation" (1938: 69). The driving forces, in this framework, are presidential leadership and the aggregation of interests in the legislature. The juristic conception is driven by "professional opinion" and finds its expression in the Supreme Court.

By Corwin's assessment, the juristic conception invoked a miracle because "It supposes a kind of transsubstantiation whereby the Court's opinion . . . becomes the very body and blood of the Constitution" (Corwin, 1938: 68). This "miracle" has become a common understanding because of the way the past has been interpreted and the claims of the institution evaluated. The document itself and traditional commentary is the first point of reference, or line of authority. This included Article III and early exegesis as well as the suppression of some lines of argument around the Founding period. The second referents are more political and they include increasingly bold assertions of judicial power as well as knowing responses from adversaries in other branches. This means recognition of a practice emerging. From the fact that the Constitution is a law comes the assertion that its interpretation must come from a court. As the highest court, the Supreme Court claims that authority. The success of its claim depends on the ideologies of authority. The more credible these ideologies are the more successful its claims will be. These ways of interpreting history support the "cult of the Court" that has emerged in the late twentieth century. They also provide a basis for examining contemporary interpretive practice in the last section of the chapter.

Lines of Authority

The common law commentaries and political theorists, the framers, the Federalist proponents, and the Anti-Federalist critics provided a rich mix of potential lines of authority. The range of judicial power and the authority over the Constitution that emerge from practice are constitutive of the institution.

Article III. Almost nothing was said in the document fashioned in Philadelphia about what makes a court or a judge. Article III, which concerns the judiciary, contains the shortest explication on a national institution, and even this attention is as much to the legal foundation of the Constitution as it is to the makeup of the Court. The guidelines here for national judicial power are far less precise than the description of Congress or the President. The discussions in Articles I and II concerning the other branches of government give a much more complete sense of what the occupants of these offices are by what they are expected to do, and there are also more explicit eligibility requirements that helped constitute those institutions. It is much harder to understand what the Founding Fathers might have anticipated with regard to the judiciary. The provision for holding office during good behavior is unusual for a national institution, and the fact that judicial salaries are not to be cut while a judge is on the bench is another unique feature. One of the few times the Supreme Court is mentioned outside Article III is in terms of appointment by the President, a fact also characteristic of many federal government employees and all the federal judges.

Given this ambiguous beginning, growth of the judiciary on the national scene is all the more dramatic. While the presidency has grown by the expansion of the executive departments and the Congress by the addition of staff, the Court rode the expectation of expertness to a position as guardian of the sacred text. In general, lack of detail followed considerable agreement on what comprises the separate powers. The character of these powers may indeed have become a matter of faith by the Federalist period (Handlin, 1966). However, adherence to the faith was no doubt exaggerated by the Federalists.

Judicial power to declare null and void laws inconsistent with the Constitution may have been "assumed by the leading men in the convention" (Farrand, 1913: 157), but it is not very clear. After the convention refused to recommend a veto of legislation by the judiciary in conjunction with the executive, the compromise proposal that the legislative acts of the United States shall be the supreme law of the respective states and that the judiciaries of the several states shall be bound thereby in their decision became the foundation for the power of judicial review by the Supreme Court (Main, 1961: 120). This "supremacy clause" concludes the document written in Philadelphia. Anti-Federalist resistance to the document is said to have stemmed in part from the perceived power of the judiciary (Main, 1961: 125).

The treatment of the Court's business in the Constitution is another clue to aspirations about the nature of judicial power. The power reaches "to all cases, in Law and Equity, arising under this Constitution, the Laws of the United States, and treaties made, or which shall be made under their Authority (Sec. 2)." Cases, in this context, may be either criminal or civil, while controversies indicate civil actions where "adverse litigants must present an honest and antagonistic assertion of rights" (Corwin, 1928). The case and controversy requirement defines the sort of judging envisioned by the Founders.

Commentaries. William Blackstone had portrayed expertness as essential to the activity of judging. Judges were to have acquired a mode of thinking that would make them repositories of the law. The learning Blackstone considered essential was provided in his *Commentaries* (1859: 67). The work, which collected years of judicial decisions and offered the knowledge needed by a gentleman, claimed a sort of Higher Law status itself. Through identification with English custom and as one of the few available sources of law when it was first published in America in 1771, the *Commentaries* represented not only an argument for the political supremacy of legal knowledge but the substance of that knowledge as well.

Judicial supremacy has depended on the Constitution's being seen as a Higher Law with responsibility for its meaning resting in the Supreme Court. The key to the practice of interpretation establishing the document's transcendent qualities was the claim of special competence. The idea that fundamental principles of government were set out in a legal document provided the possibility for judicial supremacy. For Alexander Hamilton, law was to be an element in the balance of forces maintaining the liberal state. Judges could handle power beyond popular control because their very independence would make them different. He described "the complete independence of the court" as "essential to a limited Constitution," which by its nature contains exceptions to legislative authority. In *The Federalist*, No. 78, Hamilton argued that "Limitations of this kind can be preserved in practice no other way than through the medium of courts of justice." In subsequent papers Hamilton reviews the tasks set down for the Court and thus reveals one conception of their nature. Justifying this grant in *The Federalist,* No. 81, he relies on the Constitution as the symbol and source of ultimate truth. The courts, Hamilton argues, are not to be regarded as superior because they can declare the acts of another void. Since the Constitution is the fundamental law, acts contrary to it are not valid. Courts do not simply substitute their view for that of the legislatures, according to Hamilton; they rely on their learning to understand things beyond the capacity of people operating in the political realm. Hamilton saw a voluminous code of laws as binding the judges: "There can be but few men in the society who will have sufficient skill in the laws to qualify them for the station of judge."

Corwin notes that the Hamiltonian argument was in response to the "Letters of Brutus" expressing concern about the role of the Court (Corwin, 1938: 231). These letters appeared in the *New York Journal* during the winter of 1788 and their author, after acknowledging that only an imperfect opinion of what the judges would be like could be formed from the document, described his belief that the judiciary would have a place "altogether unprecedented in a free country" (Corwin, 1938: 232). Brutus feared their independence and the mysterious ways of the law that limited any assessment of what the courts would do (1938: 234). This argument, democratic in spirit and possessing all the erudition we have come to associate with the founding generation, was the Jeffersonian position with regard to federal judicial power.

Claims of Authority

There is a compelling contradiction in the development of judicial power in the American state structure. The principle of constitutional government is that authority rests in the people. In spite of this deference to popular authority, the Constitution became the touchstone for a legal elite (Wood, 1969; Gunther, 1985: 16). Judges have placed legal authority in America above politics,[5] based on an idea of autonomous or relatively autonomous law. Contrary to conventional understanding, this did not occur with the early claims of Chief Justice John Marshall. The development was much slower and it is only recently that we say as a matter of social fact that the Supreme Court has the power of "judicial review."

Early Claims. A theory of shared constitutional interpretation, expressed as the difference between a juristic and a political conception of judicial review, was the basis for the struggle between President Thomas Jefferson and Chief Justice John Marshall. Marshall's tie to the Blackstonian juristic conception is well established. The American jurist had access to Blackstone and his statements are classic expositions of the conception of judging that Blackstone put forth. Marshall's decisions were the first actions tying these possibilities for authoritative judges to the Constitution. The reading of judicial prerogatives by Marshall in *Marbury* v. *Madison* was, at the time, a standoff in the political struggle for interpretive authority. The best-known disagreement from a high bench of the period was Justice Gibson's dissent in *Eakin* v. *Raub,* a case from the Pennsylvania Supreme Court in 1825. Gibson called the right to declare unconstitutional acts void a "professional dogma" and "a usurpation of legislative power." There is, in Gibson's opinion, however, a recognition of the judicial predisposition toward this power. Given minimal professional support and the Lockeian tradition of legislative supremacy, the fact that Marshall achieved a political standoff was a major accomplishment. Marshall had placed Hamilton's suggestions in an institutional context, giving them more practical significance.

The traditional foundation employed by Marshall is evident in the early portions of his opinion in *Marbury*. The Chief grounds judicial supremacy in the Blackstonian concept that, "The government of the United States has been emphatically termed a government of laws, and not of men." Law would be the key linking interpretive action to the Court. The President gains his power as an officer of the law and thus, he "is amenable to the laws for his conduct." Marshall's "separate" powers argument is described in terms of differing capacities rather than a political balance of forces: "It is emphatically the province and duty of judicial department to say what the law is. Those who apply the rule to particular cases, must of necessity expound and interpret that rule." The Court would then derive its institutional standing from its availability for settling disputes, and since these would arise under the authority of the new government, the justices would be the ultimate arbiters there as well.

Once a certain kind of rationalism is accepted, the step from the document to expert reviewer seems small. Alexander Bickel's analysis of *Marbury* ties judicial review to this tradition by pointing out that Marshall's argument proceeds "on the basis of a single textual reliance namely the fact itself of a written Constitution" (1962: 4). However implicit it was, the institutional reality of the Constitution required intentional, political action to transform the idea into dominant political practice. Marshall's "poor" reasoning may indicate the priority of political considerations over traditions of judicial authority. Preventing the decision from being overturned immediately was Marshall's coup. This action, and neither the Chief Justice's reasoning nor his authority, stands as his contribution to introducing the Court into the mainstream of American politics to develop along with the other branches of government.

There was no shift from the legislative supremacy of the English tradition with the ratification of the Constitution or with Marshall's assertion in 1803 that the power existed. Judicial supremacy would be established much later on a basis linked to the English jurists, accepted by the Founders, and institutionalized in the growing professionalism of the bar.

Growing Authority. The second claim to judicial review over Congress did not come until fifty years later, in *Dred Scott* (1857). Even then, Chief Justice Taney's reading of the document with a proslavery lilt turned out to be antithetical to dominant ideas of "progress." Rather than rallying the nation behind the Court, Taney's claim was a disaster. The successful effort to establish that Taney was wrong (the Civil War) further diminished the stature of the institution. Not until the late nineteenth century and early in the twentieth did the Court successfully begin to reassert its power.

By contrast with the nearly one hundred years prior to that time when only two declarations of the power occurred, from 1865 to 1970, eighty-four acts of Congress were held unconstitutional either in part or in their entirety by the Supreme Court (Pritchett, 1984). Students of "the politics of judicial supremacy" (Mendelson, 1960) have pointed out that successful reliance on the power of judicial review came in the period after the decline of a powerful party system in the various regions of the country and before the rise of the strong urban party system (Skowronek, 1982). The exercise of judicial review is also associated with weak parties in Congress (Nagel, 1962).

The political context thus influenced the emerging institution of judicial review. But even more directly relevant to the new institutional capacity was the rise of professionalism (Seron and Heydebrand, 1983). The founding of the American Bar Association in 1878 would ultimately provide a significant institutional basis for the ideology of judicial authority. This confidence showed itself in the exercise of judicial review. The end of the nineteenth century was a period in which the bar was engaged in heated debate over its proper role, and the early ascendancy of a group espousing the traditional republican virtues would eventually give way to a new kind of instrumentalism that would presage a shift in the ideologies of authority (Gordon, 1985).[6] Judicial review emerged as a potent weapon growing along with the legal profession as the nineteenth century drew to a close.

Institutionalization. Shifts in the ideology and competing claims have continued to be evident in such occurrences as the legislative veto controversy and President Richard Nixon's litigation of the "executive privilege" claim. The failure here resulted in the most recent statement of judicial supremacy. In *United States* v. *Nixon* (1974), the conflict over interpretation of the Constitution arose as a challenge to a severely weakened president, and the capitulation of the Richard Nixon strengthened the image of the Court. With references to Marshall's historic assertion of judicial power over the other branches, the challenge to the presidency sounded familiar. "But if the courts are the ultimate interpreters of the constitution and can restrain Congress to operate within constitutional bounds, they certainly shouldn't be empowered any less to measure Presidential claims of constitutional powers" (Jaworski, 1974). Thus, they asserted the judicial prerogative to say what the law is with less fear of contradiction than at any previous time in American history.

This decision contributed to the preeminence of the judges in such matters, yet it ought not be considered independent of the circumstances in which it was handed down. This was a "public drama" of the first order with all the symbolic meaning and cultural significance we give our big events (Gusfield, 1981: 184). The events of Watergate evolved from mystery theater to morality play with the Supreme Court slipping from neutral observer to the side of the angels as the identity of the angels became clear. The Supreme Court played a part in the "dramatic[ization] of the rule of law" (Gusfield, 1981: 184) that relied on the overall setting including the president as villain. By the point of the decision in *United States* v. *Nixon,* it was pretty clear that the Court could rely on its claim to judicial supremacy, although it made its opinion unanimous just to be on the safe side. The authority of the Supreme Court to finally determine the meaning of a written Constitution had been "placed" in the document (Bickel, 1962: 1).

Quite often those who have spoken of the implicit nature of judicial review have had a stake in the argument. Learned Hand asserted that judicial review is necessary but is an "interpolation" and not explicitly in the document (Wechsler, 1959). William O. Douglas claimed that "Once there is a written Constitution it is but a short step to the assertion of the power of judicial review" (Paulson, 1959: 65). In each case, the argument referred to the tradition of the polity for its authority and that tradition provides the interpretive scheme for political life. As stated by Louis Hartz, "judicial review as it has worked in America would be inconceivable without the national acceptance of the Lockeian creed, ultimately enshrined in the Constitution, since the removal of high policy to the realm of adjudication implies a prior recognition of the principles to be legally interpreted" (1955: 9). Yet the motivation to take a stand and bring life to certain facets of the tradition must be understood in political terms.

Political science scholarship contributes to the institutionalization by treating judicial review as if it were simply there. Stephen Wasby, among the best in political science literature for his attention to the minutiae of institutional life at the Supreme Court, focuses on the political sagacity of John Marshall as a source for judicial review, and although he recognizes that the power was not used much until the 1930s he says little about the intervening one hundred years in regard to the institution. Sylvia Snowiss, whose work on judicial review is more penetrating than Wasby's and raises more interesting questions about Marshall's contribution to the doctrine in its early years, goes no further than his tenure on the bench in examining the practice of judicial review (1981). Of course, there is extensive discussion of the propriety of this institution in a democracy (Wasby, 1984: 219–224) and there is a great deal of attention to the political uses of judicial review (Wasby, 1984: 59–64), yet in the end, as noted in the first chapter, this scholarship views the institution of judicial review as a fact rather than a construction.

Attorney General Edwin Meese challenged this understanding in the mid 1980s when he asserted that Supreme Court interpretations of the Constitution were not "the supreme law of the land" (1986). Speaking before a gathering billed as a "Citizens' Forum on the Bicentennial of the Constitution" in New Orleans, Meese began by invoking "all of the Founding Fathers" as authority for seeing the Constitution, and not the Supreme Court, as "the supreme and ultimate expression of the will of the American people." The intense criticism generated by the remarks— coming primarily from the legal profession—attest to the widespread belief in the Court's authority over constitutional interpretation (Levinson, 1986). Arguing that the Supreme Court's decisions only bound the parties to the case, Meese offered a rereading of the texts of American constitutional history from Madison to *Cooper* v. *Aaron,* where the Court in 1958 asserted ultimate authority over the law in America.

Criticism of the Attorney General and defense of the established tradition came from the president of the American Bar Association, who said that the opinions of the nation's chief law enforcement officer, if taken to heart, would "shake the foundations of our system" (Levinson, 1986). The president of the ABA was joined by the executive director of the ACLU, Laurence Tribe of Harvard's law school, Anthony Lewis of the *New York Times* (who spent a year studying at Tribe's law school) and Benno Schmidt, president of Yale University and former dean of Columbia Law School. The tone of the criticism followed that of the ABA president. Meese's speech was said to be "inviting anarchy," charting a "disastrous" course, "an invitation to constitutional chaos." While some supported the Attorney General, like the *Wall Street Journal* and Professor Levinson of the University of Texas Law School (for different reasons), the legal establishment was clearly upset by this assault on the Court as a cornerstone not only of modern constitutional interpretation but also of the legal profession's understanding of the Rule of Law.

Thus, judicial supremacy may best be understood in terms of the Higher Law backgrounds of the American constitutional law. In the name of the constitutional scheme, the Supreme Court exercises power over the other branches of government that the justices have solidified by careful manipulation of the authority given them and the mythology surrounding the law. Some manifestations of interpretive ideology that reveal how professional mysteries are linked to our understanding of Court and Constitution are considered in the next section.

INTERPRETATION

Inquiry into the authority of the Supreme Court to interpret the Constitution has obviously intensified. Widespread fascination with texts and interpretation involving scholars whose interests range from literature to psychoanalysis, the Bicentennial hoopla, and conservative assaults on the work of the Court, seem to have fed one another in this part of jurisprudence. Interpretation is a legal issue in flux. While traditionally it was assumed that a stable body of doctrine governed the decisions made by judges, more recently it has been accepted that judges make choices on idiosyncratic bases and manipulate the tradition to serve their political ends. The contemporary turmoil hints at future jurisprudential form.

Positivism in the study of law has nurtured a distinction between law and politics and the positive framework is replicated in many areas of contemporary jurisprudence. There are efforts to impose a new formalism that replicates economic calculations based on efficiency (Posner, 1985) and there is a movement to expand the political interpretations of the realists (Kairys, 1982). Neither of these serve the social scientist very well. So in the tradition of ideological sensitivity with which we began, we turn to scholars offering ways to describe an activity that is partially limited by law and partially discretionary.

Interpretive Communities

By addressing constitutional discourse rather than the rules or the behavior of judges, a new level of insight is being promised. In the ideological or ideational sphere of legal discourse, action is a function of professional practices because lawyers who speak to the Court and the lawyers who are the judges have developed a special way of speaking about constitutional rights. Claims under the Constitution have come to rely on language games steeped in professional experience (O'Neill, 1981). This "artificial reason" of the law has been around for some time but it has only recently become a predominately professional enterprise. The study of the qualities and the meanings in lawyers' "reason" need not contribute to the isolation of law, as traditional formalism has done. Nor need it degenerate into "trashing" in the manner of some modern realists (Kairys, 1982). Instead, we call for attention to the "interpretive communities" that dictate what makes sense and what it is appropriate to say.

The late Robert Cover, in a foreword to the *Harvard Law Review*'s survey of the 1982 term of the Supreme Court, offered a major contribution to debates about the nature of law and constitutional interpretation in "Nomos and Narrative." Cover's position is influenced by the realist and a response to social scientific perspectives on law. The striking thing is that he finds something "there" (in the traditional doctrinal materials). Cover's efforts are characterized by extraordinary skill. He is erudite yet relaxed in developing his view of a normative universe "of right and wrong, of lawful and unlawful, of valid and void" which he believes survives the critique of formalism. He does this with reference to foundations laid by Clifford Geertz (1973) and James Boyd White (1973, 1982).[7]

Cover's version of an interpretivist position bears on aspirations to a social science of ideology, because as a student of law he was particularly sensitive to the sources, "thickness," and force behind systems of meaning in the legal sphere. The work is described as "narrative jurisprudence" and it covers much the same territory as the ideological jurisprudence presented here. The primary difference is simply that work coming out of the law schools is strikingly inattentive to how narratives are constituted and hence constrained by communities of knowing participants. In the case of law, much of the discourse is professionally circumscribed. The doctrines and ideas of the law are open for manipulation by the lawyers, of course, but to the extent that they are grounded in social relations they have all the qualities of "artificial reason" as traditionally defined.

Robert Cover's optimism was not unlike the claims heard from the Critical Legal Studies Movement, which takes the view that after demystifying or "trashing" the law it is possible to make up whatever one wants.[8] Although the movement seems to rely on the elite law schools for the authority that is no longer expected from doctrine or argument, there have been some contributions from "CLS" to an ideological approach (Freeman, 1978) and there has been considerable soul searching about the nature of law (Klare, 1979; Trubek, 1983).[9] Alan Freeman's examination of equal protection draws attention to a perpetrator's perspective and a victim's perspective. His discussion penetrates the conventional categories to provide insight into the doctrine as social phenomenon.

Philip Bobbitt's effort goes a step beyond this, since he explores the ethical argument as a kind of interpretive tale, in order to show how it has been employed in constitutional discourse. He investigates how argument depends on tradition by looking at discrimination. Bobbitt draws attention to Thurgood Marshall's proposition concerning the poll tax, that "While a city can charge 15 cents to ride on a subway, people wouldn't want to put a dime in a turnstile to get into the voting booths" (*Harper* v. *Virginia State Board of Elections,* 1966). As Solicitor General, Marshall asserted that constitution prevented imposition of a poll tax. Bobbitt also mentions Archibald Cox's oral argument in *Shapiro* v. *Thompson* (1982: 129–131) to show how wealth discrimination exists at the boundaries of the interpretive community. The idea of protection from wealth discrimination has an ethical force for some, but it has not become a tenet of the community that knows the law unless something like voting or travel is involved.

Compelling and, in the present context, helpful discussions have come from Michael J. Perry of Northwestern Law School. Perry discusses the relation between text and intrepretation in religious communities (1984) and brings out how social relations distinguish ideas from practices. He observes that "religious tradition has ceased to live when (inter alia) the community that is its present bearer is no longer sensitive to the need to criticize and revise the community's form of life in the light of new experience and exigencies" (1984: 12). Attention to some source of meaning, even critical attention, is what constitutes a community. The focal point or, in Perry's terms, "occasion" is the sacred text with its "writtenness" and its "permanence" operating to constitute a community. The insight is not about the transcendent claims of the Higher Law tradition; it is in the necessarily communal nature of textual authority. As the Constitution has become the textual referent for such a community around the Court, the institution has grown in stature. Some would like to change that and expand the community.

Doctrines announced by this court on the Constitution have all but supplanted the text itself and certainly marginalized other authorities except those willing to give a special place to what the judges have to say. The Supreme Court has become the definitive source for the meaning of the fundamental law in America, and the judge as authority, rather than law, is as much a part of our life as streamlining and television commercials. Political scientists have begun to examine this situation. Sometimes drawing heavily on the interpretive literature in law schools and sometimes from their own authority, they have added a critical perspective to constitutional interpretation.

Neither Sotirios Barber's *On What the Constitution Means* nor Gary Jacobsohn's *The Supreme Court and the Decline of Constitutional Aspiration* nor Christopher Wolfe's *The Rise of Modern Judicial Review* accept realism. Consequently, although they were all published recently, they don't seem quite modern. Yet they ask us to reflect on lost practices, like a more general inclination and capacity to interpret the Constitution. This reflection illuminates the present. Jacobsohn begins with Frederick Douglass' view of the American Republic in 1852, which is linked to Martin Luther King's speech at the Lincoln Memorial in 1963 (1986: 1). There is also a vision of a future where constitutional discourse and attention to the constitutional aspirations of this republic become more common. Thus, they offer a great deal to contemporary law study. Yet one can hardly lose track of how different their project is from scientific aspirations for research about law.

These works share a tradition. They reflect a growing interest in institutional relations and interpretation as part of a constitutional structure (Murphy, 1986), but there are differences. The thesis advanced by Wolfe is that the nature of judicial review has changed from the initial understanding in the Constitution with a limited role for judges to a more expansive power. Barber's and Jacobsohn's position are more complex. Barber takes the Constitution seriously in a sense that is closer to Ronald Dworkin than Justice Owen Roberts. He says that he hopes "to persuade the reader that . . . a normative constitutional ideal" is presupposed in constitutional law (1984: viii). Similarly, according to Jacobsohn, the judiciary has lost its commitment "to what is permanent in our fundamental law" (1986: 145). He says we have lost our constitutional aspiration. That "growing interest" in new sources of interpretive authority and a new method and purpose represented in these works is central to this new interpretivism.

Wolfe describes the "rise" of modern judicial review through three periods. The first, or traditional era, runs to just after the Civil War. In this period Wolfe describes "a distinctively judicial power, essentially different from legislative power" in which the modern notion of judicial power was "unthinkable" (1986: 3–4). The discussion has some of the qualities of John Agresto's (1984) work but it is much more detailed and less wedded to contemporary policy questions about the role of the federal judiciary. Combining just the two pre-modern periods, Wolfe's treatment of the lost tradition of interpretation is longer that Agresto's entire book. The work, especially treatment of the transitional period, has a basis in political economy and ends with "the victory of laissez-faire due process" (p. 203). It relies heavily on established studies of conservative activism but hedges on the institutional fact that this activism, and not the

New Deal, is the foundation for the modern era. The section on the modern era, which presents the transition of 1937 as institutionally significant, seems wrong given evidence that the modern Court was in place well before 1937 and for reasons quite different from those that produced that political shift.

Barber's book is a call to look at more than cases in interpreting the Constitution. He emphasizes that "the Constitution is supreme law, not the word of the Court or anyone's opinion on the requisites for harmony within the government" (1984: 5). Like Wolfe and Jacobsohn, Barber challenges the authority of the Supreme Court by reference to the Constitution. This involves much more than mechanical jurisprudence. It is modern and does not advocate a return to a world unaffected by social research as Wolfe might encourage us to do. To do this Barber offers a new way of understanding how the Constitution can mean something independent of the Supreme Court that is reflected in Jacobsohn's look at the past by juxtaposing Roscoe Pound and the Founders. Jacobsohn does this in his first chapter in order to distinguish between what he calls community aspiration, like a "post-Watergate mentality," which might hold public officials strictly responsible for violations of the public trust, and constitutional aspiration, an embodiment in the language of the Constitution. This community aspiration is associated with sociological jurisprudence, while constitutional aspiration is associated with republican government. A consequence of this mode of inquiry is a presentation jarring at times and sometimes difficult to penetrate. Although this work does not fit into popular categories, the perspective on constitutional interpretation and the insights to be drawn from an expansive historical inquiry are important additions to public discussion of the Constitution.

By reaching beyond the dominant practices, these scholars thus illuminate some crucial issues in American politics that social scientists have taken for granted. One in particular is the nature and extent of judicial authority over constitutional interpretation. Jacobsohn devotes two chapters to judicial finality, one on Lincoln's view and another, his last chapter, that treats what he calls "the dilemma of judicial finality" in our time. The latter discusses S.158, the "Human Life Bill," drawing on legislative discourse to show the status of Supreme Court authority for Congress. This work is a model for social research on law and legal institutions as they structure social life and political discourse. Wolfe's treatment of judicial finality pervades the work, and he makes it evident by comparing present practices with those now lost. The political and economic developments of the late nineteenth century explain the "rise" of modern judicial review and these inquiries push considerably deeper than the traditional policy-oriented debates have pushed.

For all three authors the Founders matter, certainly much more than they matter to realist or sociological scholars in law. For Wolfe, the Founders had it right, the men who wrote the Constitution are "the source" and things have moved progressively downhill since they produced the Constitution. His picture of the Founders in the nineteenth century (1986: 216) is ahistorical and not as essential for saying what they meant as it is for establishing the theoretical turn he wants to make at this late date. For Jacobsohn, the Founders exemplified the crucial aspiration, but others represent the aspiration too, like Frederick Douglass, Abraham Lincoln, Martin Luther King, and maybe Archibald Cox. Very few contemporary constitutional thinkers make Jacobsohn's list—not, for instance Ronald Dworkin, Thomas Grey, or John Hart Ely. In the end, the model of constitutional aspiration like the "constitutional frame of mind" described by Barber (1984: 8) seems likely to prove more fruitful as both goal and basis for inquiry into constitutional practices beyond the Supreme Court than elevation of the Founders to apostolic status.

Another thing these scholars have in common, and I believe they all have right, is the view that realism has changed the way we see action on textual authority. Realism in law has undercut the authority of the text. Realism makes us cynical and it causes us to be self-conscious and ultimately to lose confidence in the capacity of meanings to guide and to constrain. Wolfe's historical approach is intuitively attractive. We are shown a change in practices and conceptions over time. This is easy to follow and the telling has merit until the author seems to be hoping that the eighteenth century can be recalled. Here we feel the power of the Founders for those of a certain faith. For Jacobsohn, the portrayal has a historical dimension but it is subordinate. His point is that something has been lost in the way the Constitution is treated. Yet the author gives the impression that what we lost is within our grasp, a contemporary possibility in need of nurturing. This is a little dreamy, but credible nonetheless.

The idea that meanings matter, especially in a scientific age, is the source of much of this new interpretivism in constitutional interpretation. The animus has been political as well as epistemological and one strand is conservative. We hear this refrain in the speeches of Attorney General Meese (1986) and it is diametrically opposed to Critical Legal Studies, and much of Law and Society, which still works with science at the core of its episteme. This is where Jacobsohn and Barber are so exciting and where Wolfe, with all the richness of his portrayal, stumbles on the right as Lief Carter (1985) has wobbled on the left. The work is sometimes a puzzle, but in its resistance to the poles of positivism these authors show that it is still possible to construct a viable alternative conception of constitutional interpretation.

These "interpretivists" are participants in a professional activity which assumes the fluidity of choice within a system of meaning. The application of this perspective to ideologies of authority and the relationship of these ideologies to the Supreme Court is a subject of ongoing interest. The significant interpretive communities for the Constitution see the court as the focus of authoritative commentary. The roots of modern communities, whether liberal or conservative, were evident in the New Deal struggle, but they go back much further. Changes in the Supreme Court and the ideological basis motivating it at any given time alter how we look at the Constitution. Thus, when the "Four Horsemen" of the 1930s stood against New Deal legislation, the Constitution was referred to by the conservative jurists in static terms and the justices described themselves as operating in mechanical fashion (Belz, 1978). As the Roosevelt Court broke out of this cocoon, the justices and the public developed a new basis for action, a "Living Constitution." The doctrinal contribution was the "double standard" and the standard was structurally tied to the process based justifications for institutional power. Although it changes, the Constitution is, as Karl Llewellyn noted, "an institution," not a matter of words or rules, but "a set of ways of living and doing" (1934: 17).

Process-Based Theory

Max Lerner placed the social foundations of constitutional government in "habits of mind begotten by an authoritarian Bible and a religion of submission to a higher power" that "have been carried over to an authoritarian Constitution and a philosophy of submission to a 'higher law'" (Lerner, 1937). Thus, in the political struggles of the 1930s the foundation was laid for a shift in the ideology of Supreme Court authority. Criticism of conservative formalism led to a process-based justification that would allow the Court to maintain its place as "the institutional church that incarnates the sacred document" (Levinson, 1979: 124). The debates, when the "double standard" arose, led to a new constitutional frame that would be monitored by the justices. Criticism of the "cloak of constitutional piety" and the "constitutional negativism" by which the Constitution was seen as a closed system accompanied F.D.R.'s reorganization plan and may have marked its most significant effect on the institution (Bradley, 1937: 92).

The shift, seen in policy terms as the "double standard," has affected the institution. The view that politics is part of the institution rather than something peripheral is ideologically linked to the struggles that led to a double standard. A consequence of the distinction in the Court's business between politics and economics is what Laurence Tribe referred to as "the puzzling persistence of process-based constitutional theories"

(1978). These are theories about the judicial function that justify review to keep the democratic process open. They hold that there is a legitimate basis for judicial concern at the constitutional level when some action "seems to obstruct political representation and accountability" (Tribe, 1978: 1063). A recent proponent of the "process-based" standard for judicial review, John Hart Ely, has argued that although the Warren Court appeared on the surface to be taking the "value-oriented" approach to deciding constitutional questions, theirs was actually an institutional jurisprudence. He wrote that "[T]he constitutional decisions of the Warren Court evidence a deep structure significantly different from the value-oriented approach favored by the academy" (Ely, 1980: 73). Ely points to criminal procedure as a key but brings in the Court's commitment to democratic processes, evident in activism in the area of freedom of expression and association, voter qualification, and malapportionment.

The conception of equality as a transcendent value rooted in claims about process has been described by a number of commentators as the basis for an extraordinary level of activism. Alexander Bickel's insightful phrasing of this claims as an "idea of progress" (1970) captures its essentially neutral tone. It was not, the Court asserted, a political claim in the normal sense that backed decisions like *Brown* v. *The Board of Education* (1954) or *Baker* v. *Carr* (1962). The values were in the process. Recent commentary, like that by F. L. Morton (1985) has shown the dramatic *institutional* significance of the Court's commitment in the 1960s to equality, particularly the eradication of racial injustice. Morton follows Bickel, but the power of his argument is in the extent to which it transcends doctrine and elevates the institution. Equality in the Warren period was not simply an argument in support of one side in a case before the Supreme Court; it stood as the basis for elevating and insulating the institution from the accountability we associate with "normal" politics.

The Court claims to be avoiding substantive judgment by relying on process. But there are substantive roots to procedural norms, such as the concern for privacy embedded in the Fourth Amendment. Process "determines almost nothing unless its presuppositions are specified, and its content supplemented, by a full theory of substantive rights and values" (Tribe, 1978). Due process rights, especially as they are becoming evident in the administrative context, rely on a substantive vision of what it means to be a person. Persons deserve respect and demand conscious attention. Even such a classic process-based realm as voting rests on presumptions about maturity, mental competence, and sex. Process-based justifications, while seeming simply to manifest the greater confidence in an ability to agree on processes than substance, do much more in institutional terms.

Ultimately, the greatest impact of process-based theories is the particularly strong claim they lay on the Constitution for judges in a democracy, or as Tribe puts it, "the impoverished relevance of the Constitution for everyone except judges" (1978: 1080). The theory and the "moral authority" behind it (Morton, 1985) would have us believe that judicial activism is an essential feature of democracy. Ronald C. Kahn has examined the process orientation in comparison with a claim of right (1984) and concludes that participants in jurisprudential debates generally advocate either one or the other and thus fall short in their ability to describe Supreme Court decisionmaking or constitutional theory. This analysis of the double standard in terms of the authority of the Supreme Court has tried to meet his challenge. The double standard that appears on the surface to limit the scope of judicial review actually establishes a contemporary basis for institutional legitimacy and sets the framework for substantive pronouncements on the Constitution.

Many have noted that the special place of the Supreme Court is tied to its power to declare acts of Congress unconstitutional. C. Herman Pritchett's observation on the consequences of this institutional practice is that "Recognition of the existence of this power tends to dominate all discussions of the Court, like the death's head at the feast" (1948: 72). Here we have emphasized the beliefs that give meaning to such activity. The double standard is an institutional practice that leaves economic policy to the elected branches of government while helping to assure that the Constitution will be left to the Supreme Court. Practices of this sort are the institution in operation, the terrain on which strategies for power are advanced.

In the political struggle between the President and the Court that boiled over in 1937, the authority of the Court in relation to the Constitution became the central issue (Corwin, 1938). The shift of 1937 is remembered as a turn away from the bad old politics of laissez-faire constitutionalism. In accepting this description we lose track of deeper significance for the Supreme Court. This is one lesson to be taken from looking at the ideologies of authority and the evolving justifications for judicial review. The "double standard" and process-based justifications like the enforcement of equal protection standards parallel the turn away from the myth of mechanical jurisprudence to a new myth of political jurisprudence. In accepting the view that the Supreme Court's product is simply politics, we lose track of the development of constitutionally significant doctrines like those surrounding privacy and the significance of the institution as final authority for the process of adjudication in America.

Doctrine and Action

The degree of authority to accord to comment on the Constitution by the nation's chief lawmaking body, Congress, has generated a body of scholarship probing the nature of constitutional interpretation. The growing debate in this area follows earlier work comparing the institutional authority of the Court and Congress (Pritchett, 1961). Whether or not the authority of Congress for constitutional interpretation can be established in the same sense as the authority of the Supreme Court, institutional action in Congress presents some challenges to judicial review that become obvious on closer examination. In Congress, acquiesence to the Court does not go so far as judicial doctrine suggests it should. Yet the Court's authority is generally acknowledged rhetorically.

In an article published in the *North Carolina Law Review* in 1983, Judge Abner Mikva contended that Congress lacks the political incentive and the institutional capacity to perform a meaningful constitutional analysis of pending legislation. Two years later, in the same forum, Louis Fisher took issue with that assessment.[10] Fisher, a scholar working for the Congressional Research Service, makes a strong case for a congressional role in constitutional interpretation. That case deserves consideration even though Fisher's language retains the conventional identification of the Supreme Court's view with the true meaning of the Constitution. This work shows that although the doctrine of judicial review is coherent and seldom challenged directly as legal authority, the practice of constitutional interpretation is shared between the branches with each contributing constructions. Greater recognition of the practice, as suggested by Fisher, may eventually change the doctrine, but for the moment recognition of the practice of interpretation by coordinate branches of the federal government is an appropriate conclusion to this inquiry into the ideologies of authority.

Fisher surveys a variety of instances where Congress has deliberated on matters of constitutional government. Judicial review, the Bank of the United States, slavery, federalism, treaties, and the legislative veto each provided examples of "coordinate construction," the theory that Congress can share in the process of interpretation. Fisher cites a number of grounds for the authority Congress possesses in constitutional interpretation. There is the oath of office. This involves a promise "to support the Constitution" and is particularly significant when legislation is being fashioned, but Fisher notes that here "of course" the Supreme Court has the power to "say what the law is." Another source of congressional authority for interpretation is in finding facts in the process of legislating. Deference to Congress of constitutional proportion has been evident here since

1937 in the requirement of only a rational basis for legislation in most spheres. Finally, there is the constitutional doctrine of political questions. Although not as powerful a constraint as it once was, at least in the case of Congress, from the war powers to constitutional amendments this doctrine sets out a sphere of judicial deference.

Actually, in only one of these grounds is the basis of congressional authority not still derived from judicial interpretation of the meaning of the Constitution. Debate over legislation is generally deferential, the rational basis test is a doctrinal matter, a judicial grant of legislative authority, and the political questions doctrine is one that the justices manage and are in the process of weakening of late. The oath of office lends support to coordinate authority in this area, for the President as well as for the Congress, who must decide the constitutionality of policy as it is made and well before it is reviewed by the justices. In the fall of 1986, drug-testing requirements and aid to Central American counter-revolutionaries are both examples involving the other branches in constitutional policy-making. There are other examples of this kind of practical interpretation of the Constitution revealed in the deliberations of governing institutions (Murphy, Fleming, and Harris, 1986: 184–195). But, in the area of doctrine, discourse, and argument, the Court does generally have the upper hand.

In practice, however, the situation is somewhat different. One of the very intriguing things about Fisher's analysis is its application to the legislative veto issue and the congressional response to the Supreme Court's interpretation of the matter in *INS* v. *Chada* (1983). This dramatic clash between Congress on one side and an alliance of executive and court on the other, reveals a great deal about the limited sphere in which the judicial doctrine of judicial review is authoritative. The legislative veto emerged in the 1930s as a mechanism for sharing authority between the executive and the legislature. It started with provisions for simple or concurrent resolutions but evolved to committee level. One of the most famous legislative vetoes is in the War Powers Resolution of 1973. Fisher's conclusion is that the level of debate in Congress on the legislative veto was "far more sophisticated and insightful on the constitutional issue than the simplistic and formalistic position of the Supreme Court" and his conclusion argues for "legislative confidence and judicial modesty" (1985: 725). This treatment denies either institution the "final word" and yet it leaves the authority for legal doctrine with the Court.

The result is a politics of elusion where congressional committees will continue to use legislation as well as informal and non-statutory methods to control administrative action even after their methods have been declared unconstitutional. Congress has continued to place legislative vetoes in bills presented to the President, and despite *Chada* they have been signed into law. There were eighteen such bills containing fifty-three separate legislative vetoes passed in the first year and a half after *Chada*. The result is not a constitutional crisis but an institutional reality of our constitutional system. Judicial decisions determine the legal terrain and they are part of the congressional debate. In this sense they can not be ignored, but like ideologies of authority generally, neither are they determinative.

Although it goes without saying, the Supreme Court has the last word on the judicial doctrine of judicial review. But it does not have the last word on the Constitution.. While the ideology of judicial supremacy, developed in the preceeding sections of this chapter, holds that a constitutional crisis is inevitable if the Court does not have the last word, in practice this is not the case. The very fact of an institution agreeing with the Supreme Court results in an institutional majority. When two of the three branches of government combine, the consequence is an array of political authority that is usually more than adequate to avert a consequential crisis of confidence in constitutional processes.

Because law professors have begun to acknowledge the rhetorical and ideological dimensions of their activity, the perspective from social science must be clear. By focusing attention on what the justices should or might do, the constitutional tradition is made an object of solely political consequence. Yet the tradition is much more. We ought to observe Cover's constituted nomos. We must comment on its circumscriptions. And we need to be aware of both the worlds that are lost and the new worlds that are being produced by law's authorities.[11] To do any less is to be governed by the cult of the Court. However, the conjunction of Court and Constitution, which has been a staple of modern legal ideology and political science, can be set apart. We have begun the process here by investigation of the ideologies of authority and the interpretive communities that maintain them. This foundation is central to the sociology of law (Hunt, 1983) and a basis for a scholarship about law and legal institutions that stands outside the professional projects spawned in law schools.

3

THE CULT OF THE JUDGE

B Y CONVENTION, the justices of the Supreme Court, at work behind
their bench in the courtroom, represent the institution. The picture of
the only nonmilitary government officials with distinctive dress (Frank,
1949: 254), robed and in place for oral argument or to announce opinions,
is an institutional icon. Quite often literally wrapped in institutional significance, the men and woman who have held this job were thought to grow
when in their vestments. Although other officials are elevated by their
office, when the justices are dressed to officiate at the Court, the submer-
sion of person into an institutional presence is particularly significant.
Now that tradition is changing. The justices are emerging from their robes
on occasion and their identity as political actors is widely acknowledged.

The tradition is symbolized by the "cult of the robe," a phrase used as
early as 1828 to describe the mantle surrounding the justices.[1] The cult of
the robe is entwined with the oracular myth "of the judge as a high priest
of justice with special talents for elucidation of 'the law'" (Murphy, 1964:
13). Institutional practices associated with this "cult" are the expectation
of independence and legal learning, traditions that established the special
place for the Court in American politics. As a focal point for the institution, the practice of equating certain characteristics with justices sets the
parameters for the play of interests at the Court. Here, perhaps more than
in any other aspect of the Supreme Court, the tension between an institutional practice and the interests operating in the political arena are at the
forefront. During nomination, appointment, and the evaluation of justices
seated on the High Court, the expectations we have for a justice inform
political actions.

For instance, debate over President Andrew Jackson's appointment to

63

succeed Chief Justice John Marshall, while intensely political, relied on a nascent American judicial tradition. The Democrats sought an appointment that would loosen control from Washington, or as Charles Warren put it, "curb what they termed the policy of prostration of the States" (Warren, 1937: 11/1). Not surprisingly, given the nature of two-party politics, the Whigs feared that Jackson's choice would be "purely political." The institutional reality was that the debate from both parties was conducted in terms of judicial competence rather than pure politics. In 1835, Whigs expressed their concern about Democrats' excesses according to the lexicon and practices that had already become associated with the institution.

The instant the question is asked and acted upon in the selection of an individual for that station—"Will his decisions be on the Democratic or on the Federal or on any other side?" Instead of—"Is he honest, is he capable?" that instant the majesty and utility of that great tribunal are destroyed . . ." (Warren, 1937: 11/2).

The choice of Roger B. Taney as Chief Justice was political, of course, but the choice and the debate over confirmation was tempered by concern about appearing excessively political where a justice was involved.

The iconography has been shifting from the cult of the robe. Once unknown and short on authority without their robes, the justices have been stepping out, and we can speak now of a cult of the judge superseding the cult of the robe. Just as the judicial temple in Washington reflects what is expected of justices, we see a changing institution in a changing picture of the justices. And while the debate over policy and institutional life is conducted sometimes in terms of "the robe" and sometimes in terms of politics, the institutional reality includes both. The reality today is a cult of the judge. It is not only on the cover of *The Brethren* that the robes are missing. From Sandra Day O'Connor's picture in front of the Supreme Court building in a pink dress on the cover of *People* (Oct. 12, 1981) to the Court's official publication, *Equal Justice Under Law,* which since 1975 has carried an informal portrait of the justices without their robes, a new cult has emerged to accompany the new Court.

To explore this dimension of the Supreme Court we examine the cult of the robe and of the judge, their characteristics as complex institutional practices, and the relationship of these practices to politics. We begin by examining the character of the cult of the robe and then turn to its manifestations in the appointment process and as a standard by which individuals are evaluated. The idea of a justice or, generically, a judge, is a configuration of practices relating individuals to the institution. These same practices also link the institution to the rest of the political culture when a justice is nominated to the bench and when his or her performance is evaluated. Appointment and evaluation are political processes, but they are carried out according to expectations of impartiality and learning. Prevailing all the time is not essential to the political significance of myth. Evidence of its existence as institutional practices is belief in these criteria as political parameters or constraints on action. The appointment of a new justice and the process of evaluation that continues even after he has retired is action according to what is expected of a justice. These expectations influence the daily exchanges of politics.[2]

THE CHARACTER OF THE CULT

Judges aren't accountable for what they do in precisely the same way that other government officials are. Federal judges serve during "good behavior." For the justices on the Supreme Court, this has come to mean life tenure for all practical purposes. This unique status (outside the academic setting) is tied to the cult of the robe, and this status-giving tenure for life places significant expectation on the business of judging. The conception that was institutionalized in the American judiciary of special people doing a special job was suggested in the defense of the constitutional system (Hamilton, 1788) and is evident in the tradition of idolatrous journalism that carries on into the present (Jenkins, 1983), where it competes with a new kind of pragmatic political reporting (Greenhouse, 1985).

Life tenure for federal judges had been approved by unanimous vote in the Philadelphia Convention. While it was more common at that time for political elites to serve for life, the view that this term was proper for justices we associate with William Blackstone and then, in the Founding generation, with Alexander Hamilton. Jefferson's argument that justices should hold office for six years raised some early doubts about judicial tenure, but Hamilton's conception of a term without a fixed end prevailed. In his defense of the plan of the convention, particularly in *The Federalist,* No. 78, Hamilton emphasized integrity and learning as qualities required of a justice. He proposed that in order for these qualities to flourish, a unique degree of independence was justified. This view became firmly entrenched in institutional practice over the years.

Two dimensions of the cult of the judge stand out. Both are associated with life tenure to one degree or another, and although there are any number of qualities that would be nice in these particular officeholders, two things constitute the justice as institutional practice: *independence,* including integrity and the absence of bias, and *learning,* including wisdom and knowledge. These aspects of what is expected in judges capture the dominant ideology of the judicial office. Rather than political acumen or writing ability and certainly more than speaking ability, we expect a justice to have the capacity to stand apart. In addition, we expect that a justice will have the ability to link his positions with those that have gone before. Thus we join legal learning to independence as the basis for the American legal priesthood. The cult quality captures the mystical dimension of these expectations, but it is not meant to overemphasize them. In fact, as we look to the exemplary features of the cult of the robe we can picture the new orientation taking over. The broad outlines of the traditional standard are suggested here along with contemporary developments. Application is the focus in the next section.

Independence

Judicial independence, as an institutional practice, is reflected in aspects of personality and preparation deemed essential to the judicial function. Independence, in this sense, has three elements. First, the justices can be called upon to exercise powers involving only the application of the law in decisions where differences exist. Second, the justices hold office as long as they desire. Third, "compensation" is not to be diminished during their term. These provisions constitute an independent judiciary. Without them we would not know what independence means for the judiciary. They are part of the institutional conception of American politics. They also have a significance fostering the perception that the state is at least relatively autonomous from powerful interests (Miliband, 1969: 138).

Throughout American history the concept of judicial independence has taken on its present character and became institutionalized because of the efforts of various boosters. Alexander Hamilton laid the foundation for emphasis on independent stature as a keystone of the institution. He considered the independence of the courts to be "peculiarly essential to a limited constitution" as "a barrier to the encroachments and oppression of the representative body" (1788: 575–576). Hamilton was far less concerned about the encroachments of the courts on the other branches than he was on providing a basis in the courts to balance the democratic strengths of the other institutions, and his dramatic description of this situation has stuck. The Court, he said, would have "neither FORCE nor WILL, but merely JUDGMENT." Something of an understatement at the time, this description is often turned to in explaining the significance of the unelected branch in American politics.

Sometime later in the evolution of the institution, as revealed by those who have commented on its place, Alexis De Tocqueville discussed provisions for independence as separating judicial power from the more political or corruptible institutions. He called attention to the protection of judicial salaries as a shield against corruption (1873). This concern would be even more intense in the late nineteenth century when the salary protection came to imply a distance from political controversy. According to Lord Bryce, "It is plain that judges, when sucked into the vortex of politics, must lose dignity, impartiality, and influence" (1891: 254). The institutional quality created by the Founders and developed by Hamilton had come to be a requirement of the person to hold judicial office.

In 1829, John Marshall addressed a plan for the constitution of Virginia with a plea suggesting the congruence of his vision with the present ideal: "The judicial department comes home in its effects to every man's fireside. . . . I have always thought from my earliest youth till now that the greatest scourge an angry Heaven ever inflicted upon an ungrateful people was an ignorant, a corrupt, or a dependent judiciary" (Cox, 1890: 19). Marshall's success in office contributed to the Court's independence, but not simply in the "uncorrupted" sense of the term. The boldly political nature of the Chief Justice's conduct suggests that the conception of a judge has changed substantially since his time. But the tension between politics and the cult was evident at the beginning.

In the case that exemplifies the claims he made for an independent judiciary, *Marbury* v. *Madison* (1803), Marshall as Secretary of State had set the stage for the issue in question by not delivering official letters of appointment for new judgeships nominated by the President. On another occasion, while presiding at the trial of Aaron Burr, Marshall dined with the defendant and periodicals at the time documented the conception that Marshall was later to repeat. They described his activity as "pollut(ing) the ermine of justice by coming into contact with an acknowledged criminal" (Cox, 1890: 18). The independence of most concern to Marshall seems to have been from the power of the other branches of government. It was an institutional rather than judicial independence or absence of partisanship.

Impartiality as a dimension of independence is a more recent institutional practice. The justices are expected to have had no personal involvement nor expressed any commitments bearing on the issues at hand prior to their resolution. This is a requirement unheard of in other areas of political life as revealed by the mere suggestion of corruption that threatened Justice Douglas's tenure on the bench and deprived Justice Fortas of his seat. This is also evident in the tradition of declining to participate in a case in which one has some unique and personal association. The practice is called "recusal." Some argue that by today's standards Marshall would have recused himself from Marbury's case (Wasby, 1984: 63). Yet in the modern period, justices have not always stepped down. Justice Black refused to disqualify himself in 1946 where a former law partner was involved in the litigation, and as associate justice, William Rehnquist sat in on at least one case that he had worked on before coming to the Court, *Laird* v. *Tatum* (1972). This action was one of the more significant issues to emerge during hearings on his confirmation to become Chief Justice.

Another dimension of independence is associated with excessive political zeal. Moderation of commitments and attachments appears to be part of the desired judicial temperament. Justice Douglas might have been viewed as flamboyant even if he had not been a Supreme Court justice, but against the somber backdrop of the Court, Douglas's passions shown all the more brilliantly. Frank Murphy, appointed by Roosevelt after Douglas, was even more liberal, his background more political, and his temperament more volatile. His dissent in *Korematsu* v. *United States* (1944), which upheld the evacuation and detention of Japanese Americans during World War II, was punctuated by some of the most vivid rhetoric the Court had seen. He spoke out against the majority opinion, written by Justice Black, as going "into the ugly abyss of racism" (Irons, 1983; Howard, 1968). The vision carried in this stance might have elevated Murphy in another branch of government or it might have simply set him apart. But Murphy did not fit at the Supreme Court and his relatively short tenure diminished the impact of his passion. Similarly, impassioned individuals have been some of the most controversial appointees. Brandeis and Black were strongly identified with controversial positions at the time. For Brandeis it was Zionism, for Black it was the Ku Klux Klan. Their commitments were one issue raised during the appointment process, but at least in the case of Louis Brandeis, this particular cause was probably a smoke screen for anti-Semitism (Auerbach, 1976).

The controversies surrounding life tenure provide another gloss on judicial independence in the life of the institution. Judicial service is terminated only by "An act of God or an act of Will" (Krislov, 1965). Both acts are unpredictable and the institution is affected when the continued tenure of a justice is in doubt. Some of the greatest controversies over judicial policymaking have arisen in periods of little retirement or an aging Court (Dahl, 1957). It is paradoxical that life tenure, the institutional factor most identified with independence, has been characterized quite often by the desire to "remain in harness" in order to fulfill political goals. Justices have often been attentive to possible presidential appointments in determining when to retire. This certainly seemed to be the case when Justice Douglas held on through ill health hoping to survive the Nixon-Ford regime. Whether for political purposes or out of a sense of institutional mission, life tenure has been a central part of the institutional life of the Court. Although it has been put to good use by individual justices in the short term and been a factor in how they are perceived, the significance of independence for the institution is harder to gauge. For one thing, it is difficult to separate from the other primary dimension of the cult of the robe, legal learning.

In the contemporary scene, the debate over activism and restraint has taken the place of more general concern for independence. The concepts hold that an activist judge brings himself and the interests he serves into the decision. The alternative position, judicial restraint, reveals how the debate has shifted. The issue is about how the justices chose to act and it is personal and political. Although suggesting a stance "above politics," the shift is to a judge rather than a Court above politics. Like independence at the more general level, restraint is neither liberal nor conservative, but unlike independence, the political implication of activism and restraint depend on what has come before, the body of law whether judge-made or statutory from which the judicial stance acquires its politics. A restrained judge operating from a received body of law that is "liberal," like the legacy of the Warren Court, will give the polity liberal decisions.

Learning

There was little organized legal education in the United States at the time of the founding. Nevertheless, in the *Federalist Papers,* Hamilton demonstrated his commitment to a type of "artificial reason" as a constraint on the men in service behind the bench. He noted that "a voluminous code of laws is one of the inconveniences necessarily connected with the advantages of a free government." The code, as rules and precedents, would bind the courts and keep them from arbitrary decision. According to Hamilton, "the records of those precedents must unavoidably swell to a very considerable bulk, and must demand long and laborious study to acquire a competent knowledge of them" (1788: 581–582). Ever since that time, the conception of the judge that we have has been linked to knowledge. But while the high point of Supreme Court power in the early twentieth century looked to legal knowledge, today we appear content with intelligence.

Immediately after the federal judicial system was established, an investigation into its workings was undertaken by Edmund Randolph, Washington's attorney general, who concurred in Hamilton's plan. His conclusion went as follows:

Those who pronounce the law of the land without appeal, ought to be pre-eminent in most endowments of the mind . . . a judge of the Supreme Court

. . . must be a master of the common law in all its divisions, a chancellor, a civilian, a federal jurist, and skilled in the laws of each state. (Frankfurter and Landis, 1928: 15)

Randolph concluded with what has come to be all but taken for granted today. He predicted that "Most vacancies on the bench will be supplied by professional men." This has come to be true to an extent and in ways that could not have been foreseen by the Founders.

Preparation in History. The change in legal training and the emergence of an organized bar in the life of the Court is essential to understanding the growth of the modern institution from the late nineteenth to the early twentieth century. We can assess that change with reference to justices who served for long enough to put their mark on the institution. By calling attention to justices who served for at least ten years in three distinctive decades, it is easy to see the changes that have taken place in preparation for the bench. I have chosen the Court's first decade, 1789–1799, a nearly central decade, 1870–1880, and a more recent but not quite contemporary period.

In the first decade of the republic the range of legal preparation varied, but none of it was nearly as institutionalized as present practice. The most common form of preparation was an apprenticeship to an established attorney or judge. It was also possible to attend lectures in law as part of university training. Reading the law in colonial American put young lawyers under jurists such as James Kent who had established something of a reputation. The effect of this practice combined British and local traditions, like the political system more generally. Study in England afforded an aspiring attorney an opportunity to acquire even greater depth in the common law. All these forms of preparation were grounded in the general cultural preparation required of men who would earn their living by their wits (and knowledge of tradition), and hence they were akin to acquiring the status of gentlemen.

There was no shortage of such gentlemen ready to serve the cause of federalism and the Constitution. The justices with extended service in this first period were men of prominence, and their preparation for the bench can be understood best in class terms. William Cushing had been Chief Justice of the Supreme Judicial Court of Massachusetts from 1777 to 1789, when at age fifty-seven he became one of Washington's original appointees. Cushing came from a family of jurists; his father had been a member of the Supreme Court of Massachusetts. William Paterson had been a member of the Continental Congress, a leader of the constitutional convention, governor of New Jersey, and coauthor of the Judiciary Act of 1789 when Washington appointed him to the Supreme Court. His legal preparation was a degree from Princeton and a period reading law with Richard Stockton. Another early appointee, Samuel Chase, had been Chief Justice of Maryland prior to his appointment. His background was middle class, as the son of a clergyman, and he had been a lawyer for thirty-five years before being appointed to the Supreme Court. Bushrod Washington came from more elevated circumstances. He was George's nephew and following education by a tutor at the home of Richard Henry Lee, he went to college at William and Mary. There he attended George Whyte's lectures on law in 1780. B. Washington was politically active for a number of years before his relatively early appointment to the Court.

Gustavus Myers, in his discussion of the class interests of the justices, traced the emergence of a "law making and judicial class" to the acquisition of large estates on which the gentry sustained themselves (1925: 43). More recently John Schmidhauser found that the early justices were drawn from families "rather clearly identified with the gentry class" (1979: 49). The gentry in the federal period often combined position with political and legal power but did not have the stability of a European aristocracy.[3] Although all these men had considerable experience with the law, none had the sort of "professional" education that has now come to be a prerequisite to judicial service.

Not until after the Federal or founding period did preparation approaching our present law school education emerge. It would be years before this development became typical of the preparation acquired by those serving as justices on the Supreme Court. The first justice to attend one of these schools was Levi Woodbury, who studied under James Gould at the Tapping Reeve Law School in Litchfield, Connecticut, in the first decade of the nineteenth century. Even though it was one of the most important schools of the day, Reeve's curriculum was little more than an expanded and systematized apprenticeship. Ten years later, Benjamin Curtis earned his law degree at Harvard, and although the present Harvard Law School traces its roots to those early years, law at that time was still part of the general curriculum. Another decade passed before Yale graduated David Davis and William Strong joined the Court. By the middle of the nineteenth century, future justices found their way into university law programs with greater regularity. Along with this change, they became subject to academic interpretations of the law. Only late did this setting become officially tied to the professional associations.

Following the Civil War, congressional resistance to Andrew Johnson blocked any appointments to the Court until 1870. Of the group that followed, all five—William Strong, Joseph P. Bradley, Ward Hunt, Morrison R. Waite, and John Marshall Harlan—served long enough to put their mark on the Court. Strong's father was a minister with eleven children. The future justice graduated from Yale and taught school while reading law for six months at his alma mater. Bradley came from an old farming family and was also one of eleven children. He attended Rutgers and also taught school before turning to law, where he became prominent in corporate practice. Hunt was the son of a bank cashier who attended law school at Litchfield before winning election to judicial office in New York. Chief Justice Waite was a little-known lawyer from Ohio described by Justice Field as a "man that would never have been thought of for the position by any person except President Grant" (Abraham, 1985: 130), but his father had served as Chief Justice of Connecticut. In 1877, President Hayes appointed John Marshall Harlan of Kentucky, where his father had been a United States Attorney. His law studies took place at Transylvania University.

This period was transitional. The era of corporate ascendancy would give a greater role to the professional manager over the gentry landowner, and although some would describe the members of the Court during this period as "from the 'better' classes of society" (Schmidhauser, 1960: 32), a large number who served for an extended period on the Court came from positions that were far from comfortable. The change to professional background begins to be apparent after the Civil War, but it was not until the twentieth century that the academically prepared lawyer supersedes the practitioner.

Of those justices appointed in the period 1950–1960, Earl Warren, John Marshall Harlan, Jr., William Brennan, and Potter Stewart served at least ten years. The backgrounds of Warren and Brennan reflect "humble" origins not generally associated with the Court. Here they can be explained in part by the democratizing influence of politics and by the increased status of the profession in Brennan's case. Warren had risen through public education to a career in politics, and Brennan had come to represent the combined promise of the ethnic vote in the East and the support of the American Bar Association through his endorsement by Chief Justice Vanderbilt of his New Jersey Supreme Court. Harlan was a Republican with family connections linking him to judicial service in a more traditional fashion. Originally from the Midwest, he had practiced law in New York City for twenty years prior to his appointment. Potter Stewart had been a member of a politically active Republican family and served on the Court of Appeals before his appointment to the Supreme Court.

From 1866, when Olver Wendell Holmes finished as the predecessor to the current Harvard Law School, those who found their way to the Supreme Court came increasingly to be educated according to contemporary practice rather than by the apprenticeship system of the past. It was not, however, until well over half a century after Holmes graduated that law school education became the expected form of preparation for practice. Indeed, the last judicial appointment to come from reading law was Robert Jackson, appointed by Franklin Roosevelt in 1941. He had only a year of formal law school before apprenticing himself in the fashion more characteristic of an earlier period. Since then, the expectation of professional training in law has become firmly established.[4]

Current Preparation. The contemporary Court reflects the importance of political and professional activity with little of the grand tradition in legal scholarship or practice associated with Cardozo, Douglas, or Stone. Former Chief Justice Burger graduated from a part-time law school and worked his way up through professional politics. Justice Marshall got his law degree from Howard Law School, just emerging from night law school status under Charles Houston when Marshall went there. Marshall is one of the few sitting justices who, like Brandeis, distinguished himself in legal practice before coming on the bench. Lewis F. Powell, Jr., personifies the professional practitioner, having been engaged in corporate law practice for thirty-three years before coming to the bench. In the process, his political activity included the presidency of the American Bar Association, the American College of Trial Lawyers, and the American Bar Foundation. As a corporate lawyer, Powell amassed considerable wealth and served on the board of eleven of Amercia's larger corporations. Brennan, Blackmun, and White came from either Harvard or Yale, and the newer, elite law schools count Rehnquist and O'Connor (Stanford) and Stevens (Northwestern) among their graduates.

The preparation now characterized in the cult of the judge is the ideological mold through which the members of the Supreme Court come to share the values that dominate the ruling counsels of American society. Judicial orientations are generally concealed by consonant beliefs on fundamentals with disagreement traditionally being superficial. In 1925, Myers indicated that "The influence so consistently operating upon the minds and acts of the incumbents were not venal, but class influence. . . . From training, association, interest and prejudice, all absorbed in the radius of permeating class environment, a fixed state of mind" (1925: 8). Well-established traditions determine the issues to be addressed and narrow the range of choice. The liberalism of Holmes, Brandeis, and Cardozo, for instance, was "well-contained within the framework of American capitalism" (Miliband, 1969: 139). Thus, the limited evidence of partisanship is due to pervasive agreement on the choices that are acceptable, and it is not surprising that students of the Court have found little evidence for the kind of bias that might link judicial background with particular opinions while on the Court. Professionalism has come to characterize the interpretive community. This gives new significance to the qualities of preparation associated with "Justice" and their relation to the authority of the Supreme Court.

Authority in the legal profession is increasingly shifting from learning and scholarship, of the sort associated with Holmes and Cardozo, to professional practice and institutional apprenticeship. The bar has long sought to preserve its place by the appointment of its own. Presently that means established practice as lawyer, academic, or judge. In this sense, as we shall see in the next section, the cult of the judge looks increasingly to professional standards and activity to distinguish the activity of judging from politics. Reading Hamilton's description of the Court as "having neither force nor will, but merely judgment," today we must understand judgment as an institutional phenomenon that owes a great deal to the American Bar Association.

THE CULT AS A FORM OF ACTION

Selecting a candidate for Supreme Court justice, gaining confirmation, and the evaluation that continues even after the justice has retired are activities governed by the institutional conventions defining the office. These activities have been carried out on terrain conditioned by the cult of the robe, the expectation of impartiality and learning in a justice, especially as it has been developing recently. Whether the outcome satisfies our inclinations, the mythology is significant in a political process conditioned by institutional criteria. We take life tenure and professionalism for granted so the process often appears simply political. The following discussion portrays the influence of the cult over political action. This process involves a volatile dynamic between participants, procedures, and views of appropriate action.

Appointment to the federal bench has two stages and is laid out in the Constitution. The first stage is nomination or selection by the President of the United States, which he does with the aid of the Justice Department, the FBI, and the American Bar Association. The power here is in the ability to choose, to put forth a name. With the Supreme Court the president has greater freedom than he does with the lower federal courts, where "Senatorial courtesy" holds sway. But Supreme Court appointments are a small percentage of the judicial appointments made by the President and crossover influences are inevitable. The second stage is confirmation by the Senate, which, the Constitution says, must "advise and consent." This veto power has been exercised twenty-six times, on nearly a quarter of the occasions the president has put forth a candidate.

The procedure, like the legislative process generally, begins in commit-tee, in this case, the Senate Judiciary Committee.

While the mechanism is essentially the same for all federal judges, the magnetism of the Supreme Court attracts much more attention to appoint-ments to the high bench. The appointment process, political by definition, is action designed to influence the choices and policies that are made in this country; it is also political to the extent that considerations beyond judgment come to the fore. Yet at all stages the process is informed by an understanding, an ideal of the Court and what a justice should be. This vision, this way of seeing what is possible, holds out the ideal of the impartial, learned individual sitting in judgment. Some judges are chosen, some passed over because of how they stand up to this vision. However, as we shift from the more romantic cult of the robe to the cult of the judge, evaluation has become dichotomized. The ABA employs the professional (e.g., legal criteria), and the President makes the political judgments. This, as we shall see, tends to circumscribe the role of the Senate.

Selection

The Constitution sets the framework and "usually manages to condi-tion the course and conduct" of appointment (Grossman, 1965: 21). This framework is realized through informal arrangements. The process cen-ters around presidential selection with confirmation as its goal. Appoint-ments to the Supreme Court are a subcategory of the larger process of federal judicial selection. Although the appointment of the lower federal judiciary is essentially a staff function, appointment to the Supreme Court is a policy decision left largely to the chief executive. Here, the driving elements are the bar, the press, interest groups, and the Senate as the body that ultimately decides. Hamilton argued that the possibility of re-jection "should be a strong motive to care in proposing"; but "the person ultimately appointed, must be the object of his preference, though per-haps not in the first degree" (Hamilton, 1788: 565). Since the legislative body can determine only how many choices the President must make, if they overrule his nomination the process begins again in a slightly altered context. Thus, the political symphony of selection is conducted under the authority of the President.

Assessing the Job. Without a sense of what it means to be a justice or any of the intermediate occupations along the way, no one would seek the post, accept an appointment when offered, or be in a position to serve in a "reasonable" fashion once appointed. What the Supreme Court denotes to potential justices determines the potential candidates. This perception is generally that the position is "special," the pinnacle of professional authority and a life's work. In a speech to the American Bar association, Justice Rehnquist, in 1976, expressed concern over who will want to be a federal judge given the present demands of the job. His point was that "the job description and the salary determines what kind of applicant you get." According to Rehnquist, the courts have "benefited from a perception in the legal profession that a judgeship was somehow more than the sum of its parts." This makes service on the Court something more than a job. Like professional work, generally Supreme Court service has its rewards and they stand out because they are so important to professional authority.

This has not always been so. George Washington had difficulty filling positions on the early Court because the institution had not yet established itself as a place for men of accomplishment and ambition. Five justices declined appointment during his tenure—two more than for the next one hundred years (Ewing, 1938: 15). The first Chief Justice, John Jay, was so disappointed with the job that he resigned after five years to run for governor of New York. Professionals with alternatives will of course avoid weak or declining political institutions. In addition, appointments to the Court are influenced by competition with private employment (Schmidhauser, 1976). Given the status of the Court for the last one hundred years, the response of Justice Miller appears to be the rule. Miller is reported to have rejected an offer to leave the Court for ten times his $10,000 salary (Fairman, 1938: 426).

Aspiration to be a Supreme Court justice can be characterized, at least in part, in terms of what it means to be a judge. The belief that individuals are elevated to the high bench, rather than wangling an appointment, is part of the cult of the robe; however, the extent to which the office is reached by aggressive, career-oriented political people should not be minimized. The judicial tradition does, however, set its own standards for judicial office-seeking. Unlike a presidential aspirant, one who seeks a federal judgeship never "announces." But the candidate who does not make at least a minimal effort to capture a place on the bench will not make it to the Supreme Court.

Although the appointments are political, the politics are directed at institutional practices and the setting of the judiciary in, and now above, politics. Washington's appointments reflected a Federalist vision. His choice of Jay as Chief Justice seems to have foreseen the Court in the midst of a struggle over federal power. Jefferson's appointment of William Johnson reflected the president's battle with Chief Justice John Marshall, and Jefferson must have been pleased by Johnson's emergence as the Court's first dissenter. Andrew Jackson's perspective on the Court was formed in struggles with Marshall that stand as the most heated to involve the two branches. Jackson's appointments, particularly that of Roger B. Taney, dominated the judicial system up until the Civil War. President Lincoln, although just as political as his predecessors, was a good deal more successful in getting his appointments through Congress than others were before or after. Andrew Johnson had his capacity to make appointments taken away by Congress when it reduced the number of sitting justices, eliminating any vacancies. Here, as in other conflicts, the debates were over the benefits or affects of an appointment on the institution and not the political consequences.

A series of appointments in the modern period set the standard for professional legal competence. The appointments of Oliver Wendell Holmes by Theodore Roosevelt, of Louis Brandeis by Woodrow Wilson, and of Benjamin Cardozo by Herbert Hoover, although political and controversial, nevertheless contributed to the contemporary perception of judicial competence. Political considerations are weighed against this tradition of expectations. Where politics has come into play too obviously it has been treated as a pariah. Always a factor in choosing among the possibilities, politics is kept in check by the tradition of judicial competence. Presidents Roosevelt, Kennedy, and Johnson made appointments with an affinity for friends and old political associates in the persons of such justices as Frankfurter, White, and Fortas. Richard Nixon earned a reputation for appointment by political philosophy thinly veiled as "strict construction" that was political in a less personal and more ideological sense. In his third campaign debate with Gerald Ford, Jimmy Carter expressed his preference for a justice in the following terms:

The emphasis, I think, of the court system should be to interpret the Constitution and the laws equally between property protection and personal protection. So when there's a very narrow decision, which quite often is one that reaches the Supreme Court. I think the choice should be with human rights.

President Reagan clearly balanced politics with institutional considerations in his appointment of Sandra Day O'Connor to be an associate justice in his second year in office. The pressure for a female justice was not only generally public, but it was institutional. The Court had never had one.

In the nomination of William Rehnquist to succeed Warren Burger as Chief Justice and the decision to bring in Antonin Scalia as an associate justice, the Reagan administration showed great skill in manipulating the institutional and professional factors. This gained the administration a great deal of political latitude. Chief executives with an opportunity for more than one Supreme Court appointment hear talk of a "legacy." This is particularly true where some ideology or style links the administration and the courts. One does not think of John F. Kennedy's legacy in terms of the courts because only one appointment remained on the bench for an extended period. There was so much to Kennedy's legacy that his appointment of Byron White remains linked more closely to the President than to the Court.

The second Rehnquist nomination in the summer of 1986 was initially treated by many as incapable of serious challenge, in spite of the extreme political orientation of the justice. This appeared to be true even in an environment of intense debate over the qualities lacked by the president's lower court appointments. The criteria alluded to by Attorney General Edwin Meese for the appointments were "intellectual and lawyerly capability, integrity, and a commitment to the interpretation of the law rather than being a lawmaker" (*The New York Times,* June 18, 1986). The final criterion reiterates the activism restraint consideration and articulates current qualities associated with the cult of the judge. Republicans praised the nomination, generally playing down the Senate's role in the process. While Democrats made a little more of the process of appointment, they too spoke as if confirmation was a foregone conclusion based on the nominees' "intelligence and integrity."

Proving the Rule. The rare case in which the vision of a judge, the practices discussed above, overwhelm nearly all political considerations tells us about factors that are otherwise muted. The appointment of Benjamin Cardozo to the Supreme Court was such a case. In the "purity" of its adherence to legal form the appointment reflects the cult of the judge. The appointment process begain in 1932 when Justice Oliver Wendell Holmes, Jr., retired at the age of ninety from the Supreme Court. This resignation left a large vacancy and a challenge to the President in the exercise of his choice.

The average period between vacancies has been two to three years, although recently it has been much longer. This is life tenure after all. Between 1976 and 1982, when Sandra Day O'Connor was appointed, there were no vacancies. The period has never exceeded six years. Like any vacancy to be filled, it has meaning because of what is around it. The vacancy in this story was that of the "judicial philosopher of the age," the Yankee from Olympus. He had served a very long time and had an extraordinary reputation. There was pressure to "fill" that vacancy rather than just make another appointment.

Some say there was virtual unanimity about who should be the replacement. I doubt whether that could really have been said about what went "before," but the appointment that followed was so extraordinary that one might suspect that it was somehow in the cards. The man who would make the decision, the President, was Herbert Hoover. He has been described as a "capable public servant," a great engineer, and a failure as a president. An apostle of "rugged individualism" and laissez-faire economics, he was not too popular as the stock market fell and the bread lines formed. Some say he would have made a great President at another time, perhaps in the nineteenth century. As it was he was defeated by Franklin Delano Roosevelt, and nearly forgotten. The thing he did well, more than once, was appoint Supreme Court justices. He appointed Hughes, Roberts, and Cardozo. As they say in the song, two out of three ain't bad.

The Cardozo appointment is the exception that proves the rule and demonstrates the vision that lurks in the background—the vision of a wise man, or in the sexually self-conscious language of today, a seer. The appointment was of Benjamin Nathan Cardozo in 1932, and it broke almost every rule in the judicial appointment book. The story begins with President Hoover consulting Senator Borah of Idaho. Hoover needed Borah in other respects and called him in to check out the list of possible nominees. Hoover handed Borah a list with Cardozo's name on the bottom and asked for the Senator's opinion. Borah responded, "Your list is alright but you handed it to me upside down." The involvement of Borah, the political figure, affirms a role for vision and ideology and a self-interest moderated by a belief in ideals.

First, Cardozo was Jewish. Most members of the Supreme Court have been Protestant, although there have been five Jews and six Catholics. This background was the exception at the time since two Jewish justices were appointed after Cardozo and there was already one Jewish justice on the Court. When Hoover pointed this out and argued that a Cardozo appointment might give rise to anti-semitism, the response from Borah was that there is only one way to deal with anti-Semitism and that is not to yield to it. Justice Cardozo's family had come to America in 1752. It certainly is not unusual to find a Supreme Court justice who traces his roots back to the early years of the republic. But Cardozo was also of Iberian descent, a Sephardic Jew, and all but six of the Supreme Court justices have been from northern Europe and they have been overwhelmingly Anglo-Saxon. Geographical representation has been one of the major political considerations behind appointment to the Supreme Court, and the justice from the New York Court of Appeals was not very appropriate in this sense. Although one-third of the justices have been from New York, Ohio, or Massachusetts, there is an expectation that the appointments be passed around, and there was already a justice from New York on the Court.

Another consideration, perhaps a more contemporary concern than would have been articulated fifty years ago, is family and life-style. Personally Cardozo was a very conventional man, but with the Supreme Court there is a requirement or expectation for a strong family life, and Cardozo still had his strongest family relations with his mother and his sister. Much later, one of the Court's most flamboyant figures, William O. Douglas, nearly got himself impeached for his life-style (and his politics) after he married a law student when he was nearly seventy years old. This and his ecological interests caused one conservative politician to describe the justice as a "child marrying mountain climber." The fact that Cardozo was not married emphasizes the extraordinary quality of his appointment. He lived with his sister and as a man of the law he had little time for a traditional family. The Court is not unlike the presidency in holding out the bourgeois family as an asset in attaining office.[5]

The strictly political is the last of the appointment considerations worth mentioning here. The nominee is usually a member of the president's party and in addition shares with the President those ideological proclivities that are said to matter in deciding cases. Nixon's appointees are a prime example of this. Justice Cardozo did not have these characteristics since he was a Democrat in the context of Hoover's Republican identification and very much a liberal as compared with Hoover's conservative stance.

The only way the appointment fit the political stereotype was that Cardozo was male and white (at that time one doubts whether even his extraordinary reputation in the legal community could have pulled him through if he had not been), and he was from an old politically active family. This has been more often the case than not with the justices. It is not a mere coincidence that we have had one John Marshall and two John Marshall Harlans. Sometimes the Supreme Court looks like a family business, John Marshall and Sons. There has also been a Washington and a Taft on the Court. Political people generally and especially political families have a special claim on Supreme Court seats.

Cardozo's family had had some problems prior to his appointment to the Supreme Court. Albert Cardozo, Benjamin's father, was a judicial appointment of the Tammany machine in New York, the machine of Boss Tweed and the Tweed ring. That is no disgrace in politics, but he got caught in a wave of reform and was held accountable for rendering certain favors like illegal naturalization, handing out courthouse jobs, and finally helping railroad entrepreneuer Jay Gould in a deal that allowed Gould to pick up another railroad or two. Albert Cardozo was censored and forced to resign. He died soon after when Benjamin was fifteen. This shadow of dishonor in Cardozo's background, we are told, helped to make him self-contained, polite, self-effacing, and such things that again do not help to fit him into the stereotype.

The future justice went to Columbia at age sixteen, and his record was the highest in its history. He went on to law school for two years and began to practice. He became particularly adept at difficult cases, someone lawyers turned to when they had questions about the law, a lawyer's lawyer. He was put up as a good government candidate for the New York Supreme Court and won. He rose to become Chief Judge of the New York Court of Appeals. It is his life in the service of the law and the respect he won that really explain the appointment process, not just the politics.

When Hoover was pressured to appoint Cardozo, the president pointed out there were already two New Yorkers on the Court. One, Harlan Fiske Stone, offered to resign to make a place for Cardozo. The wonder of this appointment is not that Cardozo was the most outstanding justice ever appointed. His impact on the Court was certainly not the greatest . . . perhaps because politics does in the end play the larger role, men like John Marshall, Stephen Field, John Marshall Harlan, Oliver Wendell Holmes, and Earl Warren had much greater impact. The wonder is the appointment itself, and while other choices have extraordinary facets and deserve special attention, like the appointment of Holmes or Warren, the appointments themselves are not nearly as good an example of transcending the political.

Holmes, for instance, was a war hero like Teddy Roosevelt, the president who appointed him. He was a liberal Republican like Roosevelt and he was from the same state as the man he replaced and he was white, upper class, and as experienced as Cardozo. But Cardozo's appointment was special. He was quiet and not passionately political. This is a quality I call judicial temperament, the impartial demeanor required of a justice. It is one that stands as part of the vision of a Supreme Court justice. The greatest appointment fights have been over partisans—Brandeis, Black, Haynesworth—and when it continued on the Court, it has had an affect on status, as in the case of William O. Douglas.

Another aspect of the vision is intelligence. We expect the justices to be a bit smarter than the average politician. Many were amazed, some stunned when during a more recent appointment struggle, that over G. Harrold Carswell, mentioned previously, Senator Roman Hruska claimed that Carswell's limited intellectual ability might indeed be an asset and that in fact mediocre people need to be represented on the Supreme Court. Others could argue that mediocrity is adequately represented in other institutions of government, but in any case it is not usually a criterion for appointment to the judiciary and it was not thought of as one of Cardozo's strengths.

Ultimately, the factor that best explains the Cardozo appointment is his status in the legal community. Cardozo's lectures and writings off the Court explained the law and how it worked. The most famous is *The Nature of the Judicial Process,* and his opinions are models of legal thinking used by others to explain the law. When he died, another craftsman of the law, Learned Hand, wrote: "He is gone, and while the West is still lighted with his radiance, it is well for us to pause and take count of our coarser selves. He had a lesson to teach us . . . a lesson at variance of most that we practice, and much that we profess." This was the lesson of judgment in its highest form, the tool on which the Court rested its claim to sit in determination of the nation's fundamental law. So I present this example as one that is typical in the sense that the vision of a justice informed the appointment; it is typical in its clarity and in its power, not in its importance for understanding the nature of appointment.

It is neither circumstantial nor happenstantial that this vision of a lawyer judge was appointed to the Supreme Court in 1932. This was a Court that in that year had established itself, at least up until that time, as the preeminent commentator on fundamental rights in America. This was a Court that needed a lawyer judge because it was as a lawyer's institution that the Supreme Court had come to power. It was as a professional's institution that the Supreme Court first moved into its own building, not in 1789, or 1813, but in 1937, right in the midst of Cardozo's tenure.

Professional Evaluation. A culture of professional criteria characterizes the appointment process in the modern period. The American Bar Association demonstrated, from its inception a century ago, a desire to counter the effects of democratic movements, usually in the states, to control the judiciary and thus encroach on what they contended was their prerogative (Auerbach, 1976). The ABA was formed in 1878 by the elite bar. The body matured quickly and by the turn of the century the association was able to announce that "The duty of the Bar is to endeavor to prevent political considerations from outweighing judicial fitness in the selection of judges." The ABA not only set standards but entered the selection process with their claim of special competence. In 1916, in a response to the nomination of Louis Brandeis to the Supreme Court, the anti-Semitic undercarriage of the ABA's conception of competence surfaced. A letter from ex-President Taft and six former members of the bar association protested the appointment. The attack appealed to "judicial qualities" (Mason, 1958: 33), a line that would become their stock in trade. The ABA asserted that Brandeis's "reputation, character, and professional career made him not fit to be a member of the Court." Although no formal mechanism had yet developed, the ABA was nearly successful in averting what they referred to as "the decay of Constitutionalism" and halting the "threat to old American stock" that they believed the appointment of a Jewish justice posed.

The American Bar Association Standing Committee on the Federal Judiciary was established in 1945. Its significance in nomination is tied to the standard of "professional" rather than political influences, but it has shown a conservative policy orientation. The committee instituted a threefold classification for the Supreme Court, after its embarrassment over the Haynesworth and Carswell nominations, which rates nominees as "qualified," "not qualified," or "not opposed." The weight of the recommendations is at least partially due to public acceptance of professional administration of standards. In 1956 President Eisenhower stated that "we must never appoint a man who doesn't have the recognition of the ABA." President Kennedy gave the committee less support and Nixon had a running battle with it. While Ronald Reagan had an increasingly intense struggle with the ABA, most of the action was around district court nominees. Indeed, it may have been that while the president lost a few nominees to the lower courts, the merit standards of the ABA allowed him to appoint extremely conservative justices to the Supreme Court. Although the legitimacy of the ABA's committee has varied with each administration, the tendency toward professionalism in the country suggests increasing influence for the bar.

Confirmation. The cult of the robe had an uneasy relationship with group politics in the appointment process; the shift to a more realistic cult of "the judge" makes it easier to accommodate group interests. The key has been a shift to minimum standards. Groups have been represented through influential leaders (as in the Catholic hierarchies' support of Pierce Butler); through group activity (as with NAACP support of Thurgood Marshall); through widespread agreement on group aims (as with the interest in a female appointee that let to the appointment Sandra Day O'Connor); and through obvious political advantage (the appointment of Antonin Scalia, the first Italian-American justice, in an election year). Group influence is maximized by defining the parameters of choice as early as possible. Where access is delegated to the confirmation stage, group influence is reduced to a veto of an undesirable candidate, rather than a positive selection of the group's choice. A further constraint is that presidential reliance upon the Department of Justice for information on candidates had led to a tendency to choose from lawyers who have had an association with "Justice" (Krislov, 1965).

The power of the Senate even in the case of the Supreme Court is not altogether clear. This became evident during Richard Nixon's first term.

In 1970, Charles L. Black, Jr., proposed that senators take an active role
in the confirmation process. The tradition, he said, was that "a Senator,
voting on a presidential nomination to the Court, not only may but generally ought to vote in the negative" (1970: 659), if, Black went on to say,
the senator believed that the nominee's view would make it "harmful to
the country for him to sit and vote on the Court." He emphasized that a
Senator did not have an obligation to simply follow "the President's
lead." The argument itself was part of the controversy over Richard
Nixon's appointments to the Supreme Court and part of the struggle that
arose during the hearings on the nomination of G. Harrold Carswell
(Harris, 1971: 94), indicating how understandings of the proper relation of
the other branches to the courts become involved in the ordinary play of
politics.

During the fight over the Carswell nomination, a coalition emerged
among senators opposed to the nomination. Their resources were standards of impartiality and competence; their strategy was to neutralize the
"natural pressure created by the President's backing" to get to a point
where the senators would be free to decide the issue "on the merits"
(Harris, 1971: 34). Carswell's decision reversal rate was used to create
this counterpressure. Of his eighty-four published decisions, nearly 60
percent had been reversed, "or more than two times the average rate of
the other judges in the Fifth Circuit District Courts" (Harris, 1971: 101).
And since it is generally true that "the rewards of higher professional
attainment and respect are reserved for those who have demonstrated at
least surface conformity to such regime rules" (Goldman, 1985: 73),
Carswell ran into trouble. Although resistance to Supreme Court mandates had been a local requirement in the South for a time, the reversal
rate became a measure of judicial competence. This measure is perfectly
correlated to the new institutional significance of the Supreme Court as
the ultimate authority on law.

Public activity in the confirmation process focuses on the hearings in
the Senate Judiciary Committee and the floor vote. Here, old facts are put
in new contexts. The facts become linked to the Senate and provide
points around which to rally. In the Carswell fight, an early deception in
testimony before the Judicary Committee eventually brought down the
nominee. The Rehnquist nomination showed the way nonideological or
institutional practices structure debate. Proponents of the nomination,
such as Senator Robert Dole of Kansas and Senator Orrin Hatch of Utah,
sought to tag Rehnquist's opponents as being motivated simply by partisan opposition to his political philosophy, thus implying that their concerns were not valid. Opponents like Senator Howard Metzenbaum of
Ohio spoke of the nominee's lack of "candor and integrity," referring to

the perception that the nominee had not come forth with the truth about his role in trying to keep black and Hispanic voters from casting ballots in Arizona when the nominee was beginning his political career. The integrity issue also involved evidence that Associate Justice Rehnquist had voted in a case before the Court on which he had worked as a member of President Richard Nixon's Justice Department. This violation of judicial ethics was the kind of institutional affront both to the Court and to the Senate, because it involved questionable testimony by the nominee, that opponents needed to secure moderate support in their effort to block appointment.[6]

Henry Abraham explained why the process results in the rejection of applicants, as it has 26 out of 137 times, in largely political terms (1985). Yet the politics he describes is a politics played out in an institutional context where frustration with the Court will influence appraisal of whoever the president sends down (or up?). The paradox of the cult is also evident since both political unreliability and involvement can cause difficulties with the Senate. Ultimately, however, qualifications as determined by professional standards will haunt a nominee or grease the process of appointment. The president depends on knowledge to fashion his choice. Such knowledge is provided by the Attorney General, the FBI, the American Bar Association, and sitting judges. The senators assess the candidate casually unless damaging information affecting their interest is brought out. The flaw must be both obvious and a threat to the interests of the legislator, and it must be evident in institutional terms.

The Senate is hampered in its inquiry into judicial orientation by a tradition that "Direct examination about pending issues is deemed contrary to the notion of proper role of the judge" (Krislov, 1965: 5). Recent hearings suggest some weakening in this institutional practice. During the hearings in the summer of 1986 over the elevation of William Rehnquist to the chief justiceship and Antonin Scalia to take his place on the Court as an associate justice, both Justices were pressed by opponents to elaborate their judicial philosophies. At one point in the hearings, Rehnquist offered the opinion "that a Senator should not simply say that this is not the person I would have appointed, that he does not share my views. [But rather] . . . have I fairly construed the Constitution" (*The New York Times,* Aug. 1, 1986). Of course, the political may be transformed into an institutional consideration as was attempted in the Rehnquist fight. As debate on the floor of the Senate opened, opposition senators sought to describe the appointment as institutionally divisive because of the extreme nature of the nominees' views. This would presumably be an "institutio-political" perspective.

Congressional action on a justice has its own institutional requirements, as set down by the Constitution and practice. When the Senate rejected the nomination of Clement Haynesworth, it established a new relation to the President and his appointee that affected the subsequent nomination of G. Harrold Carswell. Congress has trouble getting steamed up during the summer, especially in an election year. Thus, the early summer after the Court completes its term is the best time for the President to fill a vacancy—when an orderly resignation allows such planning. When Congress does act, like the rest of the appointment process, it is action in terms of what a justice can be. There is no institutional practice or convention whereby representation of mediocrity is an attractive consideration. The closer a nominee comes to the judicial ideal, the less significant the range of political concerns. But in any case, political interests are marshaled on a battlefield of institutional tradition.

Evaluation

The political view of the Court and the cult of the judge now dominates the evaluation of justices. But as in the case of appointment, evaluation of judicial service must come to terms with the standards associated with what it means to be a judge. The standards don't act as rules; they are part of the institutional perception and hence they ground the choices actors make. Perhaps because evaluation is generally a retrospective activity, it is more intertwined with the cult of the robe than selection. While craftsmanship and restraint are linked to success or failure on the "high bench," they mean nothing without the proper alignment to an "idea of progress." In this case, since evaluation is not presumed to be essentially political, the tradition comes clearly to the fore, setting out parameters for the political much more attentive to not backing losers than to not making waves.

Evaluation is an activity enmeshed in the institutional practices that constitute the Court. Those who study the court contribute to the cult. One survey of where scholars have placed the justices listed eight failures and twelve great justices (Blaustein and Mersky, 1972). The failures were Van Devanter, McReynolds, Butler, Byrnes, Burton, Vinson, Minton, and Whittaker, all serving in the second quarter of the twentieth century, a period deemed at the time to be an ebb in the Court's standing. The greats are more spread out, more likely to hold the Chief's chair, and much more effective politically, by the standards of 1972. They included Marshall, Story, Taney, the first Harlan, Holmes, Hughes, Brandeis, Stone, Cardozo, Black, Frankfurter, and Warren. Thus, the constituted reality of an increasingly political conception of the judge appears in these evaluations. Evaluation is sometimes a form of worship. Occasionally reverence for the institution becomes excessive, but perhaps as often, the greatest reverence for the institution supports critical evaluation, compelling discussions of the justices and of sitting justices offered in order to set them on another course (Bickel, 1970). The object of attention, with reference to the role of the cult in evaluation, is the shared vision of what constitutes a justice.

The Standards. One of the standards by which justices have been evaluated is craftsmanship. It has at least three meanings relevant to this investigation. First there is the "epigrammatic Holmesian" contribution, after Justice Holmes's impact on the images and metaphors we use to understand the law, like the crowded theater that shapes thinking about the meaning of the First Amendment. This is the least legalistic but not the least significant in its contribution to the institution. Second, there is popular contribution to the status of the law. This is the sort of quality on which both appointment and evaluation can be based; it is also the aspect of evaluation on which there will be most disagreement. Justice Warren would fit the standard for some, Justice Frankfurter for others, depending on how their contribution is viewed. Finally, there is the legal profession's determination of what constitutes a craft. Here, the emphasis was traditionally on careful reasoning, meticulous presentation, and an adherence to professional expectations. This is represented by Justice Cardozo, whose appointment has already been examined. More recently, Lewis Powell, a statesman of the ABA and a conciliator at the institution, fits this mold. These dimensions are brought together in a formulation of statesmanship associated with political science.

The initial standard for a lawyer's judge was set by Justice Joseph Story. One of only two nineteenth-century associate justices designated "great," his work on the Court was supportive of the paths laid out by John Marshall and thus was in line with the institutional ideal of reliance on the past. However, it was off the bench, in his writings and teaching at Harvard, that Justice Story established his position as a craftsman lawyers appreciated. The same was true of Brandeis, even though his appointment, like that of Cardozo, was controversial on other grounds. Justice Brandeis stands with Harlan as a man whose contribution was also to that brooding spirit of the law. Brandeis articulated seminal positions that eventually were represented in the winning side. His contribution to the law of privacy was developed in the common law context, brought with him to the Court and introduced in *Olmstead* (1928) as a dissent. His contribution to the evolution of legal practice was the notion that a legal brief need not be limited to the recitation of precedents. He offered this idea in *Muller* v. *Oregon* (1908), before he came to the bench. While evaluators will debate who fits into what, the claim here is simply that the basis for evaluation varies.

In the process of evaluation, independence is represented by two forms of mythology—judicial self-restraint and judicial statesmanship— each involving a dimension of independence relative to politics. The ideological dimension of judicial self-restraint was a reaction to the concern about the Court's conservative activism during the New Deal and an attempt to deflect the Supreme Court from its libertarian course in the 1950s (Auerbach, 1976: 259–262). Jerold Auerbach views the "advocacy of undiscriminating judicial passivity" as having taken the argument for activism out of its historical context and "elevated it to the status of an eternal verity." In 1958, Learned Hand delivered the Holmes Lectures at Harvard Law School and asserted the Holmesian version of judicial restraint in opposition to the active protection of minority rights then becoming established on the Court. Herbert Wechsler, who delivered the next series of lectures, treated the concern as a maxim that still occupies jurisprudential discussion. He advocated "neutral principles" that would transcend any immediate result that is involved (Wechsler, 1959: 19).[7] The ideology is embedded in the notion of a Higher Law, and its current significance is a function of the attack on that notion. Since professionalism could not claim special access to the law, it would have to proceed with restraint.

The continuing significance of judicial restraint has carried its founding fathers, Justices Holmes and Frankfurter, to positions of considerable esteem. Holmes stood against the Court's supervision of economic experimentation, and this position, along with his contribution to the Court's store of concepts, gained him a place of prominence. Frankfurter is more completely identified with the qualities of judicial restraint. As a reaction to the pre-1937 Court's anti-New Deal decisions, restraint became a characteristic of his jurisprudence. By the measure of judicial restraint, activists like William O. Douglas have suffered. As a political myth, the cult of the robe protects the justices by according them a certain distance from political pressure, but it has also served as a criterion for evaluating their conduct in office. In all these instances, craftsmanship has been associated with perceptible sets of values as well as a style of work and a depth of treatment (Atkinson, 1975: 353).

In opposition to the classic view of independence represented by the doctrine of judicial restraint is political evaluation that elevates the justices according to their ability to gauge the forces of change. A factor particularly relevant to evaluation of Supreme Court justices has been an ability to comprehend the demands of the polity and adjust to them. De Tocqueville described this political sagacity as *statesmanship*. He included with it the willingness "to brave the obstacles which can be subdued." The obstacles De Tocqueville observed, a little beyond the midpoint in the nineteenth century, were linked to the supremacy of the Union and obedience to law (1873: I/92). Contemporary observers have also tried to accommodate the judicial tradition to political life (Jacobsohn, 1977; Shapiro, 1977) by a conception of statesmanship. Gary Jacobsohn, following De Tocqueville, saw the capacity to account for public opinion without losing track of the traditional meaning in law as the central characteristic of statesmanship.[8] His discussion, one of the most compelling contemporary efforts to deal with the relationship between Court and Constitution, emerges from frustration with the normlessness of traditional social science and its inability to account for the role of belief and the ideal in the legal process. The work is in the tradition of Leo Strauss and Herbert Storing, and it offers statesmanship as an escape from the relativism that leaves us no basis for evaluating the justices.

Both independence and learning contribute to statesmanship, which requires thoughtful decisionmaking without the influence of "outsiders" and attention to the legal tradition within which the choice must be announced. Use of the law depends on an assessment of its bearing. Precedent must be seen in new terms, for even if the past is to be preserved, it may have to be reconstructed. Foresight is the basis for success in this endeavor and it is represented by thoughtful interpretation of tradition. Some justices have established a special place for themselves by their ability to bring the law into line with recognized social needs. Others have failed miserably.

The Results. Of the "great" justices, the first, Harlan and Black, had the "idea of progress" (Bickel, 1970). They were on the side that ultimately prevailed. John Marshall Harlan, who served from 1877 to 1911, was the other nineteenth-century associate justice who, along with Justice Story, was deemed great. He is known for his willingness to stand against the tide and for his perspicacity. Harlan's lone dissent in *Plessy* v. *Ferguson* (1896) makes him a revered forefather of the contemporary advocates of civil liberties. But this was not all he foresaw. His concern for due process was expressed in *Hurtado* (1884) and *Twining* (1908), dissents that anticipated the extension of the Bill of Rights to the states. Similarly he dissented from the inclination of his brethren to overturn social legislation in *Lochner* (1905) in a demonstration of considerable foresight. It was Harlan's perspicacity rather than his logic that carried the "great dissenter" to his present place of high esteem as justice. Hugo Black also achieved stature by his sensitivity to progress while on the Court. Although a former member of the Ku Klux Klan, soon after his appointment Black wrote for a unanimous Court in *Pierre* v. *Louisiana* (1939), throwing out a conviction by an all-white jury. His absolute interpretation of the First Amendment stood as a polar position on the extension of civil liberties as did his position on incorporation of the Bill of Rights. The Court never went quite as far in the first instance, but it went in that direction.

Thus, whether speaking for the majority or in dissent, justices whose position is ultimately favored are more likely to be judged great. While not a requirement for service on the Supreme court, judicial experience may actually be a handicap at least in terms of this sort of political judgment. The justices designated great are least likely to have such experience, and the next least likely are the near greats. Those most likely to have prior judicial experience have been designated failures (Blaustein and Mersky, 1972). It is not legal skill, pure and simple, but that skill as it contributes to the institution that colors the evaluations. Given the choice between skill and political foresight, the scholars seem implicitly to prefer the latter.

The role of political considerations is even more evident with those who have failed to correctly anticipate the nation's political evolution. In the cases of James McReynolds, William Van Devanter, and Pierce Butler, all were members of the reactionary "four horsemen" who opposed Franklin Roosevelt. This was a mistake by the light of recent history. Charles F. Whittaker in his service on the Warren Court voted against the extension of civil rights and personal liberties that became the hallmark of the modern Court and McReynolds, who was also on the wrong side historically, guaranteed himself a place of dishonor by his anti-Semitism. Van Devanter wrote little that might have saved him from the consequences of having clashed with Roosevelt and Butler may have been the least "gifted and most doctrinaire of the Four" (Abraham, 1985: 177). This won him the lowest evaluation of all the justices.

Other failures were stuck with the perception that they had been elevated to the high bench through the crony system. Friendship with those in a position to influence an appointment to the bench only becomes a real problem in the context of judicial evaluation when it is accompanied by incompetence. Harold Burton had been a senator with President Truman and won unanimous approval on his nomination, but he is generally recognized as having lacked both judicial craftsmanship and leadership capabilities, but he is nearly redeemed by his startling opposition to the president in the steel seizure case, which almost placed him above politics. Senator Jimmy Byrnes, Roosevelt's man in Congress, served for a short time on the Court and his own decision to resign after a year confirmed, if it did not lead to, the low esteem in which he was held as a justice. The last of the failures, Sherman Minton, went along in *Brown,* but that was not enough to enhance the judgment of the profession. It remained too obvious to those who observe the Court that Burton, Minton, and Byrnes would not have been on the bench if not for their relation to someone "up there."

The cult of the court, draws a group of professionals to the institution while the cult of the robe serves as a standard for appointment and a basis for evaluating their contribution. Closely connected to the state apparatus through artificial reason and the Higher Law, professional evaluation shields the justices from partisan comment while enabling them to channel the range of commentary. The very aura of mystery surrounding service on the Supreme Court functions for the state by minimizing "blatant partisanship" (Miliband, 1969; 141). Generally nourished inconspicously, defense of the tradition is always significant and sometimes quite passionate. This was evident in reactions to *The Brethren* where both the outrage from the legal community that such detail was revealed and the curiosity from the public made the book a bestseller. The passion was there when Justices Black and Harlan burned their papers to preclude scholarly assessment of why they acted as they did, which they believed might be detrimental to a traditional perception of a justice as serving only the law. The contemporary perception of a justice draws on the traditions of the robe, but it has become even more thoroughly wedded to the institution itself. The cult of the judge is a reflection of the institution, a manifestation of the cult of the Court.

4

THE INSTITUTIONAL SETTING

THE JUSTICES of the Supreme Court work in an institutional setting that is a complex social and political phenomenon; perceptions, practices, and actions constitute the Court and locate it in American politics. All these factors give meaning to the building on Capitol Hill in Washington, D.C., where justices and their staff gather. The building has come to signify political as well as physical location. For the most part, the factors that constitute the institutional setting are products of two professional interests, law and administration. These interests have been politically shaped into institutional form. And rather than stone and marble, it is the professional interests, along with the public and various political actors that delineate this structure in the American constitutional system. Judicial action on cases takes place in this setting and the setting gives meaning to that action. This chapter explores the institution by examining the forces at work in the construction and maintenance of the Supreme Court.

We begin with "construction" of the modern institution and approach it through interests and the ideologies of law and administration. The politicians who built a Supreme Court and its place in American life were craftsmen who worked with legislative detail, public knowledge, and professional interests in creating the institutional setting. As a construct linked to the requirements of the "new American state" (Skowronek, 1982), the Supreme Court's institutional setting combines professional interests with political realities. As a result it is integral to a state structure in which pluralism privileges interests over law (Lowi, 1969; 1979). The apparent contradiction, that the reign of group interests rather than law coincides with construction of the modern Court, is interpreted by further attention to emerging institutional practices that turn out not to be at all inconsistent with a politics of interests.

The resulting institutional place of the Court differs markedly from where it was before World War I. Not only have the justices moved out of their basement chamber in the Capitol to a considerably more inspiring facility; that place has become the end of the line for most legal disputes in America. This is new and it is pretty obvious. The Court has also become far more bureaucratic, inside and out, than it had been. This is not generally apparent but becomes evident when we look within the institution. Support for the Court's legal work—the Reporter, the Clerk, and the Curator, the public relations people, a legal staff *for the institution*—and the increase in policy support—the law clerks who draft more and more of the Court's product—belie the idea of traditional judicial authority and reveal a much more bureaucratic institution. The consequence, consistent with the Court's location in the governing structure, is an authority that relies less on doctrine and interpretation and more on institutional position.

CONSTRUCTION

In the Anglo-American legal tradition, courts were originally associated with both the extension of sovereign power and the resolution of private disputes (Shapiro, 1981). Reliance on fixed principles was an early feature of their authority. Medieval courts got their power from the king and took their law from the community. In the modern liberal state, courts established themselves in the political life of the country on a foundation laid by legislatures and depending upon settled political authority (Hurst, 1950: 85–86). Today the idea of a court, at least in the United States, is not easily separated from professional practices and professional practitioners, from lawyers and lawyer-judges. Yet the authority of courts in the modern American system of government has become a function of their institutional position—where they sit in an increasingly bureaucratic governing apparatus. Now, competing forces of law and bureaucracy, mediated by the political realities of American government, define and construct the institutional setting for the Supreme Court.

Law and Administration

Two professional ideologies have been central to the construction of the Supreme Court on the American political landscape, law and administration. The first, as the professional claim of an emerging group of practitioners with special competence in manipulating the rules according to which government was supposed to proceed, is an ideology of rule and a claimed practice of expertise. The second is a belief in rational management and a commitment to efficiency. Associated now with the state bureaucracy, it began as a program for the marketplace. The substantive interests contributing to the construction of the Supreme Court are law and administration.

The Legal Profession. The creation of a Supreme Court in the Constitution preceded the influence of lawyers organized as a profession, but eighteenth-century lawyers actively participated in the "Founding." Five of the most able lawyers at the Philadelphia Convention reported a proposal for judicial power out of committee (Cox, 1890: 2). A significant number, no fewer than twenty-five of the fifty-five delegates to the Constitutional Convention, were lawyers. Charles Warren reported that much of the adverse reaction to the plan drafted in Philadelphia among those who later became known as Anti-Federalists was "due to the fact that the proposed constitution 'was the work of lawyers' " (1911: 218). Lawyers continued to affect the Supreme Court as the growing press of business distinguished the Court of 1789 from the institution later in the nineteenth century.

By midcentury, because of the growth of the economy and the expansion of the population into new territory, a full-time bar emerged (Hurst, 1960: 257), and soon after that the interests of professionalism pressed for satisfactory institutional manifestations of increasing stature. These forces transformed the federal courts and provided for an extension of their powers. For Alexis de Tocqueville, the courts, which served as "the visible organs by which the legal profession is enabled to control the democracy" (1873: 289), were state courts deriving their authority from the local social and political elites. On the Supreme Court and off, Joseph Story led the movement for an increasing federal presence in the legal profession from "the institutional apex of a vast interlinked network of lawyers deployed throughout society" (Gordon, 1985: 5). In post-Civil War America, a commercially charged and increasingly bourgeois bar began to look to federal courts to thwart increasingly democratic and mass influences in the states.

Robert Gordon describes the struggle for the legal system desired by the post-Civil War bar, "one securing a formal equality of rights to own and exchange property in a competitive market," as requiring "collective action to reclaim lawmaking institutions from corruption by special interests and to strengthen their capacity for general rights definition and impartial administration" (Gordon, 1985: 38). For Benjamin Twiss, this was a dramatic intellectual and political effort to affect the governing institutions in the interests of new corporate elites (Twiss, 1942; see also Paul, 1969). Thus, the legal profession elevated the Court to a highly visible position as an expression of its political power. The institution remains dependent on lawyers as the group most attentive to its work.

The rise of the Supreme Court, along with litigation in general, is related to a peculiar modern political culture. Dispute settlement in America is highly correlated with professionalism, and once a society has a system of conflict resolution determined by a professional class, institutions tend to foster and preserve forms familiar to the profession. One characterization was offered by Arthur Koestler: "The inertia of the human mind and its resistance to innovation are most clearly demonstrated not, as one might expect, by the ignorant mass—which is easily swayed once its imagination is caught—but by professions with a vested interest in tradition and in the monopoly of learning" (1959: 427). Consequently, the number of lawyers affects the litigiousness of a society. In the United States, this group establishes the authoritative basis and the form of conflict resolution.[1]

Lawyers also play a more immediate role. They structure the adversarial process that precedes decisions. John Marshall is reported to have relied heavily on the arguments of counsel for the opinions that were purportedly the product of his pen. In the case of *Gibbons* v. *Ogden* (1824) Daniel Webster, counsel in the case, reports that Marshall himself acknowledged that he had simply repeated Webster's argument in his opinion (Chroust, 1965: II/284). The role of "law writers," the legal scholars, in formulating the principles by which the Court acts has been widely acknowledged (Jacobs, 1954). Their resistance to the development of welfare legislation was evident during an earlier discussion of institutional capacity. As noted by Benjamin Twiss, Thomas Cooley of Michigan's law school "organized the precedents into principles which by the skillful tongues of those lawyers were converted into the strongest antigovernment doctrine in American constitutional law—liberty of contract" (1942: 19). Doctrines like this on one side were balanced, politically, by developments like the Brandeis Brief, which allowed the realities of social life to be more fully presented to the bench (Krislov, 1965: 57).

The judiciary is an important group within the legal profession. They populate a rung in the legal hierarchy that is a route to the higher benches. They are also important for the attention they pay to nominations. Sometimes their views are solicited; sometimes they initiate suggestions. They have become central to the confirmation process, appearing at hearings and writing letters of support. Such was the case when Judge Griffin Bell, subsequently appointed Attorney General, supported the nomination of fellow Judge G. Harrold Carswell. The judges are often approached by the Attorney General as he gathers information on the competence and temperament of prospective appointees.

Another professional contribution to the institutional setting is the organized bar's role in the composition of the Supreme Court. The American Bar Association has exerted increasing influence upon the process of selecting justices and in determining the minimum standards of competence for appointment to the Supreme Court. The Special Committee on the Federal Judiciary, established in 1932, soon turned attention to Supreme Court appointments as a vehicle for influencing policy. The ABA's condemnation of the Roosevelt "court packing" plan in 1937 suggests that it was not the institution per se that was being defended in 1937, but rather the bar's view of good policy (Grossman, 1965; Westin, 1959). In 1986, as the debate over ideological appointments heated up, the ABA's evaluation along with judicial service, on which it is partially based, became the predominate measure of judicial competence, the primary foil for criticizing the politics in an appointment.

The bar also serves as a sounding board for institutional issues and a source of support for structural changes in the federal court system. Former Chief Justice Burger, in his annual reports to the American Bar Association, demonstrated the institutional significance of the link between bench and bar. The Chief's "Report on the Federal Judicial Branch" delivered August 6, 1973, is an example. Burger exhorted lawyers to support remedies for a system he described as "suffering from long-deferred maintenance and reliance on methods and procedures that are inefficient, outworn and inadequate to deliver prompt justice at reasonable cost to the consumers of justice." Burger's requests for additional judges in the federal system and a new level of court between the appellate courts and the Supreme Court were assured a forum for discussion and at least some bar association support. Yet the creation of the Court itself, at the pinnacle of a system of justice, is the legal profession's greatest achievement.

Bureaucratic Rationality. In the twentieth century, the move toward professional administration influences the Court's institutional setting. This has become most evident in the Chief Justice's office and the increased significance of the Judicial Conference. The ideology of efficient management has been brought to a traditional and somewhat hostile arena. Administration, an ideology like law, is, unlike law, a product of the industrial revolution, not the Enlightenment. Again, like law, administration has a professional base that organizes interests around shared principles and promotes ongoing institutional attention to these principles. They are just different principles.

As a facet of the institutional setting, administration shares many of the organizational attributes of the law. As with the legal profession, the Court provides a visible forum for the Chief Justice to lobby in behalf of the administration of justice. The Chief Justice's participation in judicial reform has become institutionalized source of change at the Court. In 1922, the Chief was designated head of the Judicial Conference. Chief Justices William Howard Taft and Charles Evans Hughes preceded Burger as conservative reformers working on structures to resist progressive influences on the judiciary. In a 1932 address, Hughes saw the purpose of the Judicial Conference as being "to diminish friction in the machinery of the administration of justice" (Fish, 1975: 130). Former Chief Justice Burger, characterized as a moderate on the Court and an activist off of it, made his mark by developing the administrative apparatus.

Burger conferred regularly with the President and Congress on the needs of the judiciary to such an extent that in 1977 a resolution was introduced in the Senate inviting the Chief Justice to address a joint session of Congress on the state of the judiciary. Congress has also considered delegating to the Chief Justice special authority in areas such as the promulgation of regulations with respect to the judicial branch on the matter of garnishing wages of federal employees (Amendment to Social Security Act, Sec. 459, 1977). The Chief's reports on the federal judiciary have praised the establishment of the ABA Special Committee on Resolution of Minor Disputes, mandatory continuing education for lawyers, trial advocacy training, higher standards for admission to practice before the federal courts, expanding duties for magistrates, abolition of the three-judge federal district courts, and screening of candidates for federal judgeships by the ABA. Recently, creation of a National Institute of Justice to further developed the administrative concerns of the judiciary as seen by the former Chief Justice.

According to an earlier generation of commentary on administration and law (Frankfurter and Landis, 1928: 7), Congress originally created "a hierarchical system of courts, not of judges." The consequence for the system was that no supervisory relationship existed among the judges in the federal system (Fish, 1973: 7). Perception of High Court leadership in administration is now an important link between the lower judiciary and the Supreme Court. A number of organizations generally established after World War II now seem to be institutionalizing this link. These organizations provide expertise, seminars, and information on the latest technical developments in judicial administration. They include the Judicial Conference, composed of the chief judges of each federal circuit, and one district judge from each circuit, with the Chief Justice of the United States presiding[2]; the Administrative Office of the United States Courts, which prepares budgets, supervises clerical personnel, and does staff work for the Judicial Conference; and the Federal Judicial Center, which coordinates education and training programs and undertakes research.

The Judicial Conference meets in the Supreme Court building. The conference has a place at the top. By setting the issue agenda and providing information, the Chief Justice has helped to create a third branch of government that reaches down to the local level. The Supreme Court also selects the director of the Administrative Office which supervises United States courts. Through this position, which is largely independent in day-to-day operation, the Supreme Court and the related administrative bureaucracy in Washington influence the issues affecting the judiciary. The Federal Judicial Center is involved in the development of computerized court management information systems, studies of sentencing, the use of jurors, and similar matters bearing on the administration of the federal courts. In this capacity, the Center has evaluated computerized information retrieval systems such as LEXIS and promoted new technology to a cautious judicial branch. Professional influence from the top is a new factor in the judicial system fostered by the prestige of the Chief Justice and is already altering the institutional setting of the Supreme Court.

Chief Justice Burger, in the tradition of his predecessors Chief Justices Taft and Hughes, aggressively applied principles of public administration to the judiciary. He did this with the help of his administrative assistant, Mark Cannon. Seen through an administrative lense, the Court's work and its institutional setting is being redefined. Cannon describes his responsibility as a careful management of institutional resources. He attributes what he calls the early difficulty with staffing the Court to the administrative chaos of the federal judiciary, in particular judicial responsibility on the circuit. Now, administrators focus on the caseload comparing the 92 case filings in 1840 with the 4,000 today. With increasing attention to matters of this sort, the Court identifies itself with its place at the top of the hierarchy of American courts rather than with its traditional product, opinions on matters of law. Thus, administration is a particular institutional manifestation of Justice Jackson's dictum, "We are infallible because we are final," but it is one that shifts the focus from traditional legal products to administrative process.

There is a connection between the claims of administrators for changes in the institutional structure and the interests they serve. Wolf Heydebrand has viewed the courts as trying to cope with a rising demand for services while being plagued by a relative decline in resources (1976). In public institutions, he observes a lag in the degree to which the work process has been "rationalized" through bureaucratic and technocratic measures for the sake of increased efficiency and productivity. The fiscal vulnerability of the modern state makes professional administrators powerful agents for institutional change. In the courts, administrative rationality conflicts with the legal-rational form of institution (Heydebrand, 1976: 2). Administrators favor the adoption of data processing, long-term planning on the basis of caseload forecasting, and changes in the organization of the workplace (i.e., the institution). Although bureaucratic conservatism is a facet of such changes, at the Supreme Court, technocratic administration redefines institutional traditions by trading off rights for efficiency. The characteristic form is more judges, more courts, more ways to deal with disputes, and less talk about rights.

These elements in the construction of the institutional setting, law, and administration have shaped the place at different times. Law dominated the institutional rise of the Supreme Court to the top of the "administrative state," and administration is transforming how the institution is known and ultimately how it knows itself. By drawing from the ways it is known and suggesting what the future holds, an ideological foundation is laid for the more instrumental political elements in construction of the Supreme Court, such as former President Taft's political clout and the boom in public building between World Wars I and II. While law is most dramatic for providing access from outside the institution thrusting it ever higher in the system of authority, especially relative to state institutions, administration operates from within the institution and the judicial process. Politics, on the other hand, is the crafting of these interests into the laws and codes, the blueprints and bodyguards that construct the institution.

Politics

The political institutions and interests that exist mediate the ongoing construction of the Supreme Court. The relation between the Court and the other branches of government fascinates students of politics (Pritchett, 1961: Schmidhauser and Berg, 1972; Scigliano, 1971) and sets the parameters for the institution. Presidential influence over appointment is only the most widely known of many factors. Other political influences on the institution appear in congressional control over jurisdiction and appropriation of the money to run the Court. These influences arise in contemporary controversies such as the attack on the conservatism of the present federal bench. They have been characterized as "any Congressional bill having as its purpose or effect, either expressed or implied, an alteration in the structure or functioning of the Supreme Court as an institution" (Stumpf, 1965: 382). Political influences generally acknowledge the existence of the institution. Yet the 165 bills designed to curb the

Court by altering its structure and the nine that passed dealing with matters of judicial review, court personnel, qualifications, the size of the institution, appointments and retirement, jurisdiction, contempt powers, impeachment, and the Court calendar (Nagel, 1973) *all* do more than etch the surface of an institution. Over time they have been responsible for the political construction of the institution itself.

Jurisdiction. Policy concerns generally appear first in the exercise of congressional power over the Court's appellate jurisdiction. In the nineteenth century, bills directed at a broad range of judicial action included the constitutional amendment that restricted the Court's power to adjudicate disputes between citizens and a state and denial of habeas corpus jurisdiction after the Civil War. Recently, legislation has been directed at specific policies such as school prayer, reapportionment, and court-enforced busing. Few of these bills, however, have become law and their policy consequences are a matter of dispute (Casper, 1976; Dahl, 1957). This change indicates the Court's stature as an independent body. Although we assume that Congress "could not so deprive the Court of authority that it loses its status as a 'supreme court' " (Krislov, 1965: 143), the legislators do have extraordinary power over what the Court decides (Hart, 1953). The more institutionalized a Supreme Court practice, the less it is subject to congressional action. But no practice is entirely immune.

Frankfurter and Landis called the steady extension of Supreme Court jurisdiction "a reflex of the expansion of Federal power, the growth of Federal litigation and the modes of its disposition" (1928: vi). The dual system of courts stems from the constitutional mandate and the Judiciary Act of 1789. In its Section 25, the act gave the Supreme Court supervision over state courts and established the "most important nationalizing influences in the formative period of the Republic" (Frankfurter and Landis, 1928: 4). Many states at that time still felt that their courts ought to be interpreting federal law, but the justices enhanced the power granted by Congress in *Martin* v. *Hunter's Lessee* (1816). There Justice Story argued that federal judicial power to make the final judgments on federal law would serve the interests of national uniformity best.

The institutional boundaries of the Supreme Court emerged as the relation between federal and state power was established.[2] Prior to that point, confusion between state and federal authority characterized the jurisdiction of the Supreme Court. The views of Rep. Coburn stated over one hundred years ago now seem to reflect a common understanding: "The United States courts are further above mere local influence than the county courts; their judges can act with more independence; cannot be put under terror, as local judges can; their sympathies are not so nearly identified with those of the vicinage" (as quoted in *Dist. of Columbia* v. *Carter,* 1973). Such wariness of the state courts, though common, is far from universal. Both in specific policy areas, like desegregation, and with reference to a more general desire for local autonomy, state courts have their loyalists, but they don't usually write about the Supreme Court.

The Court's decisions often reveal congressional influence on jurisdiction. In *Ex Parte Milligan* (1865), the Court granted a writ of habeas corpus after the Civil War to a federal prisoner tried by a military commission although he was a civilian. Congress responded by proposing to eliminate the Court's appellate jurisdiction. John A. Bingham of Ohio made the following threat in the House of Representatives:

If, however, the Court usurps power to decide political questions and defy a free people's will, it will only remain for a people, thus insulted and defied, to demonstrate that the servant is not above his lord, by procuring a further Constitutional Amendment ratifying the same, which will defy judicial usurpation by annihilating the usurpers, in the abolition of the tribunal itself. (Warren, 1925: 449)

Another bill would have required concurrence of all the judges in any opinion on a constitutional question. These responses suggest the range of possibilities. Neither bill was successful, but Congress did withdraw habeas corpus from the Supreme Court in 1869 (see *Exparte McCardle,* 1869).

In 1875, Congress gave the Supreme Court jurisdiction over civil cases under the Constitution or laws of the United States. Although the Court had claimed this authority for some time, with this congressional grant the federal courts "ceased to be restricted tribunals of fair dealing between citizens of different states." The Court emerged as a forum for the assertion of "every right given by the Constitution, the laws, and treaties of the United States" (Frankfurter and Landis, 1928: 65). The justices "further widened this domain" by their interpretation of legislation. For instance, in the *Pacific Railroad Removal Cases* consolidating a number of personal injury claims against railroads they ruled that since a federal charter of incorporation is a law of the United States, any litigation, irrespective of its nature, brought by or against a federally chartered corporation is a suit arising under the "laws of the United States" (Frankfurter and Landis, 1928: 69). The consequence was "removal" of the cases from state to federal courts.

Until 1889, capital cases could not reach the Supreme Court on anything other than a special procedure. But according to Frankfurter and Landis, "As practice became more prevalent for a single judge to hold circuit court . . . the finality of power of the single judge became particularly open to criticism in criminal cases" (Frankfurter and Landis, 1928: 109). Thus, in 1891, the introduction of criminal appeals to the Supreme Court was extended to all "infamous crimes." Responding to perennial concern about the Court's workload, Congress assured the finality of lower court decisions in most cases by leaving further review to the court's discretion (Ulmer, 1973: 124). Subsequent legislation, like the Criminal Appeals Act, "enlarged the domain of the Court's business and . . . brought to the Court each term an average of ten additional cases" (Frankfurter and Landis, 1928: 119). Decisions of state courts and circuit courts of appeals became final in certain types of litigation, and discretionary review by the Supreme Court became the vehicle for protecting national interests.

The "Judges Bill" of 1925 dramatically limited the Court's obligatory jurisdiction. The bill protected the institution's role as "arbiter of legal issues of national significance" (Frankfurter and Landis, 1928: 261) by eliminating the presumption that the Court would resolve all federal rights. Table 1 shows the changes in the Court's business that resulted from the legislation. By 1937, constitutional cases doubled those of a decade before and the Supreme Court had ceased to be a common law court (Casper and Posner, 1976: 30). The provision for direct appeal to the

TABLE 1
Subject Matter of Certiorari Petitions, 1929–30 Terms Compared with 1937–38 Terms

Major Categories	1929–30		1937–38	
	No.	% of Total	No.	% of Total
Constitutional law	121	9	232	14
Bill of Rights	9	—	12	—
Commerce Clause	0	—	20	—
Due process	103	—	147	—
Full faith and credit	4	—	9	—
Impairment of contract	5	—	13	—
Other	0	—	31	—
Statutory regulation under the Commerce Clause	127	9	88	5
Federal tax	314	22	259	15
Common law	230	16	238	14
Bankruptcy	61	4	144	9
Patents	66	5	108	6
All others	499	35	610	37
Total	1,418	100	1,679	100

Source: G. Casper, 1976: 21. Taken from Felix Frankfurter and James M. Landis, "The Business of the Supreme Court at October Term, 1929," 44 *Harv. L. Rev.* 1 (1930); *id.*, 1930, 45 *Harv. L. Rev.* 271 (1931); Henry M. Hart, Jr., "The Business of the Supreme Court at the October Terms, 1937 and 1938," 53 *Harv. L. Rev.* 579 (1940).

Supreme Court from special three-judge district courts has been a matter of more recent concern. These appeals had been possible in cases enjoining enforcement of state or federal laws on the grounds that they are unconstitutional. Judicial lobbying and a request by the Judicial Conference "to ease the administrative burden on our Courts" was successful in 1976. This legislation eliminated the requirement for special tribunals in constitutional cases and narrowed access to the High Court even further.

New federal legislation inevitably brings the Court into questions formerly left to the states. This has included suits brought by Office of Economic Opportunity lawyers against the states under 42 U.S.C. 1983. The federal code is full of examples that were once state crimes as automobile theft, bank robbery, and petty gambling. Between 1969 and 1977, Congress had passed forty-seven statutes that increased the work of the federal courts. The Burger justices, however, have shown an interest in use of the state courts to alleviate the pressure on the federal courts (*Preiser* v. *Rodriguez,* 1973). *Wilson* v. *Garcia,* decided April 17, 1985, refines this principle. The justices held that the time limit for filing Sec. 1983 damage suits against state and local officials for violation of civil rights would be whatever the state uses for personal injury suits brought under state law; this would generally be two or three years. By this sort of piggybacking process the institution shifts the locus of substantive law from Washington to the states.

Location and Composition. Although it was early in U.S. history that the Supreme Court was expected to concentrate on settling disputes rather than setting policy, what the institution would look like and where the justices would sit was less settled. During its early days, the United States Supreme Court even sat with a jury. In the case of *Georgia* v. *Brailsford* (1792), a special jury was convened to decide which of the parties could collect a debt sequestered during the Revolutionary War. After four days of argument, and having been charged with their responsibility by Chief Justice Jay, the jury returned a verdict against the State of Georgia. From the Court's initial preference for meeting in New York City to the latest wrangle over the distribution of support staff, the location and composition of the institution has been political. Today's conventions are yesterday's coups, and political action by Congress has created the institution as we know it. But because we know the institution so well (at least those who know it at all know it well), we forget how it got that way.

One boundary for the Court is the long-standing limitation on extrajudicial activities. In 1793, the justices refused to give advisory opinions and declared themselves unavailable for extrajudicial service. Thus, a unique institution developed in the United States. Russell Wheeler of the Federal Judicial Center has commented that "until the Supreme Court came to be viewed as a full-time job its members were easily drawn to other activity" (1973: 123). Ex officio assignments such as the appointment of five justices to the Electoral Commission of 1826 or the Chief Justice's position as a regent of the Smithsonian Institution are rare. The President has occasionally called on sitting justices for special service. Roosevelt sent Jackson to Nuremburg for the war crimes tribunal after the Second World War and Johnson placed Warren at the head of the commission to investigate the Kennedy assassination. It may well be that the modern Court, relying less on unique judicial claims than on institutional authority, will be drawn on more often for extrajudicial service.

Even after the Constitution had been ratified, Congress considered leaving the enforcement of federal rights to the state courts. The creation, instead, of inferior federal courts and their division into circuits dominated the institutional life of the Supreme Court for years. Beyond the transportation problems associated with circuit riding, circuit duties precluded an institutional presence in Washington. It was on the circuits that the Supreme Court was expected to do most of its work. In 1867, for instance, the justices spent a little over four months in Washington. Scholars of institutional life like John Schmidhauser report that Justice Story had many lucrative and complex arrangements that he ran back in Salem, Massachusetts, including a teaching job at Harvard (Schmidhauser, 1979: 129–132). Not only would the size of the Court be determined by the link between justice and circuit for the next century, but one can read from the events in the period that a federal presence in the states was deemed more significant than dramatic judicial institutions in Washington. In this way, the Court as an institution played a role in molding the nation.

The few cases presented to the Court in the early nineteenth century complemented their obligations on the circuits (Warren, 1911: 243). Since there were very few cases for the Supreme Court to hear, only five in the 1793 term, circuit work remained the primary judicial responsibility (see Table 2). Circuit riding was temporarily eliminated by the "Midnight Judges Act of 1801"; had the act not been repealed the next year, the Court might have been able to develop more rapidly as an institution. No doubt the arduous duties combined with low pay and the relatively primitive conditions in the new capital discouraged some prosperous and highly regarded lawyers from assuming a position as justice of the Supreme Court.

But Congress resisted elimination of circuit responsibilities in defer-

TABLE 2
The Circuit Burden

Justice	Miles	Circuit	Territory
Taney	458	4	Del., Md.
Barbour	1,498	5	Va., N.C.
Story	1,896	1	Mass., Me., N.H., R.I.
Baldwin	2,000	3	Pa., N.J.
Wayne	2,370	6	S.C., Ga.
Thompson	2,590	2	N.Y., Conn., Vt.
Catron	3,464	8	Tenn., Ky., Mo.
McKinley	10,000	9	Ala., La., Miss., Ark.

ence to the states. James B. Bowlin's arguments against a bill introduced in 1848 to eliminate circuit duties are typical.

Make your Supreme Court a fixture here [in the Capital], with no associations but the corrupt and corrupting influence of the metropolis; make them the drones of the great hive of American industry and American enterprise, and you will destroy (what is as essential in a Judge as legal learning) good old-fashioned common sense (Warren, 1925: 197).

The justices supported the bill, but Congress would not alter the structure. The Court responded by limiting oral arguments, formerly unconfined, to two hours on each side in 1849. The circuit connection was responsible for the change in Court size on seven occasions. In 1807, for instance, a seventh circuit was created to handle the frontier, and with it a new associate justice joined the Court. Increases in the membership of the Supreme Court would come periodically as "the territorial needs of the country for more circuits was met" (Frankfurter and Landis, 1928: 34). After the Civil War, as a slap at President Johnson, Congress precluded filling vacancies to the Court until the number of Associate Justices was brought down to six. A response in 1869 to the circuit riding issue was a proposal for a Court of eighteen, nine for the circuits and nine for Washington, with three shifting each year. Eventually, duty in the circuits meant little and the number of justices was set at nine.

Resources. Although appropriations are hotly contested in government, generally one seldom hears about controversy over the appropriations needed to run the Supreme Court. Like other items in the federal budget, expenditures for the Court must be presented to Congress each year. One or two of the justices and staff from the Court annually appear before a subcommittee of the House Appropriations Committee for funding to run the institution. This budgetary power is the most basic way the legislative branch exercises control over the Supreme Court. As part of the judiciary budget, money allocated to the Court (Table 3) gives some

TABLE 3

The Judiciary: Comparative Summary of Appropriation and Appropriation Estimates

	1976 Enacted to Date	Proposed Supplementals for Pay Costs	1976 Adjusted Appropriation	1977 Estimate	Increase 1977 over 1976
Supreme Court	$ 8,010,000	$ 118,000	$ 8,128,000	$ 8,371,000	$ 243,000
Court of Customs and Patent Appeals	853,000	30,000	883,000	893,000	15,000
Customs Court	2,587,000	92,500	2,679,500	2,705,000	25,500
Court of Claims	2,429,000	78,000	2,507,000	2,536,000	29,000
Courts of Appeals, District Courts, and Other Judicial Services	239,231,000	6,747,000	245,978,000	278,880,000	32,902,000
Administrative Office of the United States Courts	7,233,000	246,000	7,479,000	8,957,000	1,478,000
Federal Judicial Center	6,565,000	55,000	6,620,000	7,720,000	1,100,000
Space and Facilities	64,000,000	—	64,000,000	75,969,000	11,969,000
Expenses, United States Court Facilities	4,570,000	—	4,570,000	5,675,000	1,105,000
Total	$335,478,000	$7,366,500	$342,844,500	$391,711,000	$48,866,500

Source: Subcommittee on State, Justice, Commerce and the Judiciary, 1976.

indication of its place in the judicial system. At less than $400 million for fiscal year 1977, the entire appropriation for the judiciary was one-third that of the Department of Justice—and the Supreme Court collected little over 2 percent of the judiciary budget. These proportions have remained the same over the last decade.

The justices depend on Congress for their pay increases. These have, of late, been part of general pay packages. The justices get raises when Congress does. The legislators have not been suffering and neither have the justices. The raise of 1982 brought them up to $115,000 a year. The Constitution prohibits Congress from cutting the justices' salaries but in an inflationary economy that happens automatically. Funds for other items in the budget ranging from the Chief Justice's limousine to printing costs and extra staff have to be extracted from Congress. Justices White and Blackmun used to present the case for the Court before the House subcommittee on appropriations. White had the job for some time and reportedly was better able to tolerate questions from congressmen that some of his colleagues.

The Supreme Court is something of a bargain. Certainly by comparison with the key institutions associated with the other branches of the federal government, the Court does not cost very much to run, a little over $17 million in 1987 (see Appendix). The proportion of the budget that goes for salaries, nearly 75 percent, indicates the institution's human quality, while expenditures for printing, busts, and oil paintings demonstrate the continuing commitment in Congress toward appearances. As with its authority for the number of justices and over jurisdiction, Congress monitors the Supreme Court in its handling of the budget. Committees in Congress determine the level at which the institution will be funded. And although Congress cannot say where the money goes, the niceties of word processing systems and extra clerks, not to mention limos and police, are matters over which Congress has control.

To fully understand the setting, we need to understand the place and the workers who are the institution. In institutions, the workplace and work processes are as essential to the transformation of cases into law as the political processes are to institutionalizing the ideological thrusts of law and administration at the Supreme Court.

THE PLACE

It's simple but generally ignored: institutions are often places, especially in government in the late nineteenth and early twentieth century. Institutions were built of marble, with columns and pediments, great halls and great stairs. A story on the new building in the first volume of the

Federal Bar Association Journal by the Assistant Comptroller General of the United States at the time, Richard H. Elliott, reported that "No institution of purely human contrivance presents so many features calculated to inspire both veneration and awe" (1931: 13). Chief Justice Hughes identified the Court with the enduring American Republic, calling it "a symbol of its faith." He had less enthusiasm for the building, built during his tenure in office. Shrine and workplace, the structure itself has become the symbol of constitutional authority. Understanding the place we call the Supreme Court is essential for understanding the institution. We look at the building first and then the workers within.

From Basement to Acropolis

While the symbolic arrangements that constitute the Court were introduced through the metaphor of the building, the building has its own symbolic, even metaphorical qualities. A construction of marble, glass, and steel that "is" the Supreme Court for most people, the building was built to be a shrine. The embodiment of the Court in its own building incorporates a vision for the Court. The possibility of this embodiment, like the authority of the institution itself, is relatively recent. Its story reveals the process and the various social dimensions of institutional significance. Here, the legal shrine is explored through the almost religious aura that surrounds the building on the one hand and the orientation toward the institution epitomized by the homage to place in the familiar declaration, "all the way to the Supreme Court."

The Shrine. The Supreme Court wandered about the republic not only for the first years but until 1937, when its present home was completed. Its first session was held in New York City, in offices shared with the New York state assembly on the second floor of the merchants exchange building which was built over a market place at the corner of Broad and Water Streets. At that time, there was little reason to complain about the noise of transactions below since no cases appeared on the Court's docket for the first two terms. When the Capital moved to Philadelphia, the Court met first in Independence Hall, known then as the "State House." In 1791, even in these historic quarters, the young institution had only enough business to occupy itself for a brief two-day term. In 1796, the Court moved around the corner to the new City Hall, where the Philadelphia City Council had first priority on the chambers.

The move to a permanent capital city changed little about the institution at first. The layout of the new seat of government in Washington was to reflect the constitutional structure. There was to be a broad avenue linking the "President's House" to the "Congress' House." On L'Enfant's original map there is no mention of the Supreme Court as a separate "branch of government." There was a place for Treasury and the War Office, but all that was indicated for the courts was "Judiciary Square," a setting meant for all the federal courts and now used by those of the District of Columbia. The square received the same stature in the plan as squares for the National Bank, a national church, a playhouse, and a marketplace.

In his study *The Washington Community*, James Sterling Young commented that where the courts would reside "provided no avenues to render it accessible to either of its coordinate centers" (1966: 6). He went on to note that the square to be occupied by the judiciary was never developed, the expense being "unwarranted by the small size of the court establishment and the small volume of business handled by the judges during their brief stay in Washington each year," a stay consistent with their "minor place in the governmental community during the Jefferson era" (1966: 76–77). This situation suggests a different Constitution than the one we presently have. It reflects the greater influence of Jefferson, who was more involved in the planning of the city than such legalists as Hamilton (Caemmerer, 1970: 387). Further evidence of an early view that there were two rather than three "coordinate branches of government" was the competition in 1791–1792 to design "a Capitol and a President's House" (Frary, 1940). No plan for a Supreme Court building would be broached until 150 years later.

For the first years in Washington, the Court sat in a committee room in the Capitol. In 1810, it moved into chambers designed for it in the building's lower level. These chambers were shared with the courts of the district of Columbia in an arrangement similar to that anticipated by L'Enfant. Upon the burning of the city by the British in 1814, the Court moved to the home of its clerk, Elias Caldwell. It returned to the Capitol in 1817 and two years later began working in a basement chamber that it was to operate from until 1860 (Skefos, 1976). An observer writing in the *New York Tribune* in 1859 gave the following account of the quarters.

You walk along a narrow passage lighted with a dim lamp. You enter, and, crowded between two walls of old boxes, see a distant glass door, a general gloom . . . Descending two or three steps, you are ushered into a queer room of small dimensions and shaped overhead like a quarter section of a pumpkin shell, the upper and broad rim crowning three windows, and the lower and narrower coming down garretlike to the floor—the windows being of ground glass, the light trickling through them. (Warren, 1925: 361–362)

From these subterranean circumstances, the Court was relocated into the room vacated by the Senate on December 3, 1860. However, by the end of the nineteenth century, this too was considered substandard housing for a Supreme Court that was rapidly growing in stature. According to Charles Evans Hughes again, the Court, not the workplace, was the symbol.

Chief Justice Taft was primarily responsible for the construction of the present building in 1937. Having been the motive force behind such administrative reforms as establishment of the Judicial Conference and reduction of the obligatory jurisdiction of the Court, Taft had "little patience for the inefficiencies created by inadequate facilities" (Skefos, 1976: 27). The need for an "adequate" building was treated at the time as if it had always existed. Yet historical evidence suggests otherwise. Not only had such pressure not existed prior to the late nineteenth century, but there is little evidence that the Court was thought to need a symbolic place to do its work, in the manner of the "Chief magistrate" or the legislature. Justice, it seemed, could be administered wherever the judges were.

With "intense personal involvement," Taft lobbied Congress for authorization to construct a suitable building (Skefos, 1976: 30). The former president exercised control over the selection of the site, the architect, and the ongoing details of construction. When the building had been completed, it was described in the official guidebook as "gleaming bone-white and austere . . . its stately facade evoking the long glory of ancient Rome" (Harrell, 1975: 115). Like the other shrines in the nation's capital, the structure seemed to succeed in capturing the public imagination and stirring public spirit.

Located at 1 First St., N.E., the building is patterned after the Temple of Diana at Ephesus. The marble came from domestic sources except for that in the courtroom, for which the architect Cass Gilbert went to Italy and consulted with Fascist dictator Benito Mussolini. The massive frieze above the west entrance was described by its sculptor, Robert Aitken, in the Court's guidebook, with all the imagery that went into the new structure.

Liberty enthroned—looking confidently into the Future—across her lap the Scales of Justice. . . . On her right "Order" (the most active or alert of the two) scans the Future ready to detect any menace to Liberty. On her left "Authority" is shown in watchful restraint yet ready to enforce, if necessary, the dictates of Justice.

This is not all. There are other figures representing those who would give counsel and research. Everywhere symbol dictates form, from the massive marble halls to the massive bronze doors and the suspended stairway (no longer in use).

The bronze doors were sculpted in eight panels and like many other things about the building they were meant to convey the pomp and mystery of a tradition of legal authority. Their story is one of the emergence of the Higher Law. The Court's official guide describes the doors in the following fashion, hardly leaving an icon of the Western judicial tradition unmentioned.

First is the trial scene which the Iliad describes as being embossed on Achilles' shield. Two elders are giving judgment and a gold prize awaits the wiser. Others are: a Roman praetor issuing an edict, Julian and a pupil (the development of the law by scholar and advocate) Emperor Justinian publishing the codification of Roman Law, King John sealing the Magna Carta, the Chancellor of England performing one of his country's great legal reforms by publishing the first Statute of Westminster in King Edward I's presence, Lord Coke affirming judicial independence by barring King James I from sitting as Judge in King's Court, John Marshall and Joseph Story.

The temple is a testament to the law as a symbol for the nation. Indeed, the setting in which the work goes on demands to be assessed for its symbolic function. It is a shrine to which one million people come throughout the year, some as believing faithful, others simply as interested citizens. They climb the "Great Stairs" and pass under the inscription "Equal Justice Under Law" to disappear between the bronze doors. The building has the proportions Americans have come to associate with public shrines. Though its size is not overwhelming by comparison with other large buildings, in its nonfunctional, purely symbolic space it is impressive. The building proclaims that it is a court. The external symbolism is exceptionally detailed and the attention to phrase and figure unusual in office buildings—even by the standards of the nation's capital.[3]

Research based on public-opinion sampling suggests that a store of goodwill influences citizen evaluation of particular actions taken by the Court. "At any given moment . . . there is a general level of approval toward the Supreme Court which form(s) part of the political culture of the state" (Dolbeare, 1973: 203). This general positive feeling has been characterized as a "halo effect" that influences evaluation of individual action. Another image of the institution in American political culture is revealed in popular commentaries on Court decisions and activities. In Anthony Lewis's presentation of the Court, *Gideon's Trumpet,* the thematic image is that of the little man, in this case a small-time crook, blowing a call to freedom through (or perhaps on) this unique institutional horn.

Worship. The public also knows the Court through its actions. Supreme Court decisions rarely affect people directly unless they hold office or serve in some public official capacity. There are indirect effects, as was the case when the children in *Brown* had their schools opened to them by actions of the President of the United States enforcing the Court's order. More often, people are affected indirectly by appellate court decisions due to the influence these courts exert on issues like affirmative action. We hear what the law is or someone's interpretation of what the Supreme Court has decided.

Archibald Cox's chronicle, *The Role of the Supreme Court in American Government,* portrays American society as litigious and opens a discussion in which the author observes, "These characteristics reach their peak in constitutional adjudication by the Supreme Court of the United States" (1976: 1). Conflicts at law are perceived by many in the same way Cox describes them, as moving toward the highest court. This perception is evident in the seemingly obligatory assertion by serious litigants that they will take their case "all the way to the Supreme Court, if necessary." The expression reveals a hope for successful review as well as a belief in the ultimate legal authority of this institution.

From the beginning of the republic we can find arguments for a strong judiciary. In cases like that of Alexander Hamilton the arguments were supported by vigorous action that influenced the institutionalization of the Court. Judicial awareness of the public has existed since John Marshall first had the Court speak with one "voice" in order to heighten its authority (Krislov, 1965: 56). The Court has handed down unanimous decisions on recent controversial policy issues from desegregation to campaign financing. It has failed to achieve consensus in such controversial matters as the *Pentagon Papers* and death penalty. Consensus is only part of the struggle for judicial authority. During the Roosevelt "court packing" struggle, both the president and Chief Justice Hughes appealed to the public, one indirectly from his chambers, the other more dramatically from his "fireside." The perception is that Hughes was able to draw on a somewhat greater reserve of goodwill or support for his position. More recently, when President Nixon was brought before the Court over the subpoened White House tape recordings, the predecision politics revealed a jockeying for position relative to the public's response. When asked if he would obey the Court, Nixon said the ruling would have to be definitive. The Court, perhaps in direct response, presented him with a unanimous opinion that appealed to the institution's special claim to legal insight. Another factor, of course, was that President Nixon was not perceived as making a disinterested interpretation of the Constitution in support of his argument for executive privilege.

Not only are judicial orders felt indirectly, but the public receives secondhand information about them. The media and staff at the Court contribute to the public presentation of both cases and court activities but far less than at the White House or in the Capitol. Although it is no longer quite true that the Court "speaks once and then remains silent" (Dennis, 1974: 770), public relations have come recently. There is no TV coverage and little electronic media support in the building. Although called "The worst reported and worst judged institution in the American system of government" (Freedman, 1956; Friendly, 1978), the durability of the institution explains resistance to innovation in media coverage.

The Court's protective (legal) cloak has always stood between the public and the political institution. A decade ago most reporters were considered ill-trained because they were not schooled in the legal tradition (Dennis, 1974: 773) and fewer than five had full-time responsibility at the Court. However, high court journalism does rate a degree of specialization. Of the twenty-three reporters regularly including the Court on their beat in 1974, six had law degrees and the average time they had spent covering the institution, 2.6 years, is not an inconsequential tenure for a national reporter. Mark Cannon, as the Court's chief administrator, attributes "media ignorance" to the "great differences in style and operating methods of the Justices and the Press" (1974: 112). Where the justices work for months on opinions, reporters have them on the wires in minutes. An excessive need to show action in reports on the Court bothers staff people like Cannon. Reporters have begun to publicize the nondecisions of the Court in jurisdictional matters—no doubt changing the way the Court operates by this treatment of traditionally ignored activity.

As Chief Justice, Warren Burger instituted some changes in how the Court was reported. Soon after taking office, he solicited reporters' views on improvements he might make and was responsible for issuing headnotes to reporters, for holding an annual meeting with reporters about their concerns, the introduction of multiple decision days, and reduction of the amount of time spent on oral delivery. These changes may be responsible for discussion of televising oral arguments that have taken place since he took office (*The New York Times,* Nov. 14, 1977). Other suggestions surface when highly publicized cases come before the Court. Surprise reports that a decision in the *Bakke* case was to be announced led Fred W. Friendly (1978) to express concern that reporters did not have time to digest the opinions before they had to get the information to their newspapers. He called for prior notification. Although reporters have not been brought "inside" the institution, in the last ten years they have received considerable attention.

Whatever Court-influenced changes may be made either in the content of the information the media gets or in the methods of its dissemination, one's evaluation of events at any point will be influenced by acquired views about the Court. In this regard, Friendly's TV series, "A Delicate Balance," and the book that accompanied it tell us a great deal about how the national media wants the Court to be seen. Along with Anthony Lewis's book *Gideon's Trumpet* and Richard Kluger's *Simple Justice,* they depict in the detail of bestselling nonfiction the story that the inscription over the door of the building offers somewhat more tersely, "Equal Justice Under Law." Even *The Brethren* with its focus on revelation holds out, as a hope and the foil against which the writing is directed, the same view that the Court is where one should expect to find justice.

Staff Support

A staff shapes the business that comes to the institution and ultimately the views of the justices into "Court" decisions. A look at the staff is a study in contrasts between the public institution and the one that belongs to those who work in it, the dramatic facade and the routine tasks behind, and nine justices whose words are law and the workers who produce the words. Paul Freund relied on the traditional characterization of "Judge and Company" to suggest the assistance provided to the justices on matters of doctrine (1962: 146). The staff makes the Supreme Court more than the justices, in practice, enabling it to function and affecting how it works. The activity of the staff ranges from institutional support provided by the Marshal, through the legal work done by the Reporter and the Clerk, to the lawyers and law clerks who focus on the outcomes of cases. The personnel are links between the institutional symbol, the style of decision, and the policy outcomes handed down by the Court.

The justices emphasize that action by the Court is collegial and that the work is done by the justices themselves. Justice Harlan announced in 1896 that there were no such things as committees within the Court to which cases were parceled out, even to decide whether they would be heard; but that every justice considered and passed on every case. The end of the nineteenth century began a transition to bureaucratic operations, but the myth of judicial activity persisted, and sixty years later Harlan's grandson made the same point to members of the Bar of New York state (Westin, 1961: 8–9). The importance of the staff has been minimized and observers of the Court have continued to comment on its collegiality, lack of committees, or delegated power "except for the minor responsibilities which each justice has for his own circuit" (Hart, 1959). This inattention to the internal dynamics until recent years reflects the degree to which other symbols have protected the workplace.

A "cottage industry" perception of the Supreme Court, where the work is done by loving hands, is reinforced by comparison with the other political institutions. The extent to which the justices do their own work has set this institution off from other branches of the national government. The relatively small staff stunned Chief Justice Earl Warren when he moved to the Supreme Court from the governorship of California. Upon entering the Chief Justice's chambers, Warren found but one secretary, three law clerks, and two messengers. Consequently, the Supreme Court has a different style to its work in comparison with Congress and the President. The institution's significance is greater than its relative size or slice of the federal budget would suggest. The differential between its size and its power is due to the symbolic importance of the Court. Yet those who work at the Supreme Court, from the Clerk to the Curator, are shielded by this symbolic presence and guard it quite aggressively. The grammar school oratory about the majesty in the law and the Constitution is more significant to them than such traditions seem to be to the staff in the more political branches of government. Although the law business is widely recognized as political, it depends on institutional legitimacy that is not political. More evidently and perhaps more self-consciously, the staff makes a contribution to the institution and the institution gives us the law.

The staff appears exceptionally loyal. Many devote an entire life to serving the justices. According to Linda Mathews, who began a decade of revelations about the inner sanctum, one of the messengers, Archibald Lewis, served for sixty-three years while three generations of the Joice family worked at the Court as messengers over a period of 120 years. Identification with the institution is also due, in part, to the pace with which change has come to the Court. It had been barely perceptible relative to how much the White House has changed its operations for any comparable period. Xerox machines came to the Supreme Court in 1969. Prior to that time, internal memoranda were circulated by the author to his eight associates on carbon paper with the least senior justice receiving the weakest carbon, Subsequently, the pace has quickened. Computers were introduced in 1973 and word processing worthy of a large publishing house came shortly afterward.[4] The messenger's remain, a link to the period prior to the completion of the present building when the justices, lacking offices, worked at home (Mathews, 1974: 21).

The opening pages of each volume of the *United States Reports* record changes in the composition of the Supreme Court. Here, along with the justices, the Court lists its important officers. Looked at over time, the *Reports* show how the Court has grown as an institution. In 1870, for instance, the Solicitor General was listed, the same year in which Congress created the office. The Solicitor General joined the Attorney General and the Clerk as recognized officers of the Court. This group has since been enlarged to include the Reporter, the Marshal, and the Librarian. These officers, however, are only the more formal parts of the institutional, legal, and policy support now part of the institution.

Institutional. The number of employees of the Court has risen to over 300 in recent years. Most contribute indirectly to the maintenance of the institution and have little involvement in legal affairs or in the formulation of the judicial policy. Those who provide institutional support range from the seamstress whose job it is to keep the justices' robes tailored to a barber, secretaries, a half-dozen carpenters and electricians, janitors, fifty police officers, a nurse and retired medical corpsman, five printers, chauffers, and around fifteen messengers.

The group that runs the institution is the largest class of personnel, and their diverse duties reveal a structure more complex than conventional lore would have us believe but far simpler than those of the other institutions. The officers of the Court deserve special mention. Security for the building and for the public activities like oral argument is handled by the Marshal. Through this office one learns where to walk quietly and where one cannot tread at all, although it is still easier to wander the halls of this institution than the other branches of the federal government. The Marshal is also influential in determining access to the justices and to the records of the Court. He coordinates ceremonial events for the Supreme Court, such as the installation of new justices and memorial ceremonies for those who have died. Most evident is the Marshal's role at oral argument when he announces that the Court is in session and runs the time-clock that cuts off lawyers inclined to speak beyond their allotment.

Although the collection that was to become the Library of Congress was established in 1800, "no provisions were made for law books for the justices until the twenty-third year of the Court's existence" (Sprince, 1976: 2). In 1801, Congress even voted down a proposal for judicial use of the new Library of Congress. In the early years, the clerk was in charge of the library. Beginning in 1845, the justices had access to two sets of law books. One was kept in the Conference Room as a source of citations to support collective discussion. The other resided in the justices' homes where they did their work (Sprince, 1976: 5). The Office of the Libarian of the Court was established by Congress in 1948. The librarian is an institutional fixture identified with the maintenance of tradition and the resources required for research. The library had a staff of twenty-three people in 1984. Its research staff of five included three lawyers and one Ph.d. The services in the library include the computerized reference tools of LEGIS, WESTLAW, AND LEXIS. Located next to the Library of Congress, the Court is less in need of a general reference collection than most institutions but it has a strong one in areas such as abortion, administration of justice, and Indian affairs, in which the justices do a lot of work. It is because the library is a research library rather than an archive that the Libarian needs to be seen in terms of the institutional support he provides.

Until recently, the librarian was responsible for preserving the identity and stature of the institution in what was written about the Court. Now, the Court employs a Curator, an office created at the suggestion of the former Chief Justice Burger. Its focus on institutional history has eased the Librarian's burden of monitoring the Court's public image. The Curator sponsors exhibits in the halls that range from the traditional portraits of the justices to presentations highlighting such institutional events as the construction of the building itself. One recent display, in honor of the late Hugo Black, included tape recordings of his views on the Constitution and the role of the justices, and cartoons portraying major events that occurred during his tenure. The display on building the present structure included letters from the justices resisting placement of the new courthouse near the tidal basin because of its distance from the mainstream of political life in the capital. These displays and the office itself demonstrate a new sensitivity to the cultivation of an image that has in the past seemed to take care of itself.

Perception of the Court is attended to by the Public Information Officer. This position, formerly described as Press Officer, still concentrates on the various media representatives who cover the institution, from those ten to fifteen who "encamp" in the pressroom full-time to the close to fifty reporters who cover the Court as only one of their responsibilities. Toni House, the enthusiastic incumbent, is a professional woman with a background in journalism who reflects the modern institution. She distributes slip opinions to the press on opinion day, publishes the Court's house newsletter, and monitors admission to the Court's public hearings. She shares with her predecessors a confidence that institutional tradition is the strongest public relations. But doors that are initially more open—the outer doors—than those of other institutions can close decisively on correspondents whose articles do not reflect well on the institution.

The Chief Justice has spent more time than most of his predecessors on duties influencing the operation of the institution and the judicial branch. One of his many innovations was the creation of an Administrative Office by act of Congress in 1972. When Mark Cannon took the job as the first Administrative Assistant to the Chief Justice, he reported that his mind "boggled as the Chief Justice detailed his administrative responsibilities . . . as head of one of the three branches of government, with a personal staff smaller than any freshman Congressman's" (Cannon, 1974: 109). The staff now includes a secretary and two professionals from the

Judicial Fellows Program who work temporarily but have sometimes been asked to stay on to help with various tasks of legal administration. The office handles matters not directly related to the decision of cases, such as preparation for the budget hearings. In addition, the Administrative Assistant counsels the Chief Justice on such matters as appointment to the Judicial Conference and various regular and special committees. The staff in the office also helps to write speeches delivered by the Chief Justice at meetings of the Judicial Conference or the American Bar Association, and it assists in planning for the Courts and formulates policy for the research staff at the Federal Judicial Center.

From the Marshal to the Public Information Officer, those who maintain "the place" reflect both continuity and change in the institution. Being wedded to its symbols, the Court has been the last of the national institutions to modernize. But in a decade the institution has leaped from the nineteenth well into the twentieth century. The Curator preserves the past, but in an ever more public way, and the Administrative Assistant epitomizes the push toward management science that reflects the foundations of modern political power.

Legal. The Clerk, the Reporter, and the Legal Officers make up the legal staff at the Court. They differ from those providing institutional support in that their involvement is primarily with legal matters. Their work maintains the legal rituals of particular relevance to lawyers. The tasks range from the formal requirements for submission of a case to dissemination of the decision. Unlike the clerks to the justices and the appellate advocates, those providing legal support to the institution are not directly concerned with the policy reflected in the cases before the Court. They support the institution by influencing the way the Supreme Court handles its legal business. Evolving from informality to increasing bureaucratization, the legal support has grown in number as well as in the degree of specialization of the tasks performed.

The last Clerk, Michael Rodak, held the position for nearly three decades. He was replaced by Joseph Spaniol, the seventeenth clerk in the history of the institution. The Clerk supervises a staff of nearly fifty made up of career appointees who carry out very different functions from those of the justices' individual law clerks. The staff sorts petitions and collects the $100 docketing fee. The fee initially supported the entire office as well as lawyers for indigents, giving the institution a little autonomy from Congress. Now, the fees, totaling over $200,000 a year, go into the Treasury, and the office, like the rest of the Court, is supported out of the general budget of the United States (Williams, 1977: 46).

An appeal to the Court must be filed by a certain date after the lower court has made its decision. The Clerk's office makes the initial determination in cases of delayed appeal and can reject cases as "out of time." The Clerk's office decides whether a petition is in proper form and the person against whom an appeal is made is notified by the office of his or her opportunity to respond. In the case of pauper petitions, the response is rare, but where there is an expectation of serious consideration, often communicated by the Clerk, a response is much more likely. The petition identifies the question involved and argues that it is within the jurisdiction of the Court (Brennan, 1963: 100). When the opposing brief comes to the Court, the Clerk routes it to the justices. When the opposing petition comes in, if it is on time and carries the name and address of a member of the Supreme Court Bar, it is also entered into the Court's record.

Part of the special position of the Clerk's office has been evident for years as a function of "institutional common law." "There is much in the practice and usage of the Court not provided for in any rule . . . a sort of common law of procedure that lies outside of rules" (Garland, 1898). It is the Clerk, not the justices, who makes the initial interpretation of these practices. Most commentary on the Clerk portrays him as an agent of the justices, yet even as an agent he influences the form and to some extent the content of controversies, making him transitional between the institution and its policy. In the summer of 1952, Clerk Harold Willey telephoned counsel James Nabrit of the NAACP about bringing the case of *Bolling* v. *Sharpe* directly to the Supreme Court to be heard with the case from Kansas that would become *Brown* v. *Board of Education.* Willey told Nabrit of the justices' desire to speed the process of review to better frame the question and ease the resolution (Kluger, 1975: 539–540). The discretionary power of the Clerk and the influence of the office are as evident in processing petitions. In the summer and throughout the term, the Clerk's office collates petitions into a conference list. They share with the Chief Justice's clerks the responsibility for initially determining what cases deserve review at the Conference. The Clerk is also responsible for the records of institutional life, which have not generally been preserved.

The formal channels for disseminating opinion to the legal community have a long and colorful history. The office of Court Reporter, responsible for this task, has gone through as many changes as the buildings in which the institution has been housed. His office and its publication, *The United States Reports,* emerged from one hundred years of practice. The "institutionalization" of this office paralleled the rise of the Court as an institution (Friedman, 1973: 283).

When the Supreme Court first met there was a Clerk and a Marshal but no Reporter on the staff. In these early years, opinions were announced from the bench primarily to inform the parties about the outcome. More careful reporting and broader dissemination was a response to interest from the bar in what the Court offered to explain the actions it took. Later, the reports were organized and sold to interested members of the bar. Although the central motivation of these early reporters was financial gain, growing institutional sensitivity to the Court's product came to press for a higher set of values. Reporter Alexander James Dallas was described by historian Gerald T. Dunne as responding "to that mysterious combination of love of law, self-satisfaction, private gain, and public spirit" that he says moved the occupants of that office to produce reports that were called by Edward Coke "a publike relation or a bringing again to memory cases judicially resolved . . . with such causes or reasons as were delivered by the judges" (Dunne, 1976: 62). Like the other early reporters, Dallas's primary interest was in state law; reports of Supreme Court activities were a secondary matter. The next reporter, William Cranch, began his life in the new capital as a real estate speculator. From 1801 to 1815, while also serving as a district court judge, he reported Supreme Court opinions from manuscripts made available to him by the justices.

The office became more institutionalized in 1816, when the first official appointee, Henry Wheaton, brought suit that established the status of the Reports as public property. *Wheaton* v. *Peters* (1834) pitted two of the early reporters against each other in a struggle over control of the reports. In these years, the Reporter was sometimes the subject of the intrigue and struggles that took place between members of the Court. According to Charles Warren, Justice Joseph Story considered resigning over the appointment of General Benjamin C. Howard to replace Richard Peters (Warren, 1925: II/105). Peters had served since 1828 and did not get along with some of the justices. Delayed publication was something they attributed to him as well as a reluctance to facilitate newspaper publication of opinions for fear of his job.

The Reporter's job has become more mechanical since the office was linked directly to the institution. In the early years, leaks were a problem and one of those leaks, the *Dred Scott* decsion in 1857, had a devastating effect on the institution. Anti-slavery papers attacked Chief Justice Tane for the comment reported to be coming out in the opinion, that "the negro had no rights which the white man was bound to respect." According to Warren, the attacks on the Court that followed "were due far more to Taney's alleged statement than to the point of law decided by him" (1925: 303). The correction was not publicly circulated until 1886, when it was reported that the phrase came by way of narration concerning a period prior to the adoption of the Constitution. Though there is a marked difference between what appears in the official reports and what reaches the public today, this is not so directly tied to the Reporter and is more accurately associated with newspaper reporters.

There had been thirteen reporters by 1977, when Yale Law School graduate Henry Putzell took the job. In addition to preparing the reports, the Reporter runs the printshop with two typesetting machines, checks the opinions for accuracy of citation and comformity to standards of legal style, and prepares the syllabus, or headnote summary, of the case. These notes, one of Warren Burger's innovations as Chief Justice, contribute to the capacity of newspaper reporters to get the decision in a form that they can use (Keefe, 1975: 1511).

Since 1972, the Court has employed three Legal Officers. Two function as generalists. They assist the justices on emergency applications and motions, analyze jurisdictional and other special problems raised by certiorari petitions, review legislation of possible interest to the Court, and advise the Clerk and staff on legal issues. They are appointed for four years or more and are described as providing "a measure of continuity to the Court's revolving door law-clerk system" (Williams, 1977: 86). Another lawyer has been shifted from these duties to full-time Special Assistant to the Chief Justice on Judicial Matters.

The three lawyers providing legal support are a bridge between the institution and its policy. The Clerk was one of the first members of the Court's staff and his contribution is that of orchestrating the pace of the work. The Reporter has grown the most in stature and contributes greatly to the reach of the Court's holdings. The Legal Officers are the newest members of this group and their significance has yet to be measured, or even widely discussed, for that matter. The legal staff reflects a trend toward increasing support and delegation of power to specialists.

Policy. In addition to institutional and legal support, the justices have assistance in formulating the policy that is part of each decision. Policy support comes from lawyers who are associated either with the individual justices (clerks) or a particular case (counsel generally and the Solicitor General). Whether behind the bench or in front of it, these men and women of the bar support the justices in crafting the legal expression that arises from the decisions passed on by the Court as law. These are the people who help decide what issues will be given the full treatment, who will win, and how a judgment will be explained. Describing these participants, all law-trained, as policy support is an effort to integrate the legal form with policy outcomes, and policy at the Court is known through opinions.

The practice of providing assistance to the justices in the form of budding lawyers was begun when Justice Horace Gray hired a "top Harvard Law School graduate" for a years's service in 1882 (Williams, 1977: 87), although it's not clear whether this was while Gray was at the Supreme Court of Massachusetts or when he went to Washington. This practice, begun informally as one might take on a little help for a time, has become the most significant institutional practice bearing on policy formulation by the Supreme Court. Most justices now hire four clerks although in 1986 Justice Stevens hired only two and William Rehnquist hired three. Justice White chose three new clerks and kept one of his clerks from the 1985–1986 term for the next year.

Although the position is an apprenticeship, the pay is a living wage, over $30,000 in the 1980s. Selection is extremely competitive. The hundreds of applications a justice receives will already have been screened in law school, which does the primary filtering and teaches what sort of student is eligible to clerk at the Supreme Court. The clerks' legal education will most likely have been from one of a small group of schools—the Ivy League, Georgetown, Michigan, California, and Stanford—with 25 percent coming from Yale for 1986. But others are represented. Justice Brennan chose a clerk in 1986 from SUNY at Buffalo, Justice Marshall one from Georgia, and Justice White chose one from Loyola of Los Angeles and one from the University of Denver to go with those whose background was "more traditional."

The justices tend to have their channels for selection. The most famous was Brandeis's reliance on Felix Frankfurter while he was at Harvard Law School for choosing his clerks (Murphy, 1982). Brandeis had no contact with his clerks until they came to Washington. Recently, Judge Skelly Wright of the District of Columbia circuit was himself a route to the Supreme Court. For six years beginning in 1979, all his clerks moved to the Supreme Court. They came, for the most part, from the *Harvard Law Review*. Justice O'Connor chose two of her clerks from her alma mater, Stanford.

Years ago, the justices and the clerks, all male, often lived together. Much has changed in the relations between clerks and justices but both have remained predominately male until recently, and the policy end of the Court has always been predominately white. The first woman to serve as a law clerk was Lucille Lomen, who worked for Justice Douglas during the 1944 Term. No more than eight women served among the clerks, who have numbered up to thirty-three, until the 1986–1987 term, when there will be eleven female clerks, two chosen by Justice O'Connor.[5] William Coleman was the first black to serve as a clerk. He worked with Felix Frankfurter for the 1949 Term.

Confidentiality had been a ritual expression associated with a clerkship, and confidence in an individual's capacity to protect the justices and the institution was considered a prerequisite to service as a clerk. Until *The Brethren,* based largely on interviews with clerks, there were only occasional and generally sympathetic leaks (Wilkinson, 1974). Even before the book came out, Chief Justice Burger had warned his clerks that he would fire them on the spot if they talked to reporters on any subject (Mathews, 1974: 20). The furor that followed the publication of *The Brethren* may have created some tension in the building but it only enhanced recognition that these underlaborers are a very significant part of the institution.

As recent law school graduates, the clerks are familiar with the dominant traditions and the areas of development in the law. The clerks have all clerked somewhere before, usually in the federal system and more often than not in the District of Columbia circuit. The clerkship attracts a particularly aggressive and gifted group of lawyers who significantly improve their careers, and former clerks go on to positions of considerable power in law, business, and government. At least four have held Cabinet posts, more than twenty have gone on to high-level posts in the executive branch, and from the academy to the judiciary the higher levels of the legal profession generally share the experience of having clerked. Of the present justices of the Supreme Court, one-third were clerks earlier in their career.

Accusations of undue influence on Court policy are of course denied, but the justices are sensitive to criticism over the significance of the clerks. Justice Jackson himself recalled some lawyers' suggesting that "the Senate no longer need bother about confirmation of the Justices but ought to confirm the appointment of law clerks" (Westin, 1961: 28). Influence on policy is through the justices. Although Justice Brennan reportedly reads all petitions to the Court (Totenberg, 1975) and all the justices claim strict supervision, the indications from former clerks, including one who later became Chief Justice, is that the clerks play a major role in all aspects of the policy process outside the conference, from the initial decision to grant review to the formulation of an opinion (Rehnquist, 1957).

The main contribution of the clerks is widely thought to come in two forms, the preparation of memos on appeal to the Court and in drafting opinions. Review of the mass of material coming to the institution is a less problematic form of influence and a widely defended practice. Here the clerks function in a traditional delegated capacity. It is during the process, where their perceptions, knowledge, and even their words contribute to the final product that their influence is most guarded by the justices. In Felix Frankfurter's dissent in *West Virginia State Board of Education* v. *Barnette* (1943), in which he voted to uphold the compulsory flag salute against a shifting majority on the Court, the justice drafted a long rationalization in which he argued that his origins made him particularly sensitive to minority rights. It was a moving testimony written in the midst of the

Second World War as knowledge of the Holocaust was just becoming evident, but his clerk tried to dissuade the justice from including the personal statement. Frankfurter is reported to have replied, "This is my opinion, not yours." And although that may still be how the opinion is remembered, the increasing significance of clerks may alter the way we perceive opinions from the Court.

Institutional practice is still to refer to Supreme Court opinions as if a person actually wrote them. This is not true for *per curiam* decisions, but they are treated differently and not studied the same way. Joseph Vining has called the contemporary situation an internal bureaucratization. He sees what the Supreme Court produces as "bureaucratic writing" and believes that this is "not just writing that appears under the name of one who did not write it. In its fully developed form it is writing that is written by many hands" (Vining, 1986: 47). One might compare how the Supreme Court operates in this regard with commentary on presidential speeches. With the President it is commonplace to attribute a good speech to the speech writer and the same is true of most political figures. But the influence of underlaborers matters less in those settings, because they are explicitly political.

In the case of the Court things are different. When we read biographies, especially intellectual ones, and find whole treatises on the intellectual life of a man with little or no attention to who wrote "his" words, we may begin to wonder about such practices. J. Woodford Howard's biography of Frank Murphy pays explicit attention to this issue, wondering whether Murphy's reliance on his clerks was excessive. He calls the problem "ghosting" in government and considers the issue one of "whether the work of the subordinate reflects the views of the superior" (Howard, 1968: 474). Although Howard absolves his subject of excessive delegation, it is not the individual but the institutional significance of the ghosting that is most significant.

The most challenging protrayal of internal workings is in *The Brethren*. But Woodward and Armstrong cite no examples where a Supreme Court clerk actually wrote an opinion that later appeared verbatim in print. Instead the portrayal is of clerks writing drafts and influencing the internal exchanges among the judicial offices. They portray one clerk for Justice Marshall producing such a devastating memo on a Stewart opinion that Justice Powell was said to exclaim, "Who is the Justice down there?" (1979: 258–259). In the case of Muhammad Ali's resistance to the draft, one clerk's research into the teachings of Elijah Muhammad are said to have changed Justice Harlan's views to support for the former heavyweight champion's appeal (1979: 137). In other cases the authors cite "legal and moral interchanges" that facilitate the judicial process

(1979: 118–119; 269). No contribution during the years they studied rivals the influence of Harlan Fiske Stone's clerk, Louis Lusky.

Lusky's impact was on one of the singularly most important pieces of legal text produced by the Supreme Court in the twentieth century, Footnote 4 in *United States* v. *Carolene Products Co.* (1938). The influence of Lusky was reported by Alpheas T. Mason, Stone's biographer. The first draft of the second and third paragraphs of the note were reportedly written by Lusky and adopted "almost as drafted" according to the clerk (Mason, 1956: 513). In this case, Stone is reported to have used footnotes in his opinions as vehicles for his clerks to try out their ideas. This biographer, like most others, ultimately defends the actions of his subject as exercising the final authority. In the end, however, that assurance may not be enough to keep the myth of individuality alive in an institutional setting where opinion, like choice and decision, becomes increasingly bureaucratized.

The lawyers who present cases also provide support in the formulation of policy. Lawyers who practice before the Supreme Court, like all attorneys, are technically agents of the Court. They are required to be members of the Supreme Court Bar or appear with a member. Admission to this group, though honorific in most cases, does have meaning for the few who actually return to the institution repeatedly.[6] This bar's association with the Court ranges from the few attorneys who have appeared regularly such as John W. Davis, whose 140 appearances ended with his unsuccessful stand against desegregation in the *Brown* litigation, to the private attorneys who hang their certificate of admission to the Supreme Court Bar on their office wall back home and never present a case to the Court.

The Court appoints counsel when a petition has been accepted *in forma pauperis*. The lawyer's role in such situations is described in *Gideon's Trumpet* (Lewis, 1964). The attorney chosen to present the appeal of Clarence Earl Gideon, Abe Fortas, was well known to the justices. Fortas was a member of a prominent Washington firm who had argued the landmark *Durham* case for a new criminal insanity rule and had worked on the federal rules of procedure as well as being intimate with the newly elevated president, Lyndon Johnson. His research and his presentation in the *Gideon* case was a model of the sort of assistance that justices depend on in formulating policy. It was keyed to cues from the justices as to what they wanted to consider.

In appointing counsel for a case before the Court, the institution is not simply looking for a competent advocate for the plaintiff because, by its nature, such a case is more than an individual lawsuit. In Clarence Gideon's case it was not simply, perhaps not even marginally to provide the appellant a full hearing that Abe Fortas was appointed. Fortas never met his client. Rather he served as an agent in the policy process. In this case, he was an agent for constitutional development. Since the power of the Court's decision is a function of how it is received, it is influenced by the justifications offered. Traditionally, much of this rhetoric has been contributed by counsel.

There is, of course, considerable difference between the clerks who approach policy through the confidence of the justices and the counsel who approach it from the outside, as representatives of the interests and individuals involved in litigation. But in both cases, the effort is one of assessing and refining the legal claims on which institutional policy is made. Success of both roles depends on knowing the propensities of the justices, their concerns about the law, and their inclinations in a particular dispute. These are the actors most clearly serving the institution in the formulation of policy.

An agent of federal power created by Congress and influencing what cases reach the Supreme Court is the Solicitor General. The government's chief litigator decides which governmental issues the Court will be asked to decide and is surprisingly influential in the determination of what it chooses to decide. It is not ordinary or even institutional perception that makes the solicitor general one of the support personnel; it is expert commentary. Paul Freund has called him the tenth justice. When the government loses a case, the appellate section at the Justice Department—with the aide of the trial attorney and other interested parties—makes a recommendation on whether or not to appeal. This recommendation then goes to the Solicitor General's office for review, and he decides whether to take it to the Supreme Court. He may even decide that the government should have lost a case that it actually won and he can file a "Confession of Error" with the Supreme Court, asking that the decision be overruled. Acceptance of such writs is likely. Once the Solicitor General has decided to take an appeal, the government's rate of access to the Court for review is exceptional, 50 to 75 percent as compared with less than 10 percent for private litigants. The conventional wisdom on this success rate is that it is "due to the fact that Government cases are likely to be of more general public importance and to the strictness with which that office screens the cases lost below . . . attempting to apply the Supreme Court's own standards" (Stern and Gressman, 1978: 261). Some have criticized this special relationship as leaving the government's counsel too closely connected with the institution and not the government (Krislov, 1965: 49), yet it is equally important to point out this special relationship as an element of institutional support. In *Clark* v. *Kimmitt* (1976), the Court asked the Solicitor General to file a brief with the awesome task of "expressing the view of the United States" on the issues raised in a petition by former Attorney General Ramsey Clark while a candidate for the United States Senate from New York that challenged various provisions of the campaign-financing legislation (*New York Times,* May 25, 1976: 24). The relationship works both ways.

Thirty years ago institutional practice was already being described as less collegial than it had been (Jackson, 1955). Now, the justices of the Supreme Court may not work much with each other but they do not work alone. They share their tasks with other officers and staff. This assitance has been described in terms of different spheres of influence, different kinds of support. The place, its legal work, and its policy contributions are all part of what we call the Supreme Court and all have been affected by changes in the institutional setting. To see this in terms of governing practices is to be forced to acknowledge the emergence of a new institution.

5

COURT BUSINESS

THE VOLUME of disputes from which the justices may choose and the kind of legal issues given full treatment distinguish the Supreme Court today from the institution of only one hundred years ago. The number of cases coming "up" has transformed the Court, providing the opportunity to comment on just about any issue in public life. In addition, the disputes that are taken for authoritative action aren't the same kind as they used to be. These changes in the docket make the Supreme Court a different institution today. "Agenda" issues and the interaction between form and substance, along with the lively debate on the workload of the Court, provide a perspective on the institution through the way it handles legal business.

Modern commentary portrays the Supreme Court as a "constitutional court" and identifies it with the big cases. In Robert McCloskey's narrative, constitutional evolution and institutional life at the Supreme Court are joined in the story of what he calls "a constitutional tribunal" (McCloskey, 1960: ix). For Henry Abraham, the story of "the Supreme Court in the governmental process" is told through the constitutional language of due process, equality, and freedom of expression (1977). Others follow this pattern, emphasizing the Court's role in fundamental policy issues not because that is all the Court does but because it is how they see the institution (Murphy, 1979: 114–233). Increasingly this activity is less important than the Court's position as the final arbiter of legal disputes.

The business of the institution covers more than disputes in constitutional law (Shapiro, 1964). In this chapter we examine the Court's business as a whole and in all its forms with attention to the institution as the last word in American law as well as a source of distinguished constitutional commentary. For the substance, we rely heavily on aggregated cases. The model for this investigation is the work of Felix Frankfurter and James Landis, *The Business of the Supreme Court*. Written in 1928, this treatise told the story of how the institution changed when it was able to choose its cases. Now, with its authority firmly established and its significance as a national institution generally recognized, we can review the work with Supreme Court handles.

The chapter moves from the legal form that identifies Court business and the Court's place at the top of the litigation flow coming out of American life to the substantive changes that have occurred in what the institution does. The Court's business as a whole is less well known than the big cases, but the bulk of its work rather than the headlines helps us understand the institution. This activity operates beneath the roles associated with juridical behavior or rules we sometimes think constitute the institutional reality. The institution is never merely "there" nor does it simply resolve disputes (or serve as a trumpet as suggested by some chroniclers). As an institution it exists in the business coming before the justices, and this business reveals its character. A look at what the Supreme Court does shows that its role in American politics has increased as institutional discretion has grown. By the middle of the twentieth century, judicial authority, capped by the Supreme Court at the pinnacle of a consolidated judiciary, played its most important constitutional role by offering a semblance of authority over the federal bureaucracy (Belz, 1985).

LITIGATION AND THE COURT

The Supreme Court needs cases to decide as the President needs legislation to sign and Congress needs bills to vote on. All political institutions have their own forms of action and agendas. The Supreme Court is no exception. Counting the prisoner petitions, the Court has a massive number of cases from which it can chooose and a capacity to stimulate appeals because of attention to what the justices are thinking. This enables the institution to play an active role in the policy process. The number and kinds of cases it deals with are a function of the decisions made by the justices and the perception of the institution. This comes out in two aspects of institutional significance addressed in this section, litigation in its institutional forms, as practice and as product, and the workload issue that is used to justify increasing the number of courts and has been linked to calls for an intermediate court of appeals. The relationship here is less straightforward than might be expected.

Litigation

Cases decided by the Supreme Court are at the apex of a pyramid of legal disputes arising in America. Like the ancient pyramids, this structure is constructed according to the design and interests of the sovereign. Table 4 demonstrates the nature of this pyramid for a representative kind of case. The base is composed of disputes over tax matters. Any factor that affects the subset of human action involving questions of federal sovereignty and federal law "can affect the number of applications for review filed in the Supreme Court" (Casper, 1976: 28). We do not look at society as a whole to observe the pool of cases. The legal process and institutional considerations of the federal system are the greatest influence on the pool of cases that flow toward the Court.

Yet, the litigation that feeds the Court is affected by social and economic conditions (Grossman and Sarat, 1975), the state of the law as perceived in the Court (Lewis, 1964), and the political culture (Jacob, 1969). Although much less pervasive as an influence on social life than it was once thought to be (Friedman, 1985), litigation is still the raw material on which the Supreme Court works. With such material the justices have a choice of cases and adequate material for wide-ranging comment on American life. There is an interactive relationship between Court and society. The Court affects and is affected by social life. What the Court decides on matters like criminal procedure (*Miranda,* 1966), school desegregation (*Milliken,* 1974), and abortion (*Roe,* 1973) alters social life. That context is cause and consequence of Court action as new groups of justices react to what their predecessors have done.

In addition, the form cases must take and the way the institution is situated in the government further determines the events that the Supreme Court will face and the impact it will have on them. Current developments have been articulated from two very different angles by Wolf

TABLE 4
The Legal Pyramid, Tax Cases

Tax Cases	No.
Civil cases decided by Supreme Court	4
Civil cases decided by courts of appeals	363
Civil cases docketed in trial courts	9,932
Civil cases received by appellate division (of the Internal Revenue Service)	18,569
Returns examined	2,030,655
Federal tax returns filed	121,609,260

Source: G. Casper, 1976: 28. Taken from H. Todd Miller, "Comment: A Court of Tax Appeals Revisited," 85 *Yale L.J.* 228, 233 (1975) (1974 data).

Heydebrand and Carroll Seron (1987) on the one hand and Joseph Vining (1986) on the other. Heydebrand and Seron, in a forthcoming book, focus on administrative reform in the courts and discuss this phenomenon as the characteristic institutional development of the twentieth century. As they describe it, relying on Weber and the classic texts in administrative process, the traditional "Rule of Law" organization of the courts is under seige from newer forms of bureaucratic administration. Vining, from a more rhetorical and less data rich perspective, discusses the accelerating bureaucratization of the United States Supreme Court and its impact on how law is taught.

In the discussion of litigation that follows, we examine the interaction of legal form, institutional practice, and the raw material worked over by the justices for a picture of Court business that will tell us a little more about the institution's place in the American state structure.

Legal Form. The Court's business comes in official categories that frame social and political issues in institutional terms. The five paths by which disputes enter the institution are original jurisdiction, certification, extraordinary writs, appeal, and certiorari. The legal forms into which disputes are crafted are not unlike the steps in front of the building. Like those steps, legal forms lead to the institution. Actually, they lead to the docket. The docket is the Court's agenda or official calendar of business, and it lists the issues that are coming up. The institution divides these issues along lines reflecting the nature of the Supreme Court. A distinction in the Constitution between original and appellate jurisdiction has been read, since *Marbury* v. *Madison* (1803), to stipulate the sphere of congressional power over what the Court does. A miscellaneous docket was developed by Chief Justice Hughes for "noncontroversial matters" that would be disposed of as the Chief Justice recommended, unless another member of the court objected (McElwain, 1949: 5; Krislov, 1965: 57). This docket comprised more than half of the requests to the Court until recently and was made up mostly of *in forma pauperis* petitions for review. Increasing discretion and summary treatment of most cases "before" the Court has led, since 1970, to creation of the "5000 Series" taking the place of the miscellaneous docket.

"Original" actions do not have to be considered by a lower court and involve "all cases affecting ambassadors, other public ministers and consuls, and those in which a state shall be a party" (Art. III, Sec. 2). In a dispute between Maine and New Hampshire involving lobstering grounds, the Court rejected the proposal offered by the late Justice Tom Clark sitting as a master, and accepted an agreement worked out by the governors of the states involved. This jurisdiction testifies to the ultimate authority of the Court. According to Alexis de Tocqueville, "When the

Clerk of the Court advances on the steps of the tribunal and simply says, 'The state of New York versus the state of Ohio,' it is impossible not to feel that the court which he addresses is no ordinary body'' (1873: I, 191). The sort of actions that can be brought against a state were limited by Amendment XI, and the number of original petitions has decreased continually as a percentage of the Court's business. These now constitute a tiny fraction of the Court's work and even then the justices do not sit as in traditional appeals but instead appoint a ''master'' to receive evidence, find facts, state conclusions of law, and recommend a decree that is subject to approval by the Supreme Court. Thus, although a small amount of its workload, the Supreme Court's original jurisdiction is a measure of national sovereignty and the enduring problems of a federal system.

Certification is a seldom used avenue to the High Bench and consequently it has minimal significance. Certification is technically an ''inquiry or request to a higher court from a lower one'' for clarification. The Supreme Court rules provide for hearing questions or propositions of law from a court of appeals or the court of claims. A recent case involved a court of appeals request concerning whether the governor of Mississippi needed to be provided with a jury trial on a contempt citation issued by the court of appeals. Because certification has been used so infrequently in recent years, in 1972 the Freund Commission recommended that it be abolished.

Extraordinary writs allow the Supreme Court to intervene in lower court proceedings or in the orders of other courts (28 USC 1651). They include a *common law writ of certiorari,* the *original writ* or *habeas corpus* (distinguished from a habeas corpus petition to a lower court that has been appealed), *mandamus* orders to compel judicial action, or *prohibition* to limit the actions of a lower court. In 1973, 124 of these writs were filed. When they are reviewed they fall into the common denominator ''cases'' and plenary review was granted in only three of them. Both because of their association with emergency situations such as executions and because of their timing since come during the summer, the extraordinary writs receive considerable attention. The announcement on October 5, 1976, that the Supreme Court was lifting a ban on executions came ''with no fanfare and no drama.'' But the decision heralded renewed attention to the death penalty and a rash of extraordinary writs were filed. In a little over a month Justice Powell issued a temporary stay of execution until the whole Court had the opportunity to review a case in which the man scheduled to die had petitioned that the Court ''turn down any appeal filed in his behalf.''

The Writs of Appeal and Certiorari are easily distinguished in the ''black letter law.'' In practice the distinction is less marked and less significant. The Writ of Appeal arises when (*a*) a state court of last resort has ruled in favor of a state law or a provision of the state constitution against a challenge that it conflicts with a provision of the federal Constitution, a federal law or treaty; (*b*) a state law or provision of a state constitution has been ruled unconstitutional by a court of appeals; (*c*) the United States or one of its agencies is a party and the cases come from a court of appeals, a district court, or other federal courts. The writ is technically a matter of right, yet since 1928 an appeal must raise "a substantial federal question." The power to determine whether such a question exists is the basis for the Court's discretion over this form of appeal. Even in cases accepted as posing such a question, the Court only notes "probable jurisdiction," reserving for itself the option to indicate, even after oral argument, that jurisdiction had been found lacking. In 20 percent of the cases that are acted upon the judgment of the lower court is vacated and the case remanded for further consideration in light of a decision by the Supreme Court while in 50 percent of the cases the decision of the lower court is summarily affirmed (Gunther, 1985: 62–69).

The writ of certiorari is the more common kind of appeal and literally asks the Court to "make the decision certain." Acceptance of a petition for "cert" indicates a willingness of the justices to review a case. Supreme Court Rule 19 indicates that the ground for accepting "cert" petitions is that they raise substantial questions and suggest a conflict either among the lower courts or with the inclinations of the Supreme Court. It takes four justices to decide to hear a case presented under the provisions for certiorari, the same number required to establish jurisdiction for an appeal. These petitions constitute 80 to 90 percent of the requests for Supreme Court action, but only 5 to 15 percent are accepted for review. The number is substantially lower when prisoners' petitions are included, but without them it is very close to the number of appeals accepted. An appeal may be regarded as a petition for *cert* under 28 USC 2103. By this provision Congress has ratified conventions that indicate there is little practical difference between an appeal and a writ of certiorari as a form of controversy before the Court. Although there is no distinction between the two major writs in terms of some manifest obligation, there are consequences that follow from the practice of formally maintaining the distinction.

Denial of a petition for certiorari, like a holding of "insubstantiality" in an appeal, means that the litigant has lost, but because of the different institutional status the implications of losing differ. Some justices, like Robert Jackson, have viewed denial of certiorari as confirmation by the Supreme Court that the lower court decision should stand. More commonly, we attribute no authority to the denial of *cert* other than that the appellate process has reached its end. Summary disposition of an appeal for "insubstantiality," however, affirms that the lower court was right (Gunther, 1985: 64). Consequently, some practical distinctions result from the difference. In *Ross* v. *Moffitt* (1974), for instance, the Court decided that there was no entitlement to appointed counsel on discretionary state appeals or petitions for certiorari but that there was such an entitlement in appeals that were a matter of right. In addition, an appeal found "insubstantial" has value as precedent while a denial of cert has none. Thus, while the distinction means less in practice than the legal forms suggest, the distinction between cert and appeal still has institutional meaning (Wasby, 1984: 160–167).

These are the traditional forms into which a controversy is shaped in order to enter the Supreme Court. They are not political forms in the traditional sense but they necessarily shape interests since the Court would not see a case without them. In each case, once meaningful legal distinctions have been losing significance and in their place have arisen institutional meanings that are much less formal and much less closely linked to the idea of a rule of law. Original jurisdiction has been bureaucratized, and although its majesty does reveal where the Court stands, the "law" is more often a negotiated settlement. Extraordinary writs, once arcane legal niceties, are now a way to get to the justices when the Court is not in session. And the distinction between *cert* and *appeal,* once a key to Supreme Court practice, is now an artifact of institutional life with limited practical significance. All these forms are part of the institution but the shift on their practical significance indicates a shift in the Court's authority.

Institutional Practice. Practices in the operation of the Supreme Court like jurisdictional statements, retroactivity policy, and *amicus curiae* briefs reveal the explicit political character of the modern Supreme Court and, like legal form, these practices are becoming less formal. This shift is part of the larger transformation of the institution from a political institution relying on the law as a basis for its legitimacy to a political institution whose legitimacy rests on its institutional position as the final arbiter. And the shift as it has taken place since 1970 is also a conservative move to limit some forms of court use.

Statements of the Court's jurisdiction over a particular issue, including the determination that a justiciable controversy exists, lie at the nexus between the institutional setting constituted by tradition and practice and the uses to which sitting justices can sensibly allow the institution to be put. Jurisdiction, as the legal boundary of Court business, traditionally excludes some issues like foreign policy and some forms of action, like advisory opinions, from consideration.[1] Other requirements include mat-

ters such as ripeness for review, the standing of the litigants to bring a
case, and whether legally protected interests are at stake. The "case of
controversy" requirement addresses the *court* dimensions of its business,
while jurisdiction involves the place of this *supreme* body in the national
system of justice. Long recognized as a way for the justices to nurture the
limited resources of the institution, jurisdictional statements make less of
the claim to a judicial practice distinct from politics. These statements are
also widely recognized as part of a discourse between the Court and
Congress over what the justices should be doing.

In other areas the Court has gone even further to indicate that its place
as a governing body in the policy process rather than as a governing body
in the policy process rather than as a distinctively legal institution will
determine institutional practice. Pragmatic consideration of retroactivity
is a case of legal forms deferring to the demands of policy. Traditionally,
decisions were fully retroactive (Gunther, 1985: 29). As interpretation of
the law they drew their authority from the claim that the decision had
been found, not made. The implication was of continuity with the past.
Here, the mythology of judging had important policy implications in com-
mitting the Court to full retroactivity no matter how many new trials
might have to be provided. But since 1965, decisions on retroactivity have
taken into account the implications on the criminal justice system of
retroactive application for all manner of relevant parties.

The extension of federal constitutional rights to the states in the 1960s
gave rise to prospective application of judicial decision and dramatically
shifted the nature of the decision. In *Linkletter* v. *Walker* (1965), the
justices of the Warren Court authorized the new practice thus confirming
that cases have come to represent interests in a political sense. The character of the decision aims beyond the parties immediately involved and
operates outside of the traditional legal framework. This "non-Hohfel-
dian" dimension has followed transformation of the substance of Court
business and it may well ultimately change the perception that the Court
settles disputes in a distinctly legal way. Calculation of the interests is the
most obviously political dimension of the business attended to by the
Supreme Court (Peltason, 1955: 44).

The increased use of the *amicus curiae* brief is another institutional
accommodation to political or representational litigation. Once a case gets
to the Court and is accepted for review, interests begin to align themselves on the particular controversy and they seek official ways to participate in the decision process. However, prior to 1939 there was not even
an explicit rule in the Supreme Court explaining how to file *amicus* briefs
(Krislow, 1965: 43). The transformation of a case from simple controversy

to a public issue around which interests may coalesce is now a function of the institution. The justices have limited use of the *amicus* brief, recognizing it as a pressure group tactic different from the tradition of disputes before the Court. According to the justices, "The traditional function of an *amicus curiae* is to assert an interest of its own separate and distinct from that of the parties whether the interest is private or public" (*United States* v. *Barnett,* 1964). They have asked for reasoned argument and sought new angles from these briefs. But these have been minor adjustments acknowledging more than limiting this new development. The *amicus* brief transcends the individual disputes in a case and its use is indicative of the modern institutional role (O'Connor and Epstein, 1981–1982).

Pleading requirements determine what the Supreme Court will decide and their manipulation is part of Court politics. The Supreme Court uses its power over what it decides to limit access to the institution for certain kinds of cases. Over the last decade, changes in the Court's business have been accomplished by what some have referred to as a turn "from the substance of justice to the niceties of pleading" (Wicker, 1976). Included as "niceties" were actions on institutional practices like tighter standing requirements and constraints on class action suits. With other requirements of deference to state court rulings and fewer remedies *de novo* in federal courts, the institution is turning from traditional discussions of substantive issues to its position at the top of the legal pyramid where the work of the justices has become a focal point (Vining, 1986: 86).

The practices examined here, jurisdictional statements, retroactivity policy, and *amicus* briefs have immediate significance as part of a Burger Court reaction to Warren Court decisions, but they have a much larger significance. Both legal forms and institutional practices influence the business of the Supreme Court. Both constitute an institutional reality that changes, albeit slowly, as the communities familiar with the institution accept new forms and learn different practices. In some circles, knowledge of these institutional practices has superseded legal doctrine as a source of professional privilege without reference to the learning traditionally associated with the law (Cover, 1983; Fiss, 1982). Together, the practices reveal a trend away from confidence in discursive authority to a more pragmatic policy focus where the authority of the Court comes from the finality of its pronouncements. This political dimension of the judicial process combines with bureaucratic exigency to diminish the focus on judicial discourse that has been the hallmark of the constitutional product of the Supreme Court. In this situation, it is becoming evident that "the absence of a producer of texts would mean the absence of work on language" (Vining, 1986: 87), the Court's most significant modern product. The place of the legal profession in fashioning decision material from which the Court works and the changing nature of that material further reveal the place of the institution in the policy process.

Decision Material. Lawyers, as the link between "the climate of social, political, and economic opinion" and "the judicial decisions comprising American constitutional law" (Twiss, 1942: 3), filter social action into cases capable of a hearing before the Supreme Court. The constraint and the guide is the "artificial reason" in the law. Lawyers are trained to determine what is possible according to convention and to identify "the controlling rule enunciated by the Court" (Scheingold, 1974). The Court's business is affected by the legal profession's view of what is possible as it is applied in the controversies that erupt in society and are handled by lawyers.

Former Chief Justice Burger articulated a professional concern in the late 1970s for the amount of litigation generated in the United States. This concern was linked to his belief that the Court had become overburdened by all the lawsuits being filed. In 1985, the justices nearly upheld an Ohio attempt to limit lawyer advertising in the belief that advertising by lawyers led more people to sue. Justice White argued a strangely controversial position: "we cannot endorse the position that a lawsuit, as such, is an evil . . . our society has settled upon civil litigation as a means for redressing grievances, resolving disputes and vindicating rights when other means fail" (Greenhouse, 1985). Yet the business of the Court is subject to what lawyers do and there is a increasing attention on the institution to professional activities.

The 1970s revealed a dramatic increase since World War II in the number of cases filed. The greatest growth was in petitions appealing criminal convictions. These jumped from 48 percent of the docket in 1956 to 62 percent in 1973 (see Table 5). This characteristic holds up even when the *in forma pauperis* petitions, which do not have the same professional status, are excluded from the calculation. The Warren Court's interest in extending rights to criminals was one factor in this increase. Another factor was changes in the criminal law such as the Criminal Justice Act of 1964, which provided for appellate representation (Casper, 1976: 41).

The civil caseload did not grow nearly as fast as the criminal caseload, but the matters comprising it changed. Over the last thirty years, common law cases have essentially disappeared. Jurisdictional issues, tax suits, admiralty, and bankruptcy declined, until recently. There was also a decline in railroad and maritime industries that had accounted for important cases, as well as a decline in the enforcement of antitrust and FTC statutes that had been a significant part of the Court's business in the preceding fifty years. Growth in the civil docket reflected new substantive rights

TABLE 5
Civil-Criminal Composition of Supreme Court's Caseload, 1956–73

| | Civil Cases | | | Criminal Cases | | | Total |
Term	Paid	Indigent	Total	Paid	Indigent	Total	Cases
1956	825	120	945	181	700	881	1,826
1957	688	50	738	158	750	908	1,646
1958	720	100	820	180	820	1,000	1,820
1959	695	40	735	187	960	1,147	1,882
1960	658	70	728	222	1,020	1,242	1,970
1961	686	150	836	215	1,130	1,345	2,181
1962	771	80	851	228	1,320	1,548	2,399
1963	757	140	897	269	1,130	1,399	2,296
1964	766	140	906	268	1,100	1,368	2,274
1965	844	140	984	379	1,380	1,759	2,743
1966	866	130	996	338	1,370	1,708	2,704
1967	939	190	1,129	366	1,610	1,976	3,105
1968	926	210	1,136	413	1,600	2,013	3,149
1969	1,014	190	1,136	473	1,680	2,153	3,357
1970	1,075	220	1,295	534	1,530	2,064	3,359
1971	1,120	290	1,410	594	1,620	2,214	3,624
1972	1,153	420	1,573	607	1,540	2,147	3,720
1973	1,391	210	1,601	706	1,860	2,566	4,167

Source: G. Casper, 1976: 35.

introduced in the 1960s and 1970s and closely associated with the Supreme Court, such as those providing protection against nondiscrimination and more recently private antitrust, SEC, and other economic regulations. Stephen Wasby points out the decrease in immigration and Federal Employer Liability Act cases over the last twenty-five years while emphasizing "the wide variety of particular issues explored by the Court in any single term" (Wasby, 1984: 152).

A number of studies discuss the litigation activities in the lower federal courts. From these we can form a picture of the decision material the Supreme Court has to work with. David S. Clark, building an early work of Heydebrand and Seron, has portrayed the Federal District Courts as shifting the basis on which they resolve disputes "from adjudication to administration" (Clark, 1981: 67). By this he means that the traditional concern for "right or justice" that is the legacy of Magna Carta "frequently takes second place to considerations of efficiency" (1981). This development is aptly characterized as a consequence of the ideology of administration. District Court work processes are changing and these same ideological shifts have effects up the legal pyramid.

In J. Woodford Howard's study of the second, fifth, and D. C. circuit courts the picture of the case material dealt with by the Supreme Court, at least relative to the courts of appeals he studied, was "selective, scattered, and issue specific" (1981: 57). The High Court rendered full opinions in 1.3 percent of the cases decided in the courts of appeals. Across the circuits, this amounted to much of the Supreme Court's workload but an insignificant exercise of oversight authority. The resulting picture of the relationship between the two higher levels of legal authority is of the shared oversight function and a sharing of some of the autonomy we associate with courts of appeal. The distinctive feature of the Supreme Court, at least relative to the courts of appeals in Howard's study, is that the Supreme Court, between 1965 and 1967, disturbed over two-thirds of the circuit decisions it heard while the intermediate federal tribals affirmed two-thirds of theirs (1981: 59). Even during this period, the Supreme Court made only 32 percent of its decisions in constitutional cases. Finally, the Supreme Court's special visibility draws it away from the correction of "errors" in the circuits (1981: 80).

The constitutional ground was no anomaly; in 1982, 70 percent of the cases the Supreme Court decided with full opinions were principally constitutional cases. These figures are not without fluidity, but drawing from the compilation of the *Harvard Law Review,* the trend toward increasing reliance on the constitutional ground has not subsided. The meaning is equally contestable, but according to the analysis of litigation developed here the continuing significance of constitutional grounds bears noting. They are, after all, the distinctive feature of this institution.

The legal product is the basis from which this docket is fashioned. S. Sidney Ulmer summarized the relevant considerations in the decision to grant review as the petitioning party, socioeconomic status of both parties, the political direction of the decision in the lower courts, and the makeup of the Supreme Court. He suggested turning more attention to "systemic" factors such as conflict in the legal system when a lower court decision is inconsistent with a Supreme Court decision (Ulmer, 1984). For D. Marie Provine, the choice by the justices about what to decide is based on what they believe to be "the proper business of the Court" (Provine, 1980). Although a minority of four justices can force a decision on the merits, 70 to 80 percent of the decisions to hear a case are unanimous. Provine has pointed out the misleading impression left by a focus on disagreement and emphasized "the influence of shared norms derived from legal and professional socialization" (1980: 333; see also Perry, 1985).

Court decisions suggest legal possibilities and judicial inclinations. They influence future business. Unlike ordinary courts or even the pre-Civil War Supreme Court, the modern institution is not tied to any legal arena that it must develop and maintain. Since the Court has been able to range widely, its decisions have had greater significance. That significance is evident in the use made of the Supreme Court's product. The impact of these decisions has been amplified far beyond their explicitly legal authority by their significance for teaching and learning in the law. As Joseph Vining demonstrates vividly, the texts of decisions by the Supreme Court have been the focus of a hermeneutic activity that has helped to constitute the substance of constitutional authority in America.

With this special place and with control over its business, the Court is able to act with a latitude characteristic of the other branches of government. The modern Court has a unique capacity to make issues of whole new areas, such as pornography or abortion, and the justices may also turn away essentially at will, as they have done in the field of privacy. With this in mind, we turn to the more purely administrative matters surrounding the workload controversy.

Workload Issue

The Court's capacity to influence public policy and shape the fundamental law is linked to how it handles the caseload. The relationship between institutional capacity and policy is long-standing. The changes in how the Court worked that took place in the 1920s facilitated attention to questions of fundamental law. These changes were justified by a "new insistence" on efficient administration of justice (Frankfurter and Landis, 1928: 217). Efficient in this sense meant discretionary, and discretion over what it dealt with allowed the Court to turn to "matters of national concern" (1928: 257). The Court today, a creature of those changes, continues to generate interest in institutional changes tied to its workload.

Capacity is an issue in the ongoing controversy over the workload of the Supreme Court. Those who favor increasing the capacity of the Court point to the caseload and say it is too large. Others see no significant increase in the amount of work done by the justices and object to changes that would increase the institutional capacity of the federal appellate courts. The push given to the issue by Chief Justice Burger maintained its saliency through his years on the Court. Burger made his arguments at American Bar Association meetings in 1983 and 1985 and in other gatherings throughout his tenure. In one such plea near the end of his term, the sixteenth annual State of the Judiciary speech at the American Bar Association's midwinter meeting, Burger pointed to the increase in the docket and called for an intermediate court to handle cases involving conflicting rulings issued by the courts of appeals, which averaged forty-eight in the preceding three terms (*The New York Times,* Feb. 18, 85). Here, his plea made an analogy with the need for more traffic courts since the invention of the automobile. What he failed to account for is the institutional significance of *one* Supreme Court. In the area of motor vehicle enforcement, traffic cops are more like traffic courts and in law enforcement the cops are about as far from the chief executive officer, the president of the United States, as the traffic courts are from the Supreme Court. Yet in some quarters it has become an article of faith that the Court's caseload is overwhelming (*Harvard Law Review,* 1983). Here, belief that the work-load is excessive fosters proposals for change that threaten to alter the place of the institution in American politics. An institutional perspective on this issue takes a more conscientious accounting of proposed changes and their consequences for the Supreme Court.

Workload. Professor David O'Brien, of the University of Virginia, argues that "[T]he evolution of the Supreme Court from the least danger-ous branch to a co-equal branch in national politics is directly related to the increasing and changing nature of the business brought to its docket" (O'Brien, 1985: 33). Although the percentage increase in the caseload is not as dramatic as O'Brien suggests (see Table 6), his point is important. Following a gradual increase from the founding of the republic, applica-tions for review actually declined at an average annual rate of about 2 percent during the last decade of the nineteenth century. Then, in the first half of this century they increased at about 2 percent a year, accelerating to more than 5 percent annually by midcentury (Casper, 1976: 6). Some scholars, finding evidence of a crisis in this increase, propose that if the justices were busy in 1935 with only 983 applications for review, they must be overwhelmed now with nearly five times as many cases (Casper, 1976: 7). It was this view that prompted the Chief Justice to appoint the Freund Commission, a group of academics who would advocate changes in the Court's structure. The commission analyzed the caseload, inter-viewed law clerks and justices, and concluded in 1972 that "the Court is

TABLE 6
Average Increase in Number of Cases Filed in Supreme Court, 1880–1974

Decade	Average No. Cases Filed Annually	Average Annual Rate of Change in 10–Year Moving Average (%)
1880–89	472	—
1890–99	383	−2.0
1900–09	449	+1.6
1910–19	561	+2.3
1920–29	737	+2.8
1930–39	940	+2.5
1940–49	1,223	+2.9
1950–59	1,516	+2.2
1960–69	2,639	+5.7
(1970–74)	3,683	+5.0

Source: G. Casper, 1976.

now at the saturation point, if not actually overwhelmed. . . . In one way or another, placing ever more reliance on an augmented staff, the Court could perhaps manage to administer its docket. But it will be unable adequately to meet its essential responsibilities." For the 1983 Term, the Court was described by those who believe its workload is heavy as having "disposed of" 5,100 cases. Thirty years before, they say the justices dealt with only 1,463 cases. Approximately 300 are decided "on the merits," where the Court makes an authoritative ruling on the controversy. Nearly half these cases get a full hearing followed by detailed opinions discussing the issues (see Table 7). The remainder are typically handled by a short unsigned *per curiam* opinion or by a "memorandum order" such as an order to dismiss, affirm, vacate, reverse, or remand (Goldman, 1985: 33).

In speaking of workload issues, Chief Justice Burger aggregated the Court's written work and argued that signed opinions increased on the average of ten every eight years since 1953. There is little dispute over the general trend toward increased opinions, especially when dissents are included (see Table 8). However, a study by Gerhard Casper and Richard Posner compared these data with similar statistics for the courts of appeals and concluded that "There is no statistical basis for a definite inference that the growth of the caseload has as yet substantially impaired (the) ability (of the Court)" (1976: 8).

A study based at New York University called the "Supreme Court Project" has reported a number of caseload-related findings that also belie the claim that the Court is overworked (Estreicher and Sexton, 1985). The NYU study evaluated the proposition that the Supreme Court does not have the opportunity to decide all the cases that it should be able to decide. Focusing on the 1982 Term, the "Supreme Court Project" looked at the 165 cases that the Court agreed to hear and the nearly 2,000 cases in which the justices denied review, and reports that nearly one-fourth of the cases granted review had no legitimate claim on the Court's time and that an additional 28 percent of the cases granted review in the term merited it only if the justices had excess time and energy to spend on them. Finally, the NYU study held that only 12 of the 1,860 cases denied review presented conflicts among three or more federal appeals courts or highest state courts, or otherwise fell into the category of cases the justices ought to have heard.

Proposals. Proposals to reform the Supreme Court's place in the structure of government are based on conceptions of the workload. There is little to indicate that elevating the institution to even more rarefied heights is more than a response to the press of business. Little, that is, but the relatively poor assessments of the way the Supreme Court's work is done. The few minutes for each case identified by Professor Hart (1959)

TABLE 7
Supreme Court's Workload

		Terms		
	Cases	*1983–84*	*1982–83*	*1981–82*
Paid Cases				
1	Cases from prior terms	520	545	522
2	Cases docketed during term	2,168	2,165	2,413
3	Cases on docket	2,688	2,710	2,935
4	Cases granted review and carried over	107	123	96
5	Cases denied, dismissed, or withdrawn	1,902	1,892	2,100
6	Cases summarily decided	71	113	114
7	Cases granted review this term	140	169	203
8	Cases acted upon	2,220	2,297	2,513
9	Cases not acted upon	468	413	422
***In Forma Pauperis* Cases**				
10	Cases from prior terms	344	317	350
11	Cases docketed during term	2,050	2,035	2,004
12	Cases on docket	2,394	2,352	2,354
13	Cases granted review and carried over	5	2	6
14	Cases denied, dismissed, or withdrawn	1,968	1,995	2,014
15	Cases summarily decided	10	6	12
16	Cases granted review this term	9	10	7
17	Cases acted upon	1,992	2,013	2,039
18	Cases not acted upon	402	339	315
Original Cases				
19	Cases from prior terms	14	16	17
20	Cases docketed during term	4	1	5
21	Cases on docket	18	17	22
22	Cases disposed of during term	7	3	6
23	Cases remaining	11	14	16
24	Total cases on docket	5,100	5,079	5,311
Argument Calendar				
25	Cases available at beginning of term	113	126	102
26	Cases made available during term	149	179	210
27	Cases reset for argument	4	3	4
28	Original cases set for argument	3	4	2
29	Total cases available for argument	269	312	318
30	Cases argued	184	183	184
31	Dismissed or remanded without argument	5	16	8
32	Total cases disposed of	189	199	192
33	Total cases available (67 hrs.)	80	(96 hrs.) 113	(111 hrs.) 126

TABLE 7
Supreme Court's Workload (cont.)

		Terms		
	Cases	*1983–84*	*1982–83*	*1981–82*
Decision Calendar				
34	Cases argued and submitted	184	183	184
35	Disposed of by signed opinion	174	174	170
36	Disposed of by *per curiam* opinion	6	6	10
37	Set for reargument	4	3	4
38	Total cases decided	184	183	184
39	Cases awaiting decision	0	0	0
40	Number of signed opinions	151	151	141

Source: *U.S. Law Week* 53: 3028.

was certainly not an adequate period for deliberation, but rather than look at how the court did its work, and there were justices who said that much time was being wasted, the findings inevitably led to calls for changes in the institution.

The most important proposals were made by the Freund Commission and the Hruska Commission, created by Congress in 1972. They recommended a National Court of Appeals that would screen cases going to the Supreme Court. This intermediate court would transmit approximately 400 cases from which the Supreme Court would then select one-third for decision. After a decade of discussion, the Chief Justice sought to revive

TABLE 8
Oral Arguments and Opinions

Term	Oral Argument	Cases with Signed Opinions	Cases without Signed Opinions	Per Curiam
1935	—	187	803	72
1940	—	195	790	86
1945	—	170	1,122	45
1950	129	114	1,088	77
1955	123	103	1,527	127
1960	148	125	1,786	136
1965	131	120	2,545	218
1970	151	137	2,968	232
1975	179	181	3,805	175
1980	154	159	3,967	115
1984	185	175	4,269	91

Source: Fruend et al., 1972: 47; *Harvard Law Review*.

interest in an intermediate federal court of appeals in 1983. Termed an "intercircuit panel," this body would resolve the conflicting rulings of the thirteen federal courts of appeals and construe federal statutes. Burger's plan would build the new institution from representatives of each of the courts of appeals, who would sit for four weeks each year. (The Chief Justice was accused of planning to choose the justices himself and did not allay all fears of judicial aggrandizement when he assured his critics that the whole Supreme Court would make this choice.) A bill to create such an institution was introduced in 1983 and never emerged from the Senate Judiciary Committee.

The spirit behind proposals being debated in Congress draws heavily on concerns for administrative efficiency. "One of the main functions of appellate court," according to Representative Robert W. Kastenmeier, Democrat of Wisconsin and a sponsor of bills in the House of Representatives to add another level to the appellate process, "is to insure uniformity and consistency in the law by resolving conflicts in decisions between or among trial courts or lower appellate courts" (Greenhouse, 1983). The premise here is one not drawn from experience with American practice but rather out of a vision of administrative rationality and a yearning for reform. The federal system has never been able to resolve all conflicts of its own making, much less those coming from the state courts, and until recently it has not shown an inclination to do either.

Disagreement with proposals like those of the Freund Commission or more recent legislation rely heavily on reconceptualization of the workload issue and in some cases are simply reactions to the institution itself. Rather than proposals for change from the outside, the NYU project looks within and examines whether the Court is using its time effectively. The project takes up some of the specifics of the argument that the Court has inadequate time to perform its tasks and looks at the claim that the Court is unable to resolve conflicts among decisions of the various circuit courts and that it is unable to adequately supervise the areas of federal law that "are crying out for authoritative rulings which the Supreme Court is unable to render" (Estreicher and Sexton, 1985). The NYU team concluded that the Supreme Court is wasting its resources in case selection. They offer a number of original recommendations, the most significant of which are

1. Abolishing mandatory appellate jurisdiction.
2. Setting new criteria for case selection based on a refined "federal question" doctrine.
3. Providing sanctions for frivolous filings.

4. Limiting forum shopping to minimize the effect of intercircuit differences.

There is of course much disagreement over what the High Court should look like. The implications of the different views tell us a great deal about the structure and purpose of judicial authority in the United States.

Implications. Of major concern is that the proposed changes would isolate the High Bench by introducing another level of review. Justice Douglas not only disputed the claims that the Court was overworked but he saw the process of filtering through the petitions for review as necessary to the larger deliberative process of reviewing developments in the law. He is quoted as saying, "The review or sifting of these petitions is in many respects the most important and, I think, the most interesting of all our functions. Across the screen each term come the worries and concerns of the American people—high or low—presented in concrete tangible form" (Westen, 1973: 32). Douglas's view had been noted in dissents through the years (*Warth* v. *Seldin,* 1975; *Tidewater Oil Co.* v. *United States,* 1972). It sets off inquiry into the implications of reform proposals for the institution and perhaps the existence of one court at the top of the judicial structure is more important than how much work it gets done.

Former Chief Justice Burger, as we have seen, can be compared with his predecessors who took an interest in judicial administration. Burger himself pointed out that in the 1920s, when Chief Justice Taft "proposed that the Supreme Court be given some control over its docket by the writ of certiorari, the same cries went up that the 1925 writ—like the proposal in 1891 for intermediate Courts of Appeal—would be 'a wall between the people and the Court' " (Westen, 1973: 12). The comparison of the modern Chiefs on administration is instructive. To the extent that it would free the justices from "mundane" tasks and allow them to concentrate on the most troubling issues, the proposals are consistent with past institutional innovation, but unlike past instances of institutional change the present proposal would eliminate rather than broaden discretion (Ulmer, 1973). According to the NYU study, at the heart of the workload issue are conceptions of the institution. They propose that the ideal of the Supreme Court as the nation's court of last resort is outdated and that the Supreme Court can better serve as manager of the federal judicial system and monitor the state courts. Another possibility is that decisions on major policy issues have come to be seen as more important to the Court's authority than a highly rationalized system of federal courts.

In an inquiry into the implications of "Authority and Institutional Arrangement," a recent study by Joseph Vining has turned the workload issue around and tried to consider "Law without a Supreme Court" (Vining, 1986: 63). By this the author meant simply to extrapolate from developments we have been observing with reference to litigation and the workload. The justices are actually doing a smaller percentage of the Court's work, the institution is becoming bureaucratized, and it may be reasonable to consider what the loss of the Supreme Court would mean. For Vining, the absence of the Court would mean greater attention to existing texts and to legal method, but probably not much greater. And the absence of the Supreme Court would "flatten the formal hierarchy that produces legal texts" (Vining, 1986: 65), just as a special intercircuit tribunal would elongate this hierarchy with perhaps the same damaging effect on the institution as a source of authoritative finality.

ISSUES AND THE INSTITUTION

Robert McCloskey, in his study of the Court's business, proposed that "the Court's claim on the American mind derives from the myth of an impartial, judicious tribunal whose duty it is to preserve our sense of continuity with fundamental law" (1960: 20). The wonder of the Supreme Court's institutional history is that this claim "on the American mind" was made in the resolution of economic and political controversies. The interests served by the institution came increasingly to be covered by an institutional legitimacy tied to specific policy areas. This section examines the substantive changes that have taken place in the business of the Supreme Court and their influence on the institution. The present focus, in the literature about the Court, on constitutional cases will be put into perspective by looking at the "double standard" for constitutional adjudication.

Historical Periods

There are three different Supreme Courts, considering the business the justices have undertaken throughout American history. The first "Court" lasted nearly one hundred years, until just after the Civil War. The second ran into the present century. This "Court" focused on business enterprise through supervision of the common law and a growing willingness to intervene in state lawmaking. The result was the modern Supreme Court. The present period begins in the Progressive Era with contests over the structure of legitimacy, but a widely acknowledged claim that the Court had the capacity to declare acts of state and national government beyond the fundamental law. In these periods, we can trace shifts in the nature of the issues before the institution by comparing some key years within each period.

1789–1865. During its first historical period, the Court shifted in size and in the business it handled. The growth of the institution was linked to an emerging sovereign, the United States of America. In its initial three-fourths of a century in operation, the business of the Court reflected the status of the national government and its concerns. Like that government, the Court began fitfully and as it grew sectionalism and slavery became its greatest challenge. The Court would ride the success of the national idea after the Civil War to its next institutional manifestation.

In 1801, half the Supreme Court's cases involved disputes in admiralty, another third came under its diversity jurisdiction, and there were a few cases where the United States was both a plaintiff and under federal statutes (Goebel, 1971: 807). In each of these areas the institution was assuming power in a vacuum (admiralty) or in a domain newly constructed in the jurisdiction given the Court by Congress (diversity). The importance of property questions for the new nation is evident in the one-third of the docket composed of disputes between debtors and creditors, over title to land, and arising from commerce at sea.

By 1825, the Court's docket was beginning to be large enough to permit aggregate comparison with the institution in subsequent years.[2] The justices in 1825 were hearing cases that combined private matters, emerging federal legislation, and national controversies such as the slave trade. Some things familiar today were absent. There were no challenges of state laws based on the Bill of Rights, for instance. Other matters that have disappeared from the institution were common in 1825. Ten of the twenty-six cases heard during that term involved common law topics. Another four dealt with the interpretation of statutes and three settled disputes emerging out of the slave trade. Because institutional practices materialized in this period, its landmark cases have become part of the lore of the modern Court. These special cases, however, were not typical of what the Court was doing at the time and they simply tie the present institution to the past. *McCulloch* v. *Maryland* (1819) asserted the power of the nation over the states and a broad interpretation was given to the commerce power in *Gibbons* v. *Ogden* (1824). While the nation was coming into existence during John Marshall's tenure in the first part of this period, the second part, under Taney, was a mixed legacy. Scholars such as Robert McCloskey present the Court by picking out the great constitutional cases, emphasizing a continuity with earlier judges in areas such as commerce and contract. The "mistake" in *Dred Scott,* the "self-inflicted wound," is offered to explain the break that came with the Civil War. The business of the Court before and after the conflict is so different that we have to place the resolution of sectional issues as the foundation for the modern institution.

Court Business

The number of cases decided by the Court in 1825 were barely 10 percent of those decided a generation after the Civil War. Not only were the numbers small in the first years, but the cases constituted an insignificant portion of the problems in the American courts. Of the seventeen subject areas covering those in which Supreme Courts have worked (see Table 9) in the last 200 years, the institution in 1825 decided cases in only seven areas, while the Court of fifty years later would work in all but three of these fields. The Court was more involved with private disputes over land and property than it is today. Many of these had implications for national politics. This was certainly true of the slave rebellion aboard the ship *Antelope*, which came to the Court during the 1825 term. The case, which set national policy on the slave trade and involved international property issues, was decided as an admiralty issue in the context of international law and international agreements.

Changes in the Court ought not be seen as overly determined by social and economic changes. By life tenure, institutional tradition and uniqueness the Court is relatively isolated. Most important, the Court sits apart. From 1789 to 1875 sixteen pieces of legislation had a major affect on the institution and its business. Beginning with the Judiciary Act of 1789

TABLE 9
Comparative Analysis of Supreme Court Business

Legal Subjects	1825	1875	1925	1975*
Admiralty	2	5	8	1
Antitrust Law	0	0	2	5
Bankruptcy	0	13	9	3
Bill of Rights (Not Process)	0	2	3	56
Commerce Clause	0	2	34	40
Common Law	10	81	11	—
Due Process				
Economic Issues	0	2	20	0
Rights of Accused	0	0	3	34
Indians	0	0	7	2
International Law, War and Peace	2	5	6	0
Jurisdiction	4	30	29	1
Land Legislation	0	11	3	—
Misc. Stat. Interp.	4	16	15	28
Patents and Trademarks	1	8	4	—
Slave Trade	3	0	0	0
Contract Suits	0	12	17	—
Taxation	0	5	27	3
All others	0	1	12	0
Totals	26	193	209	171

Source: Frankfurter and Landis, 1928: 302; *Harvard Law Review*, 1976; G. Casper, 1976: 13; O'Brien, 1985: 32.
* Full opinions only.

establishing the federal judiciary through the Act of 1866 expanding jurisdiction over civil rights and the Act of 1867, which expanded jurisdiction
over habeas corpus and amended the Judiciary Act of 1789 providing for
review of state court decisions, Congress solidified the institutional structure in conjunction with federal and institutional interests. The significance of the institution in its own growth is in the members' expression of
needs and possibilities as well as congressional interpretation of national
needs through visions of the institution. This activity has been more fully
documented for the next period in the Court's history.

   1866–1918. After the Civil War, the business of the federal courts
changed quickly once the relation between nation and the states was
decided militarily. The development of business and transportation, infra-
structure and commercial questions delineating the nature of the national
economy occupied the institution. The new railroad system, for instance,
facilitated both the territorial and commercial expansion of the nation.
The Court, far from being autonomous or the creature of unmediated
social pressure, assumed a new authority over federal law. By its interpretation of statutes, the Court began to reflect what Frankfurter and
Landis called quantum jumps in the "assumption of authority" (1928: 60).
The institution was not yet capable of authoritative decision on matters of
fundamental law without considerable support from the other branches.
In 1875, at the midpoint of post-Civil War industrial expansion, disputes
in which the Court was fashioning a national common law remained the
largest category of business, increasing somewhat over the preceding fifty
years.

   The "common law Court" characteristic of the institution in the nineteenth century (Casper, 1976: 12), would all but disappear by the end of
the period. New issues like bankruptcy litigation, due process claims,
land legislation, patents, taxation, and suits against the government became more common. This increase was also evident in the construction of
statutes and the delineation of jurisdiction for the expanding federal court
system (see Table 6). Formerly the business of the state judiciary, commercial matters in a growing economy were taken on by an expanding
federal judiciary. Bankruptcy, absent from the docket in 1825, would
become 5 percent of the Supreme Court's work fifty years later and common law cases concerning private economic disputes even increased to
half of the institution's business by 1875. The variety in the 1875 docket
suggests the transitional nature of this Court. The institution remained
involved in admiralty, jurisdictional, and international issues as it began
to emerge in its more modern form with attention to due process, the Bill
of Rights, and taxation.

   In the Age of Enterprise, the federal courts were securely attached to
a ruling class. They did not have to fear the sectional controversies that

cut so deeply into their authority before the Civil War. After the war the tension came from another source, conflicts between classes, between capital and labor. The Supreme Court became involved, particularly when state legislatures sought to block the emerging practice of unregulated economic activity. Justice Stephen J. Field, dissenting in *Munn* v. *Illinois* (1877), suggested the way for the Supreme Court (Paul, 1969: 8–10; Swisher, 1930) by proposing a constitutional basis for eradicating state legislation regulating economic enterprise. It was a way suggested during the period by lawyers (Twiss, 1942) and "law writers," those intellectual craftsmen whose ideological product can become part of the landscape with the proper institutional imprimatur (Jacobs, 1954). This the Court provided in *Lochner* v. *New York* (1905).

The importance of *Lochner* is not that it was a case characteristic of the period and not that its conservative philosophy dominated the Court (Lasser, 1985), although judicial conservatism was a feature of the federal judiciary during the period. The importance of *Lochner* is in what it symbolized about the stature of the institution, for *Lochner* came to mean that the Court *could* stand against the popular institutions, even for those who believed it ought not. On this basis, the courts would emerge as forums of public litigation after the turn of the century (Baum, 1984; Chayes, 1976). The shift toward federal restrictions on state legislation first affected business, but this power laid the foundation for attention to other fundamental rights. The institution that grew to serve capital would turn to other constitutional rights while the economy was shifting to administrative management.

1918–Present. Soon after the turn of the century, the Court would shift its attention more completely to constitutional law. In 1925, enabling legislation gave the Court far more complete judicial discretion, and trends that would come to dominate the Court in the next generation began to emerge. While the traditional private law or "landlord and tenant" cases still made up a large portion of the Court's business,[3] an increase in federal statutes had transformed such areas as regulation of the economy, taxation, and antitrust. This activity would mean a decline in the common law questions and such peripheral issues as land legislation and patents (see Table 6). Thirty-four constitutional questions were before the Court in 1925 in a total caseload of 209. This nearly equaled the number of constitutional cases heard over the institution's first seventy years. Decisions based on the Constitution continued to increase in the twentieth century so that by 1970 they constituted over half of the Court's docket and increased to two-thirds in the next five years (Casper, 1976: 51).

In J. Woodford Howard's study of the courts of appeal this phenomenon of Supreme Court work is examined for the extent to which it serves as a check or supervisory institution for the intermediate levels of the federal judiciary. Although his work involves the Supreme Court only to the extent that it bears on the work of the intermediate courts, it still contains valuable material about the last step in the appellate process, and what makes that step different. According to Howard, although the Supreme Court and the courts of appeal share much of the same jurisdiction, "the business of the Supreme Court was not a reflex of circuit activity or of external pressures" (1981: 57). As was mentioned with regard to the workload, the High Court was more likely than the courts of appeal to overturn cases that came to it in the mid-1960s, and the Supreme Court was over three times as likely to decide constitutional questions than the intermediate federal courts. Before 1937, the Supreme Court had reached a level of constitutional policymaking and catholic taste in business distinguishing it from the institution prior to the legal consolidation of capitalist industry (Paul, 1969). After 1937, emphasis on constitutional cases increased geometrically, but according to observers of institutional practice, the increase came on a much narrower policy agenda. This was due to emergence of a "double standard," a vivid example of judicial influence over its business and the link between that influence and the nature of the institution, to be discussed in the next section.

The Double Standard

After the struggle over legal supremacy waged by Franklin Roosevelt, the Supreme Court began to be seen as a political institution. The temple that the lawyers had instantiated into American governmental practice over the preceding fifty years and finally erected behind the Capitol in 1935 was no sooner finished than its foundations were being challenged by democratic claims and the political jurisprudence that came with them. The political attack on economic due process reached into the scholarly community and thoroughly demystified the formalism and neutrality of the constitutional tradition (Lerner, 1937). This shifted the jurisprudential, and hence institutional, foundations for Supreme Court action. One consequence was the "double standard."

The "double standard," an institutional practice, distinguishes the economy from politics for the purpose of review by the Supreme Court.[4] This practice of distinguishing is triggered when the Court reviews a law passed by Congress or a state legislature on economic matters, something like a minimum wage law, for instance. According to the practice, the justices merely ask that there be a reasonable basis for such laws. A higher standard of review is required when fundamental social and political issues, like discrimination, are considered. As a matter of convention, since 1937 the Court is said to have turned away from supervision of the economic realm in favor of attention to politics. By using two standards for review, the justices have announced that fundamental political freedoms will receive closer judicial scrutiny than economic freedoms. After describing the nature of the distinction we will consider some of the questions it has raised.

The Distinction. The "double standard" has been described in various ways by the commentators and although the language varies, the existence of the practice has been confirmed by observers of the Supreme Court. According to Henry Abraham, "what the post-1937 judiciary did was to assume as constitutional all legislation in the propietarian sector . . . but to regard with a suspicious eye legislative and executive experimentation with other basic freedoms" (1977: 15). Abraham calls these basic freedoms cultural and he associates them with the Bill of Rights. To Gerald Gunther, "The modern Court has turned away due process challenges to economic regulation with a broad 'hands off' approach . . . Only on a few occasions have some Justices expressed doubts about the Court's stance of extreme deference to economic regulation" (Gunther, 1985: 540). The language used by Willard Hurst to describe the double standard is another variant, but Hurst maintains a distinction between the economic sphere, referred to as "private markets," and the political sphere, which deals with or affects "values not tied primarily to allocation of economic resources" (1980–1981: 459).

The practice of distinguishing between economics and politics in employing judicial review can be traced to the period just prior to the New Deal struggle over the orientation of the Supreme Court. Justice Oliver Wendell Holmes advocated abandoning the general deference to legislatures when he was confronted with basic "non-economic" rights. Dissenting in *Truax* v. *Corrigan* (1922), where the Court struck down an Arizona statute forbidding injunctions against peaceful picketing, Holmes insisted that courts are not competent to scrutinize social goals or prevent "the making of social experiments that an important part of the community desires." Justice John Marshall Harlan's call for restraint was evident even earlier in *United States* v. *E.C. Knight Co.* (1895), a key economic case, where all of his colleagues declared the Sherman Anti-Trust Act unconstitutional. A suggestion of the distinction is evident in his contrasting willingness to intervene in *Plessy* v. *Ferguson* (1896), a question of political or social rights in his view, and declared the state legislation unconstitutional.

But the struggle over the New Deal and President Roosevelt's "court packing plan," announced following his second inaugural in January 1937, launched the double standard. The plan followed two terms where McCloskey described the Court as tearing "great holes in the New Deal program of recovery legislation" (1960: 167). Not long after the plan was announced, with its prospects for adding up to six new justices to the Court, the justices began a retreat from strict supervision of the economy. In *West Coast Hotel Co.* v. *Parrish* (1937), on a Washington State minimum wage law for women and children, the Supreme Court turned away from the doctrine of liberty of contract, a cornerstone of its laissez-faire ideology. As the story of the emerging standard goes, "Gradually the Court embarked upon a policy of paying close attention to any legislative and executive attempt to curb basic rights and liberties in the 'non-economic' sphere" (Abraham, 1983).

The standard took shape in *United States* v. *Carolene Products* (1938), the case containing Justice Stone's crucial footnote four, which was used to support "increased judicial intervention in non-economic affairs" (Tribe, 1978: 450). The Stone note claimed special basis for judicial intervention where legislation appears on its face to be within a specific prohibition of the constitution, where it "restricts those political processes which can ordinarily be expected to bring about repeal of undesirable legislation" like voting, or political assembly, and where legislation is prejudicial to discrete and insular minorities.

Here the Court suggested that it "would sustain regulation in the socio-economic sphere if any state of facts either known or reasonably inferrable afforded support for the legislative judgment" (Tribe, 1978: 450). This level of judicial deference was understood as abdication from the field. In discussing the *Carolene Products* footnote, Gerald Gunther said the Court had turned away from "commercial transaction" the year before and relied on the footnote to explain its "growing interventionism regarding legislation which restricts political processes" (1985: 535). He concludes: "The 'double standard' suggested by that footnote . . . has had a pervasive influence. . . . [T]here can be no doubt that the modern Court has been characterized by a notable activism on behalf of fundamental rights and interests outside the economic sphere" (1985: 542). The attack on economic due process had been a stunning institutional reversal. The Court's standard for constitutional review shifted from aggressive review of the legislative prerogative in the economic area to almost total abdication to legislative will on such issues in under five years.

Thus, in *Olsen* v. *Nebraska* (1941), Justice Douglas was able to assert that the presumption of constitutionality in the economic sphere was "no longer debatable." Robert McCloskey said that later decisions such as

Day-Brite Lighting v. *Missouri* (1952) and *Williamson* v. *Lee Optical* (1955) made it "pellucid" that no claim of a deprivation in the domain called substantive economic rights would be sustained by the Supreme Court (1960: 38). But the Court never repudiated jurisdiction over economic questions in clear and unequivocal terms (McCloskey, 1960: 40); rather, it was out of a footnote that the double standard emerged from the old framework for reviewing legislation and took shape in practice.[5] J. Willard Hurst described the Supreme Court as practically withdrawing "from the function of judicial review affecting statutory regulation of private market dealing" (1980–1981: 456; Tribe, 1978: 233–239, 434–455, 994–1000).

The consequences were dramatic for those who would seek help from the Court in this area, and the peripheral results were nearly as important. The institution became associated with a policy position, and institutional support (Lewis, 1964) as well as critique was built around it accordingly (Bickel, 1970). The withdrawal has meant a "marked disinclination of the Supreme Court of the late twentieth century to involve itself . . . in legislative determinations concerning the distribution of wealth or income" (Bickel, 1970: 457). The Court has led the national agenda away from the contentions and dangerous matters of material well-being and focused attention on the equally contentious but much less dangerous issues of social and political life.

The Challenges. The idea that the Supreme Court could or should distinguish economics from politics was not well grounded and it did not go unscathed. In the beginning, challenges revealed juridical doubts about the formulation, but they were doubts that became increasingly irrelevant as the distinction became institutionalized. In a law review article titled "Chief Justice Stone's Conception of the Judicial Function," written in 1946, Judge Learned Hand wondered "Just why property itself was not a 'personal right' "; nobody, the judge lamented, had taken the time to explain this. According to Hand, Stone's conception comes from the teaching of James Bradley Thayer that a pluralism protected by law is preferable to economic due process. To Hand, however, judicial review required deference to all forms of legislation, and he feared Stone was trying to establish a new form of activism, one that would have the Roosevelt Court wielding the Bill of Rights in the interest of political and social minorities.

The double standard was investigated by Robert McCloskey in the belief that the justices might have "a coherent apologia" hidden somewhere for their retreat from "economic supervision" (1962: 45). The arguments McCloskey uncovered "for demoting economic rights to their modern lowly Constitutional status" were of two sorts: judgments about the nature and importance of the rights themselves, and judgments about institutional competence as it bears on different kinds of questions. Judgments of the first sort consider laws limiting free expression a greater affront to the social order than laws curbing economic liberty. To those who ground the special place of political rights in the benefits of an open society, McCloskey points out that while the participatory open society is undeniably compelling, it is not, without more, an argument for downgrading the status of economic rights. When McCloskey takes up judgments of the second sort, institutional competence, "economic order" (1962: 53), he finds the Court unable to effect its will against a determined population. The persistent volatility of the abortion issue reinforces this observation. In fact, it is easy to suspect that political rights are more volatile than a good many economic matters, and that in the present climate the legitimacy of the institution is inadequate to settle them. McCloskey states that "we are perhaps justified in concluding that the policy of abstention was never really thought through" (1962: 54).

Whether it had been adequately thought through or not, the double standard is closely tied to the present political view of the Supreme Court. Roosevelt's attempt to "pack the Supreme Court" challenged the view of the Constitution as "Higher Law." For Phillips Bradley, a participant in that struggle, the Constitution as symbol was hiding the instrumental reality of the document as used by the Supreme Court. Others, like Edward S. Corwin, aware that the higher law view of the Constitution was an artifact, cautioned against judicial insensitivity to popular will (Johnsen, 1937). The view that the Court was "deciding economic questions" required that the myth of the justices above politics be destroyed. The temple on the Hill that the lawyers had built was no sooner standing than its foundations were altered by political jurisprudence. The destruction of formalism in the scholarly community changed the institutional foundations for the Supreme Court while flashing the "double standard" as a screen.

The growth of judicial behavioralism was heightened by the policy change in 1937. The movement, begun by C. Herman Pritchett (1948), showed the political nature of Supreme Court justices and, while some scholars of this persuasion remained attentive to economic policy,[6] most commentary for the next thirty years focused on political rights. Because of this orientation, decisions were ignored and, well into the modern period, textbooks on constitutional law and many students of the Court and the Constitution proceeded as if nothing had happened in regard to economic issues since 1937. The double standard was institutional practice, but plenty of economic business continued to be done by the nation's highest court.

Economic Policy

Extrapolating from the public law tradition represented by McCloskey and realists such as Martin Shapiro, we uncover policy orientations that are barely noticeable because they are not what we expect of the institution. The Supreme Court has been very active in economic policy through statutory interpretation and in association with constitutional provisions like those in the "Privileges and Immunities" or "Commerce and Import-Export" clauses. In these areas, as McCloskey noted, "Since 1937, the Court has been rebuilding its constitutional dwelling place" (1962). Economic policy issues reviewed by the Supreme Court take the form of statutory interpretation of federal and state legislation and review of administrative agency action.

The Federal System. An ongoing issue in the relationship between the states and the national government is "preemption," the doctrine that where the national government has legislated, the states must defer. Preemption is associated with constitutional protections for interstate commerce and the hierarchy of laws protected by the supremacy clause. It was evident, for instance, in *Arkansas Electric Coop* v. *Arkansas Public Service Commission* (1983), where the jurisdiction of the state public service commission over wholesale rates charged by a rural electric cooperative to its member retail distributors was held not preempted by the Federal Power Act.

The commerce clause has been cited in economic cases before the Court such as the one from Massachusetts over an executive order requiring all construction projects funded by the city of Boston to have a work force of at least half city residents. The Court allowed the order to stand (*White* v. *Mass Council of Construction Employers, Inc.,* 1983). In another decision, the Court held that the minimum wage requirements of the Fair Labor Standards Act could be applied to a public mass-transit authority (*Garcia* v. *San Antonio Metropolitan Transit Authority,* 1985). The majority overturned a holding in *National League of Cities* v. *Usery* (1976), which had set a standard of local immunity from federal regulation. In *Garcia,* Blackmun declared the *Usery* standard "unworkable and inconsistent with established principles of federalism."

Another kind of economic policy involved a lawyer who lived in Vermont and wanted to practice law across the Connecticut River, in New Hampshire. The Court held that a state bar rule prohibiting admission of attorneys who are not state residents violated the Constitution's "Privileges and Immunities Clause" (*Supreme Court of New Hampshire* v. *Piper,* 1985). Regulation of the professions as well as other licensing practices is an important economic function that the Supreme Court has continued to monitor since 1937.

Congressional Legislation. A substantial number of the economic policy cases to which the Supreme Court gives a full hearing, such as *Bank of America* v. *United States* (1983), require statutory interpretation. In the Bank of America case, the attorney general's office had brought test suits to elicit an interpretation of federal law on interlocking directorates between competing banks and other financial institutions. The Court rested its decision on the Clayton Act, which it held did not bar interlocking directorates between banks and insurance companies.

The willingness of the Court to enter the economic sphere is also evident in its handling of the dispute between the NCAA and colleges resisting NCAA control over broadcasts of college sports (Easterbrook, 1984). The propensity to decide interesting cases where they might be avoided is evident in the challenge by Universal City Studios to the production of video cassette recorders. The video company wanted the electronics company to make up some of the losses that were due to duplication of copyrighted material. The Court applied patent law concepts to these problems and thereby expanded the fair use doctrine in copyright law.

Economic cases decided in just one year, 1985, cover a variety of statutory issues such as the "maritime employment" provision of the Harbor Worker's Compensation Act and its application to welders who worked on fixed offshore oil-drilling platforms (*Herbs Welding, Inc.* v. *Gray,* (1985); the enforcement of arbitration agreements under the Federal Arbitration Act (*Dean Witter Reynolds, Inc.* v. *Byrd,* 1985); a trademark dispute between Park 'N Fly, Inc. and Dollar Park and Fly brought under provisions of the Lanham Act; and a controversy between a publisher and the heirs of Ted Snyder over royalties for the song "Who's Sorry Now," which was written by Mr. Snyder in 1923 (*Mills Music, Inc.* v. *Marie Snyder,* 1985). These cases testify to the Court's ongoing involvement in economic matters.

Administrative Decisions. Since the Supreme Court supervises the regulatory process, its role has expanded as these instruments of national power have increased (O'Brien, 1985). In administrative law, supervision of the legislature's delegated powers is ultimately more akin to the "ordinary" processing of disputes than the articulation of constitutional rights. This shift was portrayed in Frankfurter and Landis (1928) with its emphasis on the policy significance of discretion over the caseload. For the last fifteen years, the Court has looked cosely at agency action, and in *Motor Vehicle Manufacturers Association of the United States* v. *State Farm Mutual* (1983), the justices endorsed the "hard look" doctrine. The decision struck down the National Highway Traffic Safety Administration's decision to rescind its regulations requiring new motor vehicles to be equipped with passive restraints. The National Labor Relations Board has offered many opportunities for Supreme Court review. In one, the Court allowed New Jersey to regulate the qualifications of casino industry union officials (*Brown* v. *Hotel and Restaurant Employees,* 1984). In another, the board had challenged a building supply company's effort to get out of collective bargaining agreements while it was going through bankruptcy proceedings. In an example of "judicial deradicalization" of labor law, the Court backed the company (*NLRB* v. *Bildisco and Bildisco,* 1984).

Picking up on the dearth of commentary on the Court's role in economic policy, Robert L. Dudley and Craig R. Ducat studied voting patterns on the Burger Court in economic cases (1985). In a factor analysis on the 1981–1983 terms, which pointedly distinguishes its methodology from ones concerned with justification, the authors base their explanations on federalism as well as economic liberalism-conservatism. Federalism, like legislation and administrative decisions, is a factor that illuminates the nature of the policy context and helps to explain judicial choice. These institutional considerations—federalism, review of administrative decisions, and factors associated with the legitimate authority of the federal government—reveal the Supreme Court's significance as an authoritative voice where it is less conspicuous, in economic policy. In these cases, the Court's claim to authority draws on its place in the institutional hierarchy of American law. In doctrinal development a practice like the double standard can divert attention from the Court's work even on Constitutional matters because that work does not fit into larger institutional expectations.

Property Rights

Traditional liberal theory linked property rights and personal rights. With the industrial revolution, came the idea that property and liberty could be separated. By the early part of the twentieth century, reform movements attacked property as protecting elites and large concentrations of economic power. Property rights came to be considered an obstacle to liberty. The attack on the judiciary in the 1930s with its distinction between political and economic life further helped excise property from constitutional protection for the individual. Its status as a civil liberty, a constitutionally protected right of every citizen, has been played down or avoided with exclusion of property from treatises on civil liberties (Abraham, 1983).

Contemporary developments in constitutional property reveal the paths of economic and political right converging. On the one hand, public prerogatives over economic interests have expanded with the growth of government, planning, and environmental concerns. On the other, public obligations to holders of statutory entitlements have been recognized by the federal courts as property. The consequence is that the rights associated with "real" property are less comprehensive and protection of entitlements is more substantial than is generally realized. This is the basis for the present discussion, and it joins a considerable commentary from the law schools (Baker, 1984; Radin, 1982; Michelman, 1981). Now, "real" property seems to be drawing on the support for civil liberties that has come from two generations of activism in the federal courts and, to the extent that property is associated with promises of constitutional government, it need not return to its status as a tool of the corporations.

The Tradition. Although the term "property" is initially used only in the Constitution's Fifth Amendment: "nor shall private property be taken for public use without just compensation," the early Supreme Court protected property by reference to various constitutional provisions. In *Fletcher* v. *Peck* (1810) and subsequent cases, Chief Justice John Marshall relied on the contract clause to prevent governmental whim from denying legitimate expectations. Before the Civil War, slavery and franchises to do business constituted important forms of property. After the Civil War property valued in the market (Commons, 1924) made the right much more appropriate to an expanding industrial order. The common quality, according to Laurence Tribe, was a model of "settled expectations." To Tribe, the model is composed of "restraints on government power" that vest rights in property on the grounds "that certain settled expectations . . . should be secure against governmental disruption, at least without appropriate compensation" (1978: 456). Property in the Constitution is a matter of expectations rather than possession of tangible things.

Expectations, in order to be considered "settled," must also be legitimate. This was evident in *Penn Central Transportation Company* v. *New York* (1978). The decision subordinated state power over historic preservation to a reasonable expectation of profit. Yet the City of New York was permitted to restrict development of historic landmarks. The legitimacy of the expectation depended on whether restrictions applied to the Grand Central Terminal constituted a "taking," that is whether economic injuries caused by public action must be compensated. Justice Brennan indicated that although takings are more readily found where there is a "physical invasion" by government, the Constitution recognizes a broader understanding of property. A taking must interfere with interest "sufficiently bound up with the reasonable expectation of the claimant."

The Court held that Penn Central had insufficient loss to constitute a violation of legitimate expectations and hence the city's action was not a taking.[7]

The compensation question had become a matter of balancing rights to determine when property could be expropriated. One of the traditional requirements was that property could be taken only from private hands "for public use." This issue arose in the 1984 case of *Hawaii Housing Authority et al.* v. *Midkiff,* where the state had instituted a land condemnation program to transfer property to those who had been leasing from the island's large landowners. According to Justice O'Connor regulating oligopoly and the evils associated with it is a classic exercise of a state's police powers. Frank Easterbrook (1984), writing in the *Harvard Law Review,* linked *Midkiff* with a case involving the disclosure of trade secrets held by Monsanto Co. (*Ruckelshaus* v. *Monsanto Co.,* 1984). Easterbrook sees the double standard here and these cases as completing "a trend toward placing takings largely outside the realm of judicial review" by treating expropriation "as simply another form of socioeconomic regulation" (1984: 226).

One doesn't need the double standard, however, to understand legislative prerogatives over property. It is only necessary to remember that "the unexceptional fact of limits" on property ownership are the norm, or, as Justice Jackson noted, "Rights, property or otherwise, which are absolute against all the world are certainly rare" (*United States* v. *Willow River Power,* 1945). Adjudication of traditional property rights has involved weighing expectations that are protected by the Constitution through the "just compensation" provision. For some time, the Supreme Court has acknowledged that "Property . . . may be construed to include obligations, rights, and other intangibles as well as personal things" (*Fidelity and Deposit Co. of Maryland* v. *Arenz,* 1983). The range of protected expectation and the Court's contribution to legitimation in the welfare state are issues surrounding the "new" property. Here, the Court's economic business took the form of a change in the reach of constitutional property.

"New" Property. A distinction between individual rights surrounding "real" property and "privileges" adhering in government largess goes back to *McAuliffe* v. *Mayor of New Bedford* (1892), where Judge Holmes of Massachusetts distinguished between "a Constitutional right to talk politics" and a job as a policeman to which no constitutional right applied. At the Supreme Court, the justices had, in the same vein, distinguished "real or personal 'property' " (Tribe, 1978: 509) from entitlements to licenses, goods, or services provided by government, and placed minimal constraints on revocation of entitlements (Tribe, 1978: 510). This distinc-

tion began to break down by the mid-twentieth century (Van Alstyne, 1968).

Initial application of constitutional protection to entitlements involved Social Security. The program had been held constitutional in 1937, but it was not until 1960 in *Flemming* v. *Nestor* that the justices addressed the status of benefits. Hearing a due process claim, the Court allowed payment to be denied to a family (following their deportation). But in 1961, the Court held that when benefits were withdrawn there had to be an unusually important government need to outweigh the right of a beneficiary (*Cafeteria and Restaurant Workers Union* v. *McElroy,* 1961). In an article published a few years later, Charles Reich argued that the welfare state had altered the status of individuals so that benefits like unemployment compensation, public assistance, and old age insurance urgently "need the concept of right" (Reich, 1964).

The case that recognized statutory entitlements as property, *Goldberg* v. *Kelly* (1970), pitted welfare authorities against a beneficiary in New York who had been cut off without a hearing, because he refused to accept counseling for drug addiction that he denied having. In the Supreme Court, Justice William Brennan noted that since much of the wealth in the country, such as tax exemptions, employment security, and unemployment compensation, "takes the form of rights which do not fall within traditional common law concepts of property . . . It may be realistic today to regard welfare entitlements as more like 'property' than a 'gratuity' " (*Goldberg* v. *Kelly,* 1970: 262). Property in statutory entitlements had become law and it was amplified by Justice Potter Stewart, who held that "a person's interest in a benefit is a 'property' interest for due process purposes if there are such rules or mutually explicit understandings that support his claim of entitlement to the benefits" (*Board of Regents* v. *Roth,* 1971: 601).

The "new" right replaced minimal protection with a presumption favoring continuation of the benefit. In *Goss* v. *Lopez* (1975), the Court found property interests present where high school students were suspended from their classes without a hearing. The deprivation was held to be substantial enough to overcome concern about the educational process. Although there were many dissatisfied plaintiffs at the Supreme Court level in the decade after *Goss,* including a foster family desiring to remain intact, a state prisoner being transferred, and a medical student who claimed to have been unjustly dismissed from school, there was also recognition that expectations constitute property. Some of the claims that were upheld by the Court combined sensitivity for the powerless with economic issues. In *Memphis Light, Gas and Water Division* v. *Craft* (1978), the utility company claimed an absolute right to discontinue service when bills had not been paid. But the Supreme Court saw an exception when the bill was the subject of a "bona fide dispute." The company would be liable for damages if the dispute turned out to be legitimate. Here, state protection against termination, except for cause, amounted to a property interest the Court was willing to recognize.

Not too long ago (in the history of property) Justice Stewart expressed doubts in *Lynch* v. *Household Finance Corporation* (1972) about the "double standard." Stewart wrote, "[T]he dichotomy between personal liberties and property rights is a false one. Property does not have rights. People have rights." Stewart wrote of modern sensitivity to due process protections of "new property" and called to mind the poor, rather than coporate managers, in describing property as a "welfare check, a home or a savings account." Stewart had noted "a fundamental interdependence" between the right to liberty and the right to property in an effort to enhance constitutional protections for homes and savings accounts. He associated them with "established" rights to travel and to the continuation of welfare benefits.

The Court continues to draw on civil rights to protect economic interest. The opinion in *Logan* v. *Zimmerman Brush Co.* (1982), by Justice Harry Blackmun, boldly restated the definition of property as "an individual entitlement grounded in state law" and ruled in favor of a shipping clerk with a short leg who claimed that he "had been unlawfully terminated because of his physical handicap" (*Logan,* 1982: 4248–4250). The protected property was a traditional common law entitlement, a "cause of action" provided by the Fair Employment Practices Act. The opinion reveals an enthusiasm for protection of the powerless very different from that expressed by the Supreme Court 150 years earlier when it viewed the poor as a "moral pestilence." The concern is now for civil liberties as much as traditional protection for economic interests. In this sense, property is a modern concept institutionally wedded to the Supreme Court.

The meaning of the Court and Constitution is captured by the shared phenomenon of institutional practices. The material in this chapter has looked at the Court's business including the institutional contributions to the property right and what the justices have been doing in economic policy. Here, institutional product draws on both traditional doctrinal authority and the more modern authority of institutional location. Economic policy has existed in both decision and doctrine and both have also been affected by institutional practices at the Supreme Court. In the political struggle between the President and the Court that boiled over in 1937, the authority of the Court in relation to the economy was the central issue and the shift of 1937 is remembered as a turn away from the bad old politics of laissez-faire constitutionalism. In accepting this description of the institution scholars lost track of the economic policy made by the Supreme Court.[8] This is one lesson to be taken from looking at the business of the institution. Of equal consequence for the institution is the turn away from the ideology of Higher Law to a new ideology of political jurisprudence. In accepting the view that the Supreme Court's product is simply politics, we neglect the base of that politics, the institution that gives meaning to the decisions of judges. The next chapter examines the production of doctrine by the institution.

6

PRACTICES IN ACTION

JURISPRUDENCE HAS traditionally dichotomized judicial choice around the poles of law and behavior, or the formal and the political elements in judging. An institutional perspective bridges this dichotomy, linking the Supreme Court and the Constitution and bringing the common elements of law and behavior to the foreground. The common elements are practices. This chapter examines the institutional and doctrinal practices that turn disputes into Supreme Court decisions (or nondecisions).

As noted in Chapter 2, formalism in law, commonly known by the aspiration to be a government of laws and not of "men," proposed that when the judge decides a case, the decision really comes from somewhere else. Formalism, with the authority of William Blackstone's *Commentaries* behind it, was the basis for claims of judicial supremacy during much of the nineteenth century. In America, lawyers carried this myth to a new pinnacle of political power for Anglo-American courts. But as courts reached their zenith their authority was being transformed. Near the end of the century, English jurist John Austin attacked formalism as resting on "the childish fiction employed by our judges, that judiciary or common law is not made by them, but is a miraculous something made by nobody, existing . . . from eternity, and merely deduced from time to time by the judges" (1885: 634).

By the time Roscoe Pound announced the American version of Austin's positivism and brought down the authority of form by referring to it as mechanical, the modern Supreme Court had been built. Once built, the system of legal authority began to be seen another way. Elegantly described by Holmes and developed in the 1930s, Realism characterized judging as behavior. By ridiculing the conception of eternally cast and judicially discovered law as a "judicial slot machine" (Pound, 1921: 170–171), realism debunked claims that the justices "lay the article of the Constitution which is involved beside the statute which is challenged and decided whether the latter squares with the former."

The Constitution stands in relation to the Supreme Court neither as a matter of rules nor behaviors. The justices say what they can about the Constitution as a function of the sense that has been made of that document over the years. What can be said about free speech or presidential power is bounded much as the choice of a new justice or the role of a clerk is bounded by institutional practices. Although law pervades the Supreme Court, realist and behavioral scholars lost interest in the institutional setting in favor of psychological categories and political explanations. Yet cases before the Court are queries about the meaning of some doctrinal tradition or other. In the case of the Constitution, that tradition is uniquely constitutive. Judicial action on expression, for instance, can no more operate without regard to the Constitution than the president can appoint justices without regard to the Senate. The capacity to judge, to understand the equal protection clause, for instance, and what responses are possible is thus an aspect of institutional life (Will, 1974: 310). Practices incorporating the "compulsion of the beaten track" (Pritchett, 1948: 58–71) join the institutional tradition.[1]

This chapter examines that synthesis in three parts. The first, Constitutional Sense, outlines the limit on interpretation and the standard for judicial choice. The discussion shows that what has been seen as rules and behavior is characterized more aptly as discourse. The second part dissects the institutional practices that transform the interests of individual justices and their staff into decisions of the Court. We end with conflict evident in the attitudes of the justices and institutional factors. This conflict, or Constitutional Politics, produces a conceptual ground for action on the basis of exchange of drafts. Here, focus on discourse incorporates judicial politics without letting them totally dominate.

CONSTITUTIONAL SENSE

In reading opinions from the Supreme Court on the Constitution and comparing the views of the justices, we see various sides of the dispute. This is the inevitable result of an adversary system, where both sides in an appeal are expected to present at least reasonable arguments for their position. Similarly, the opinions of justices in most instances also make sense. As Veronica Geng pointed out in a satire on constitutional discourse published in *The New Yorker,* there is no constitutional right for a twelve-year-old girl to audition for the Clint Eastwood part in a sequel to

"Dirty Harry." Even if the justices felt that the director's refusal to give the little girl a chance was "rotten, beastly, a crying shame," they would not hear an appeal on this basis (Geng, 1978: 31).[2]

The discourse to which the justices must relate has structure and meaning. It has been wrongly characterized at the hands of some realists and behavioralists as completely up for grabs (Carter, 1985: 9). Ill-formed, ambiguous decisions bordering on the limits of "good sense" exist. But pure nonsense—action with no previously agreed to or even comprehensible foundation—is rare. Even *Dred Scott,* a prime candidate and a politically stupid as well as morally bankrupt decision, had the constitutionality of slavery, among other things, on its side. Pure "constitutional" nonsense is rare on the Supreme court because of the constitutive relationship between sensible communication and the institution.

The tradition of sense in the law has been recognized as a constraint on the justices among sophisticated students of the judiciary for some time (Pritchett, 1967). The literature on judicial interpretation attentive to the "sense" in the law goes back to Edward Levi's reasoning by example (1949). Later, Julius Stone described the skills of the lawyer and the judge in terms of a rhetorical tradition that placed constraints on reasonableness (1968), and Ronald Dworkin has modernized positivism by linking its definitive nature to institutional expectations (1977). Still, few contemporary scholars have paid much attention to how doctrine influences what judges decide.[3]

Legal sense is evident in successful appeals and appears in conference, in opinions, and in oral argument.[4] It is the basis for the political maneuverings that characterize the work of the Court. In order to incorporate "sense" in a description of judging, we draw on convention. The constitutional practices making up the tradition of discourse are unique and structurally interrelated. As developed in the following pages, the tradition is shown to be more akin to discourse than rules, hence more than mere rationalization, and capable of evolutionary growth or decay.

The Tradition as Discourse

The justices of the Supreme Court, like other judges, hear, speak, write, and think in the language of the cases before them. To the extent that there is a social intelligence informing their action, the conditions under which this intelligence operates are characteristic of human discourse, or language. For a petition or appeal based on the Constitution to be heard it must contain reasonable claims and be capable of eliciting a sensible response (Murphy, 1964; 160–161). This sense has already been characterized as the artificial reason that initially led to the political stature of courts. For the "reason" of justices about some area of law like the

Constitution to function in this way, it must have available ideas "laid down in advance of action" (Read, 1938: 51) by habitual interpretation. Edward Corwin, the Princeton government professor who dominated constitutional scholarship in the first part of this century, in describing the peculiar freedom open to the justices characterized the structure and limits on their action as "jural freedom . . . which the Court has built up for itself piece by piece by its own past practices and precedents" (1934: 182). For the Supreme Court, constitutional law is a distinct tradition associated with the institution. Although other traditions have a bearing on interpretation carried out by the justices, constitutional law is the subject of the present treatment because the commingling of Court and Constitution is such a distinctive characteristic of American government.

Precedent is the traditional constraint on judicial action and it is a guide to the practices on which the court operates. But precedent must be distinguished from the present description of a tradition of discourse. As an explicit statement in a legal tradition, precedent is a signal, an indication of what has made sense, rather than being the "sense" itself or the actual Constitution. Use of precedent is much like use of words in a language, and it presupposes knowledge of the place or grammar within which it is to be used. Understanding the tradition precedes knowing the meaning of a precedent. Just as learning the name for court requires more than pointing to the word and pronouncing it, learning a precedent involves more than associating a title with a situation, although as with words we sometimes act as if ostensive definition is the basis for knowing the meaning of a precedent.

As authority for how concepts have been used, references to precedent show judicial discourse as subject to the constraints of sensible communication. This is particularly true in the case of oral arguments. In the argument of July 8, 1975, over the Nixon tapes, Leon Jaworski brought in prior cases when he argued that "if there is any one principle of law that *Marbury* v. *Madison* decides it is that it is up to the Court to say what the law is." Jaworski invoked *Marbury* as authority for his position and as a point of clarification rather than an order. Its power came from the sense it made. The justices, as students of the Constitution and practitioners in the Supreme Court, understood the claim.[5]

Case citations call up a stream of concepts. Tied to social relations through communities of interpretation, citations may even identify individuals with particular ideas. These social foundations of constitutional ideology also appeared in the Nixon tapes argument when Jaworski drew on an earlier case, *Doe* v. *McMillan,* where "Mr. Justice White pointed out that . . . the separation of powers doctrine has not prevented this Court from reviewing acts of Congress, even when . . . the executive branch is also involved." The authority of the special prosecutor's argument did not preclude compelling points on the other side, but law does not compel in that way. The law, and references to precedent, are what is involved. Law, as a tradition of sensible discourse, is the form of the activity and the outcome. Law determines what a dispute is about and how we will know it.

When John Marshall first used the concept of "commerce," he introduced ordinary meaning into constitutional discourse. The formulation he gave became a part of the institution and a basis for continual development. A claim based on the concept of "commerce" that did not make sense in terms of this tradition might be heard as something else, but it would not be heard by the Court as a "commerce" case. Intelligible use of traditional constitutional concepts involves an intuitive recognition of their qualities or what is essential to the Constitution. Jerome Hall noted, for instance, that "The concept of anything is the articulation of it in a context" (1963: 46). Similarly, Felix Frankfurter proposed that "words may acquire scope and function from the history of events which they summarize or from the purpose which they serve . . . They bear the meaning of their habitat" (1947: 213–237). The justices have the final say on their doctrinal habitat, even if they don't have the last word on the Constitution.

Charles Black described structural factors that exist beyond, or perhaps beneath, precedent (1969: 35). He viewed the decision in *Barron* v. *Baltimore* as resting on the relationship between the federal government and the states rather than any provision in the Constitution. Similarly, the First Amendment cannot be used formally to protect a President's right to speak, although ordinarily he might deserve a courteous audience. The structure of the document precludes some form of review by the Supreme Court. "Independent state grounds" take a case beyond the purview of the High Court. This was characteristic of the *Mount Laurel* decision, which rested on the New Jersey Constitution. In *People* v. *Anderson* (1972), a case decided by the California Supreme Court that voided the death penalty on the basis of California's constitutional provision against "cruel or unusual" punishment, the attorney general of the state was precluded from taking the case to the Supreme Court of the United States because the California decision was grounded in state law. There is no reading of the federal Constitution, three-fourths of the way through the twentieth century, that would compel California to keep the death penalty.

Given the nature of constitutional discourse and judicial review, a claim against the Constitution may be legally wrong and still make sense. Gideon's assertion that he had a right to a lawyer at his trial was such a claim. It had not been established by a lawmaking body, yet it fit into a doctrinal tradition suggested by the Court and, it terms of that tradition, it made sense. This was true with most of the revolution in criminal procedure advanced by the Warren Court. Usually, claims presented to the justices will have been filtered through a lawyer and various other courts, thus assuring consistency with the tradition.[6] With the prisoner petitions like Gideon's, the Court selected from among the multitude of petitions for ones that were of interest.

The Character of Tradition

By responding to the conceptual possibilities of the tradition, the justices associate ideas with the institution. By that action the ideas become the basis of litigation. "Clear and present danger," offered as a felicitous phrase, became central to constitutional adjudication of the First Amendment. In this process, "the mental set . . . and the development of an effective syntax is the result" (Garvey, 1971: 19). The tradition is linguistic to the extent that its concepts and structure constitute a social world (Brigham, 1978). The trade of the judge is not plied by the means of theoretical science; the syntax is descriptive. The conceptual tools and the relations that follow from them are useful and reliance on them shows a capacity rather than a compulsion.

The possibilities include a great many general social meanings brought together in an essentially unique sphere (Scheingold, 1974; Shklar, 1964) where issues of politics and social life are seen in terms of professional practices (Foster, 1976: 5). Claims before the Supreme Court rely on the fabrication of ideas through professional experience. Doctrine evolves through manipulation of doctrinal possibilities in the service of interests. Lawyers and justices force such evolution when their range of action is limited and the tradition changes through their arguments and justifications. New ideas are gradually incorporated and relatively minor conceptual leaps must be accepted by increasing numbers to establish a concept.

One doctrine revealing this process is "liberty of contract" (Twiss, 1942; Jacobs, 1954; Paul, 1969). Edward Corwin traced the concept back to its Higher Law foundations, the tradition of vested rights from which a reading of liberty as protection of less tangible interests emerged. The related idea that liberty in the Fourteenth Amendment might protect privacy is based on the commentary of Thomas M. Cooley (1888). Cooley presented a systematic statement of interpretations by state courts that worked its way into the federal Constitution one hundred years later. Such suggestions were not always accepted (see *Slaughter House Cases*, 1873), but their introduction to the discourse of constitutional law (Twiss, 1942; 42–62; Corwin, 1948: 120) was as a possibility that would continue to be "pressed by the Bar more and more insistently" (Corwin, 1948: 129). Explicit mention of the concept by a justice was in the dissent by Justice Field in *Munn* (1877). Here, in the case of "liberty of contract," a period of "suspended animation" followed as refinements were made and the concept gained wider acceptance (Corwin, 1948; 134–137).

Corwin accords special significance to the founding of the American Bar Association two years after the Court refused to throw open the door of due process to property interests in the Illinois case, characterizing the association as a "sort of Juristic sewing circle for mutual education in the gospel of laissez faire" (1948: 137–138). Acceptance by a majority of the Court constitutes authoritative recognition, and with *Allgeyer* v. *Louisiana* (1897) liberty of contract becomes more than a possibility. Yet others attentive to liberty of contract could not help but be as struck by its demise as its ascendance. Walton Hamilton observed, "Its legal insecurity may rest upon personnel . . . or it may be due to the older and established doctrine that the state might intervene with regulation to promote public safety, public health, public morals, and public welfare" (1938: 190). Although some speculation suggests the limits of attachment to ideas, in fact, it is simply easier to turn away from a doctrine than to establish one. The lawyers and judges that put liberty of contract to rest had a program (Auerbach, 1976; 191). The Roosevelt appointees chose not to act on the "possibility" of liberty of contract. Although they undercut its appeal, they did not erase it as a sensible claim. Rather, they attended to other doctrinal developments, particularly in the area of political liberties. The elevation of contract to a constitutional claim limited the powers of political institutions. Subsequent activity relied on constitutional limits to maintain the place of the Court in American politics while changing the policy it made.

In the modern era, the incorporation of privacy also exemplifies conceptual evolution. In 1896 and for nearly a half-century thereafter, the justices could not have ruled that prohibiting abortion, or any number of other regulations, violated a constitutional right to privacy. There are many reasons for this, not the least of which was the absence of privacy as a constitutional right. By the mid-twentieth century, strange as it might have been to those outside the constitutional sphere, abortion was one of the class of actions and conditions with a particularly close relationship to the constitutional version of privacy.

Judge Cooley provided the seed, the still evident phrasing of a right "to be let alone" (1888: 29). The conceptual foundation was further extracted from the common law by Samuel Warren and Louis Brandeis in 1890. They proposed that libel and slander provided limited protection and described a broader right to be derived from the tradition of private property and "an inviolate personality" (Warren, 1890: 141). By treating the concept as "privacy," a protection in its own right rather than an attribute of other rights, the writers advanced the legal status of the concept.

Brandeis brought privacy to the Supreme Court expressing concern, in his dissent, about wiretaps as a "subtler and more far-reaching means of invading privacy" that violated an implicit constitutional guarantee, "the right to be let alone" (*Olmstead*, 1928: 473). Justice Murphy took the concept a step further by association with the Fourth Amendment (*Goldman*, 1942: 136), and Justice Frankfurter, of all people, gave it a substantive cast when he indicated that "Security of one's privacy against arbitrary intrusion . . . is therefore implicit in the 'concept of ordered liberty'" (*Wolf*, 1949). In 1951, Justice Douglas claimed in dissent that constitutional liberty "must mean more than freedom from unlawful government restraint; it must include . . . The right to be let alone . . . the beginning of all freedom (*Public Utilities Commission*, 1951: 467). In a little more than another decade, the authority of the concept was established.

By the time it captured a majority of the Court, privacy would be talked about as a right "older than the Bill of Rights" (*Griswold*, 1965: 486). Of the subsequent privacy decisions, none more firmly demonstrate its new status than the 1973 abortion rulings (*Roe*; *Doe*). In *Roe* v. *Wade*, privacy was a familiar part of the justices' tool box and the opinion treats the *Griswold* case as one in a series that had recognized the privacy right. Justice Blackmun seemed to care less where he found it than that it was "there."[7] Although not without criticism for the lengths to which he took the right (Ely, 1973), Justice Blackmun felt that the use of the concept had been such that it covered the abortion claim.

The constitutional idea of "state action" in the privacy right and the implications of constitutional privacy's "association" with the First Amendment distinguish this concept from the statutory privacy originally suggested by Brandeis for inclusion in the laws of the states. Where the common law right had been a limitation on the press, constitutional privacy developed as a complement of the First Amendment and thus is not a weapon against media instrusions. In *Time, Inc.* v. *Firestone* (1976), the plaintiffs turned to common law privacy in confronting constitutional protections for freedom of the press. Similarly, for structural reasons in the Constitution, such as its application to individuals and not the government, it would not make sense to apply constitutional privacy to presidential papers.

Use, to be sensible, most conform with the structure of constitutional doctrine. This conformity is evident in cases where the traditional measure of law has suggested purely political action on the part of the justices. In *Brown* v. *The Board of Education,* for instance, the very structure of the argument was carefully grounded in past experience in order to minimize the Court's leap. When the justices chose to consider the claim, their response would be influenced by the decision that had rationalized Jim Crow, *Plessy* v. *Ferguson.* They would put a gloss on equality that would pay homage unconsciously to the disjunction of the constitutional meaning by emphasizing nonseparation or integration without attention to the quality of the treatment. The promise of quality treatment, after all, had been the ruse in *Plessy.* It would not be reaffirmed. The structure of the decision is remarkably similar, although the outcome is reversed. Yet in the reversal, the justices would introduce a new kind of authority to indicate that the world had changed. This was, of course, the social scientific data provided by Kenneth Clark (Rosen, 1972: 228).

A feature of judicial discourse is its reliance on possibilities. Anything that has not yet found a place in the conceptual structure can't be the basis for institutional action. However, once a sensible claim has emerged it may be treated in a variety of ways. The claim may or may not be used. Its popularity may increase or it may be ignored. Privacy was exceptionally popular after it had surfaced in the Constitution. Thus, ideas get their institutional meaning, their authority through use. By the mid-1970s, privacy claims, though still numerous, were beginning to be far less successful in gaining a majority of the Court. A claim may make sense or have been a subject of recent interest, but the justices still choose whether or not to accept further cases or decide them in a particular way. The use made of a right is a function of the predispositions of those on the Court, while its status as a basis for sensible claims is a function of the active memory of constitutional discourse.

The erosion of rights does not merely reverse the evolutionary process. Once privacy had been introduced into the Constitution, its status like that of contract might be disavowed. Or a justice who is hostile to a particular concept can refuse to use it. In this situation, there is an element of choice absent when a concept has not yet been incorporated. Justice Rehnquist's privacy decisions suggest this development (*Rakas* v. *Illinois,* 1978). Yet negation, if it is forceful enough, may be just the thing to keep a concept in the judicial mind. The whole panoply of institutional disaffection from liberty of contract gave it a status in American thought and made it part of the institution. The excessive zeal in protecting "contract" warns future justices about acting on their economic theories, especially when those theories are contested elements of a policy debate.

In order to be eliminated, a concept would have to be stricken from memory. This is not impossible, since institutional viability requires use.

The lawyers and justices who work with the Court must call upon the ideas in the tradition of constitutional interpretation in order that they remain viable. The *United States Reports,* although comprehensive, is also undiscriminating. Thus, cases like *Patterson* v. *Colorado,* an early free speech case, have dropped from use, superseded by the more consistent expression of ideological hegemony associated with "clear and present danger." *Patterson* has been upstaged by *Schenck* as the first modern free speech case and is nearly forgotten except for a disclaimer by Justice Holmes in *Schenck.* Still, cases decided by the Supreme Court generally have more vitality than those never mentioned in the constitutional context at all.

INSTITUTIONAL PRACTICES

When we say that a decision is "in" or "of" an institution, we mean it is linked to a set of practices. The Supreme Court decided *Marbury* v. *Madison* in 1803, *Dred Scott* in 1857, and the 1978 case of *Regents* v. *Bakke.* The decision in each case came from a somewhat different set of procedures or institutional practices, but if the practices had been too different we would not say the cases had been decided by the Supreme Court. These practices, for all their perceived neutrality, intensified by the pomp and mystery at the Supreme Court, necessarily serve political interests. President Jefferson, struggling against the myth of the impartial judge as John Marshall was trying to develop it, liked seriatim opinions because they served his interests. Yet practices such as the opinion of the Court, the seriatim opinion, the majority and dissenting opinions, oral argument, and the conference are also institutional channels to which interests are subjected and inevitably transformed.

The following material will examine how institutional practices shape the choices or opportunities open to the justices. Like legal ideology, institutional practices operate at a level that channels politics. The practices seldom determine the outcome in a case. Which side the justices will choose in a particular case has the most serious consequences so most attention to institutional practices is about their influence on judicial choice (Murphy, 1964). Practices like oral agrument or the *amicus* brief determine more than who wins and who loses. They affect the substance and the quality of the Court's work, and because of the relation between Court and Constitution, the practices influence what we take to be the law. (See Schmidhauser, 1979: 113.)[8]

At the risk of anthropomorphizing this inquiry, we can note institutional qualities similar to those expected of a justice. Like life tenure, the working environment is expected to insulate the justices. In 1928, when

Felix Frankfurter and James Landis examined the "methods and practices in the discharge of business" before a Supreme Court that had begun to assume its modern character, they listed the following conditions as requisites of a sound judgment: oral argument without oratory, a vibrant conference session where every matter would be considered by well-prepared justices, assignment of opinion after a conference vote with subsequent consideration of drafts both individually and at conference, discouragement of rehearings, and more generally, judicial tenure and public scrutiny of the institution. This is a picture of institutional, or institutionalized, judiciousness that, for Frankfurter and Landis, was the key in the relationship between Court practice and product.

As the business has increased in volume, the Court has streamlined its deliberations and taken on increasing staff assistance. The justices now sit only in Washington and, compared with past practices, they sit there quite often. Collective deliberation in conference has been maintained with cutbacks on oral argument and an increase in the institutional discretion to choose what the justices will consider. Summary decisions and technological assistance, resisted for quite some time by the Supreme Court, are now characteristic practices. With the increasing recognition that judges and justices are political and the shifting foundation of its legitimacy, institutional practices are also shifting from legal to bureaucratic forms. The nature of this surprising shift is evident in all areas of institutional practice, the term, the winowing of cases, full hearings, and the decision.

The Term

The decisions issued by the Supreme Court will come during the "term" since official action requires that the Court be in session. Running from the first Monday in October through the following June, and quite often into July, the term has taken on its present character as the institution has become more integral to the federal system. At the turn of the century, an increasingly modern Court met from October until May, but before that, institutional obligations like riding the circuits meant that the members of the Supreme Court were barely considered part of the "Washington Community," because they were in town so infrequently (Young, 1966: 76–77).

Now, in the first week the justices decide which of the accumulated cases they will hear. Public sessions begin officially with three days of oral arguments, and for the next seven months, the Court hears oral arguments for two weeks, recesses for two weeks, and then returns to arguments. On argument days, the justices sit from 10:00 to 12:00 and 1:00 to 3:00. One of Chief Justice Burger's innovations was to increase the lunch break by one-half hour. The tradition of not hearing cases on Wednesday afternoon or on Friday cuts further into the brief time the Court has to conduct its public business. These periods are reserved for discussion of cases by the justices in conference. May is also left largely free from public sessions so that the justices can prepare their opinions. By then, the focus is on the more controversial cases heard during the term. In the mid-twentieth century, the justices often extended the term into the summer for important cases like the one involving President Nixon's tape recorded conversations (*United States* v. *Nixon,* 1974).

Part of the summer, however, is reserved for individual review of petitions to be acted upon in the fall and for the occasional petition for temporary action, like a stay of execution, which is taken pending review by the whole court. On rare occasions, the justices convene a special term during the summer recess. There have been seven of these "summer sessions." One dramatic instance affirmed implementation by President Eisenhower of the decision to desegregate the public schools in Little Rock, Arkansas, *Cooper* v. *Aaron* in 1958. This decision shows the justices' willingness to work a little longer in order to establish their authority over the Constitution where it is ostentatiously flouted (Gunther, 1985: 32). The summer of 1972 also presented circumstances of enough moment to call the justices back from their recess. *O'Brien* v. *Brown* resulted from consideration of an emergency petition for certiorari on July 7 concerning the seating of delegates at the Democratic National Convention scheduled to convene July 10 (Stern and Gressman, 1978: 3).

Sifting

The justices deliberate together in the conference. This is the end of the line, the heart of the institution. Once the justices have had a chance to look over the petitions for review, the process of choice begins. Through the secret group conferences and private consideration of petitions, control is exercised over the business at hand. The justices determine both the number and the content of cases that the Court will treat fully. This capacity to set its own agenda, called "the most striking feature of the modern Supreme Court" (Schmidhauser, 1979: 158), means that the institution is "no longer the passive institution 'with neither force nor will'" (Provine, 1980: 2) that it once was.

During each conference the justices consider between eighty and one hundred petitions for certiorari or appeals to decide whether to grant plenary review and hear them argued later. At the conference, the Chief Justice's greatest impact is over the initial filtering of cases. This prerogative has been exercised to some degree or another since Hughes's time (Danelski, 1968). Once simply an opportunity to decide what would be considered for rejection, filtering is now much more significant since the Chief's office makes the initial determination of which among the four to five thousand cases coming up the justices will see. Each justice at the conference has the right to add to the Chief's list, but those cases without at least one justice in support are denied further consideration. New motions, appeals, and petitions are considered in the same manner each week. Since 1972, five of the justices have relied for their information on a memo prepared as part of a "cert pool" system. A clerk from the chambers of each justice participating in the pool takes a turn at preparing these memos.

Four justices are necessary to grant a full hearing on a case, and any case warranting consideration in the opinion of four justices will be docketed for oral argument. The procedure depends on considerable commitment to the institution. Even in the face of substantial opposition from a majority, four members of the Court might hope for a change in the majority position as the issues are refined and the hearing progresses. But if only four vote to hear a case there is a substantial gamble on the part of the minority. The justices do have an opportunity to dissent from a failure to grant certiorari, but the records do not identify the dissenting votes unless the minority justices choose to come forth. Dissents are not revealed when review is granted.

Summary decisions on appeals, which are possible at the conference, have been given increasing weight in recent years. Long considered of less value as precedent than decisions following full hearings (Brennan, 1963), such action binds the lower courts (*Hicks,* 1975) and is final. The procedure entails action on the case without the benefit of full briefs or arguments and without written opinions. On occasion the justices have expressed concern over potential loss of prestige for the institution with the reliance on summary decision, but the numbers have continued to increase.

With nearly thousands of petitions to be reviewed, the sorting process necessarily relies on the superficial characteristics evident in requests for attention. Justice Jackson once calculated, at a time when the case load was barely half what it is today, that each of the justices was permitted on the average only thirty-three seconds per item for discussion (Westin, 1961: 25). More recently, Justice Rehnquist described a normal week as leaving nearly the same 4.8 minutes per case (1977). Clearly there is discretion to focus the Court's time on a few of the cases before it in the process of deciding what to decide, just as the process itself is a decision about what to address. For a case to reach the argument stage it must appear to a substantial number of justices as meritorious. Like the first of Edward Levi's steps in the process of "reasoning by example" (1948), the justices necessarily see the issues before them in the context of other cases with which they are familiar. The result is more likely to be one in which there is an issue at hand stemming from some balance of considerations than one in which there is clear failure to apply the law in the case below.

The setting where this "sifting" takes place is steeped in tradition. From the veil of secrecy to the handshakes all around that begin the conference, this meeting is at the center of institutional life. Although it has no standing "in law" (i.e., no foundation in statute or opinion of the Court), the conference has come to exemplify the collective process. More recently, the setting and conduct of the conference have been the center of controversy. Although the participants usually guard the secrecy of conference actions, when Chief Justice Burger sought to prolong consideration of a petition from convicted participants in the Watergate coverup by holding it over for a second conference session, he was met with a calculated leak to the media by his brethren (*The New York Times,* April 22, 1977: 1). The extraordinary leak to the public about special treatment of the Watergate case put pressure on the Chief Justice to return to institutional practice. Perhaps as significant in measuring a shift at the Court was the transformation of the conference room into an antichamber of Warren Burger's office, complete with his personal art collection, gifts from visiting foreign justices, and magazines for reading while waiting to visit with the Chief Justice.

The justices had been united in their resistance to an inquiring public eye. Except for occasional breaches, actions that took place behind the "purple curtain" generally remained secret. Some of the judicial commentary, however, was "banquet formalism." In a 1975 speech to the American Bar Association, Justice Powell denied the existence of blocs of justices and cautioned against intrusion into the internal dynamics of the institution. In the last decade the amount of information about institutional practices and breaches of practice has been tremendous. Yet, in their commentary on the internal workings of the Court, the justices set limits on access even while it is increasing. Justice Rehnquist tried to discourage greater access by characterizing the conference as "fragile" and "virtually unique." He proposed that since the justices are the only persons in attendance they are permitted a "candid exchange of views" and are forced to prepare themselves given "the knowledge that once in the Conference it is our own presentation, and not that of one of our staff which must be depended on" (1977: 20). According to Henry Abraham, conference secrecy "is entirely proper. . . . [T]he Court cannot in good conscience open its deliberations to the glare of publicity" (1977: 38–39). However, recent scholarship demonstrates unequal impact of secrecy.

Because litigants "differ in their capacity to deduce probable review criteria," the practice benefits some participants more than others (Provine, 1980: 4). The big winner in this sweepstakes is the federal government.

The justices have defended their range of choice at conference on the basis of both the quality of petitions and institutional tradition. Chief Justice Hughes observed in 1937 that "about 60 percent of the applications for certiorari are wholly without merit and ought never to have been made." Hughes felt that 20 percent were plausible and that the deserving cases were ultimately chosen (Stern and Gressman, 1978: 120). As late as 1949, the justices were still defending their discretion. According to Chief Justice Vinson, the Court's effectiveness depended on its choosing cases of such importance that they will transcend the particular facts and parties involved (Stern and Gressman, 1978: 120). Justices in recent years have been more emphatic about the necessity of discretion for the modern institution, and there have been dramatic decreases in the percentage of petitions granted to those filed. Discretion has become a part of the institution. This is evident in the response to the Freund Commission report where suggestions offered concerning formalizing discretion in all areas have met with minimal controversy. The belief that it is a reasonable possibility to "go all the way to the Supreme Court" is widespread and bears very little relation to institutional practice.

The Court has the option of summary disposition at the initial stage, and although it has in the past rarely amounted to reversal, the Court has granted petitions and vacated the lower court judgment at the same time. This is usually done when some Supreme Court decision has intervened between the time of the lower court ruling and the conference. The decision presumably would have a close relationship with the case coming up in conference (Stern and Gressman, 1978: 358). The Court also occasionally restricts review to only some of the issues that the litigants present, as in *Witherspoon* v. *Illinois* (1969), where the justices decided to review "the contention that Witherspoon had been deprived of a jury which represented a cross section of the community" by the dismissal of all those who were absolutely opposed to the death penalty. Other matters in the petition were denied review.

Full opinion still stands as the measure of institutional action, yet the process of initial decisions has been widely recognized as of political significance (Wasby, 1984; Schmidhauser, 1979). The initial decisions on appeal amount to judgments that are generally conclusive. In the final analysis, judicial choice about what to hear has become institutionally significant, in part because of the shift in the ideology of judicial authority from the reason in law to the position of the Court in the system. The conference has become a vital subject of inquiry. Provine draws from her analysis a picture of how "the top appellate court in any complex legal system must perform" (1980: 101). She sees a need for "jurisdictional boundaries," "hegemony as the final arbiter," and supervision of "non-jurisdictional conflict." It is no small paradox of American politics that the vision of fairness and disinterestedness associated with the legitimacy of the state and reflected in the Court throughout its recent history (Schmidhauser, 1979: 157) is giving way to a new view of the institution characterized more by administration than deliberation (see Table 9).

Hearing on the Merits

Oral argument, the public part of the decisionmaking process, has been reduced to less than an hour from an extended series of presentations sometimes lasting weeks and rivaling the other branches of government for its drama. Argument begins with the traditional announcement from the crier:

Oyez! Oyez! Oyez! All persons having business before the Honorable, the Supreme Court of the United States, are admonished to draw near and give their attention, for the Court is now sitting. God save the United States and this Honorable Court!

Presentation by attorneys in the Court chamber is a brief public interlude and the few cases that get this treatment become the focus of uncharacteristic attention. The excitement comes less from the oratory than from the aura of expectation surrounding the activity. More attention is focused here than on the outcome, which, for the media and inevitably for the public, is something of an anticlimax. During oral argument, we see the Court working.

The public session, presided over by the Chief Justice, demonstrates the way judicial training combines with individual perception and inclinations. For one thing, the language spoken is unique (Brigham, 1978). Here, the exchange of views is a key to judicial communication. We can observe legal discourse in the deliberative process. During oral argument we can see whether the judges understand the concepts revealed in the presentations when they respond or engage with the attorneys. Unlike the opinion itself, and certainly the conference, the justices are using the language of the law in public. Although the opinion usually makes sense, the only actual evidence of judicial competence with the tradition of law is these public arguments.

These sessions are among the most intense events in American public life. Here the link between the event and consideration of the issues by those who will decide them is very close. The "big" cases still draw overflow crowds, and the tiny gallery in the courtroom accommodates the curious by silently moving them through in a continuous stream for a view of the action. At least once every few years the nation focuses on the institution in this way. The case of *Regents of the University of California* v. *Bakke* (1978) was a dramatic example. More than any other part of the process, oral argument before the High Court galvanized the national debate on affirmative action that was going on at that time. The sense of a fight and the anticipation of a decision, which are characteristic of argument, make these presentations special. Debate slows following the decision.

For the cases to be given a full hearing, the clerk organizes the "argument calendar" at the rate of one case per hour during the Court's four-hour sessions. When a case reaches the argument stage, action reverts to lawyers and the justices become involved with them more directly than they are with emissaries from the outside at any other time. For the public event at least, and in some other respects, like their contribution to the reasoning in cases, the attorneys become part of the institution. Their contributions, of course, must be in accord with institutional practices dictating how to submit briefs and how to make an argument.

By the time the justices sit for oral argument, the issues have gone well beyond the individual participants. Yet the adversary form still dominates even at this stage of review. During argument in *Bakke,* the justices focused their numerous questions at Reynold H. Colvin, representing the white applicant to the University of California's medical school at Davis. At first the lawyer was reluctant to generalize about the policy implications of his claim, wishing instead to focus on his client's interests (Friendly and Elliott, 1984). Yet it was the challenge to the law that made argument so charged, as in the following exchanges:[6]

JUSTICE STEWART: You spoke, Mr. Colvin, of the right to admission. You don't seriously submit that he (Bakke) had a right to be admitted?

MR. COLVIN: That is not Allan Bakke's position. Allan Bakke's position is that he has a right and that right is not to be discriminated against by reason of his race. And that is what brings Allan Bakke to this Court.

. . . .

JUSTICE WHITE: Well, what's your response to the assertion of the University that it was entitled to have a special program and take race into account and that under the 14th Amendment there was no barrier to its doing that because of the interests that were involved? What's your response to that?

MR. COLVIN: Our response to that is fundamentally that race is an improper classification in this situation. As a matter of fact, the Government in its own brief makes that very point.

Rather than being of a technical nature, the questioning in this case addressed broad legal issues familiar to most who followed the controversy. A manual for practice before the Supreme Court advises counsel to prepare argument for persons who know very little about the particular case and the precedents peculiar to the case, but who know a great deal about general principles of law with which they are frequently called upon to deal (Stern and Gressman, 1978). The justices in the *Bakke* arguments tested how various legal categories fit with the case.

An issue of appellate advocacy central to the Court's work is whether the justices read the briefs prior to oral argument, in the preparation of the opinion, or not at all. Each justice receives the briefs two or three weeks before the arguments and, of course, each claims to read them (Brennan, 1963: 102). The tradition in appellate advocacy is that a tribunal that has reviewed a case prior to the proceedings is considered "hot" and an uninformed bench is "cold." Although the justices seldom admit not reading the briefs, Frankfurter is said to have ignored the briefs until he had participated in oral argument. Contemporary practice is for the clerks to prepare ten- to forty-page "bench memoranda" on cases to be argued.

Active judicial participation in oral argument shows that members of the Court are at least generally familiar with the issues being presented, and counsel realize that to address Powell on affirmative action or Brennan on obscenity is to talk with the men who created the discourse. Sometimes that discourse is particularly dense, as when Justice Harlan interrupted counsel in a case about the exercise of religion and said, "I think it would be helpful if you start with the premise that it is a religious exercise. Would you tell us whether this case can be distinguished from McCollum, Torcaso, and Engel and, if not, then are you asking the Court to overrule those cases and why?" (Clayton, 1964: 199). Such questioning consumes most of the time allotted to counsel, and the Court does not usually allow extra time to compensate for their interruptions.

Judicial attention is evident in the attempts at wit and sarcasm during argument. In a school prayer case some years ago, the counsel representing schools with prayers acknowledged that religion in the public schools was unconstitutional but he contended that reading the Bible and reciting the Lord's prayer were not religious exercises but rather were used to bring discipline and calm to the classroom. Justice Stewart suggested tranquilizers for the same effect (Clayton, 1964: 198).

The importance of oral argument for the outcome is hard to gauge. There is considerable commentary, usually from interested parties, to the effect that it does matter. According to the second Justice Harlan:

. . . .[T]he lawyer who deprecates the oral argument as an effective instrument of appellate advocacy, and stakes all on his brief, is making a great mistake. . . . [T]he first impressions that a judge gets of a case are very tenacious. They frequently persist into the conference room. And those impressions are actually gained from the oral argument, if it is an effective job (Harlan, 1955: 57).

Traditional support for oral argument as a significant practice is the fact that a justice who does not participate in this stage of the process seldom participates in the final determination of the case. Another institutional characteristic that supports this view is the fact that the conference— where the outcome of the case is informally determined—follows the argument by only a few days. Thus, argument may be important because it comes immediately before the vote. Thurgood Marshall made the point that because the conference follows argument usually within a week, the public sessions are more important than conventionally thought (Breitel, 1968: 145). One contention is that in arguments, unlike the written brief, the lawyers can answer back, giving them a chance to shape the opinion of the justices (Lewis, 1964).

On the other hand, evidence that oral presentations are not significant is their decline in the modern period. Historically, argument has been sacrificed to an increasing caseload and the preservation of the conference (Wasby, 1982). This has diminished the opportunity for the bar to influence the outcomes and for the public to witness the justices in action. Yet although shorter, arguments may have gotten more intense, and even if the justices are not persuaded by argument, they are confronted with the case. In fact, given the nature of the practice, oral argument is " 'with' rather than 'before' the Supreme Court . . . a highly political process of social interaction" (Schubert, 1974: 130).

Argument before the Court may serve in subsequent construction of the opinion (*Rathburn* v. *United States,* 1935; Jacob, 1978: 222). And argument can affect the opinion in other ways. In the case of *Jones* v. *Hildebrandt* (1977), the Court dismissed a petition for certiorari on which it had heard arguments, the justices noting "we have here then a shift in the posture of the case such that the question presented in the petition for cetiorari is all but mooted by petitioner's oral argument." In *Moose Lodge No. 107* v. *Irvis* (1972), Justice Rehnquist, writing for the majority and indicating a reluctance "to attach conclusive weight to the relatively spontaneous responses of counsel," held the attorneys responsible for what they had said in oral argument.

While it is possible to infer from these statements that appellee (Irvis) is simply not interested in obtaining any relief as to guest practices of Moose Lodge if he should prevail on the merits, it is equally possible to read them as being tactical arguments designed to avoid having to settle for half a loaf when he might obtain the whole loaf.

Thus, while the practical weight of argument is unsettled, the interest in these proceedings from the public reflects another kind of significance to the institution.[9]

The *amicus,* or "friend of the court" briefs, also present issues at the same time that they introduce other "parties" in the case (Krislov, 1985). Increasingly the participants represent larger issues that transcend the individual situation. An *amicus* brief asserts an "interest of its own separate and distinct from that of the parties" (*United States* v. *Barnett,* 1964). These briefs may be more important than those of counsel, depending on their source and their quality. The ACLU brief in *Mapp* v. *Ohio* (1961) was central to the decision because it referred to an earlier decision on illegally seized evidence that had not been placed before the Court (Friendly and Elliott, 1984). The impact of *Mapp* on American constitutional law indicates the importance of interested outsiders.

Decision

[A]s soon as we come off the bench Wednesday afternoon around three o'clock, we go into "conference" in a room adjoining the chambers of the Chief Justice . . . we deliberate and vote on the four cases which we heard argued the preceding Monday . . . on the Friday of that week we begin a Conference at 9:30 in the morning, go until 12:30 in the afternoon, take 45 minutes for lunch, and return and continue our deliberations until the middle or late part of the afternoon. (Rehnquist, 1977)

At the decision stage, the emphasis is on the merits and the conference becomes the forum. Here, individual preferences begin to shape the outcome. Reports on the proceedings come from the justices. In 1956, Justice Tom Clark reported that "ever since John Marshall's day" the formal vote in conference began with the junior justice and moved up through the ranks of seniority (Westin, 1961: 48). The vote would then be in the reverse order of the initial discussion. According to Justice Rehnquist, the Chief Justice begins with a discussion of the case and gives his proposed vote. Subsequent debate then moves to the senior Associate Justice and down the line until consideration of the case is concluded. Each justice's discussion of the case is followed by a tentative vote, although it is common for a justice to reserve judgment until the rest have had their say. The process is far more fluid than it once seemed to be (Abraham, 1977: 39).

The final lineup of the justices is not clear until the majority opinion is signed and this, of course, requires that the basis on which opinion can be expressed be drawn up. In this ongoing exchange of draft memoranda, the basis for opinion is constructed (Murphy, 1964: 82–89). A view of opinion formation was provided by Justice Rehnquist.

At the beginning of the week following the two-week sessions of oral argument, the Chief Justice circulates to the other members of the Court an Assignment List, in which he assigns for the writing of a Court opinion all of the cases in which he voted with the Conference majority. Where the Chief Justice was in the minority, the senior Associate Justice voting with the majority assigns the case (Rehnquist, 1977).

Opinion assignment is of obvious interest to political scientists, and this institutional practice has received a great deal of attention (McLaughlan, 1972; Rohde, 1972; Ulmer, 1970; Danelski, 1968). Chief Justice Burger saw opinion assignment as a means of equalizing the work and he often exercised his "managerial" authority when he was not in the majority.[10] Because the majority opinion must maintain the majority coalition, it is most often written by the justice whose views on the case are nearest to the center of the coalition (Murphy, 1964: 56–68). Inevitably, even without explicit strategic considerations, the draft around which the majority will coalesce will stand close to the middle of institutional opinion.

The justices originally each wrote short, "seriatim" statements explaining their view on the issues at hand. By the early 1800s John Marshall presented one opinion for the Court, which he usually wrote himself. This is recalled as a stategic maneuver in the conflicts between the Federalists in the judiciary and the Jeffersonian Republicans who dominated the other branches of government (Schmidhauser, 1960: 110). The one view on the law focused the authority of the institution. President Jefferson, bothered by the emerging convention of what he called "secret, unanimous opinions" expressed his concern to his first appointee, William Johnson (Morgan, 1954: 147), and President Madison called for a return to seriatim opinions so that Republican judges could record their position on the issues. The resulting practice was individual dissent and a majority opinion, with dissent, "the rule rather than the exception" (Pritchett, 1945: 43).

The exchange of drafts among the justices produces court policy. The conference vote is only tentative. Policy choice is refined when the object of the vote becomes clearer. Draft memos, once the key to this process, are being supplanted by new technologies. An internal telephone line, word processing, and an ever increasing number of clerks are altering the traditional process.

The Friday conference decides when a case will be announced from the bench or "come down." Often cases are held back for months, prompting speculation about the nature and intensity of judicial disagreement especially among attentive publics. Such speculation is a staple of the May issues of publications like *U.S. Law Week* or the *National Law Journal*. Decision day was a special event for the Court and for the press. It was traditionally a Monday until 1965, when greater flexibility and closer relations with the press made it no longer necessary. Monday is still the most likely decision day until the last weeks of May and early June, when the justices convene often during the week to announce decisions (Grey, 1968). There is no official warning when opinions will be announced, but there are clues, such as Justice Jackson leaving a sickbed to be present when the Court announced *Brown* v. *The Board of Education*.

The opinions are no longer read in full at these sessions. The author of the majority opinion gives a summary and dissenting opinions are announced. Former Chief Justice Burger hinted that even those summarizing majority opinions should limit themselves. His colleagues are not always so restrained. After Justice Stewart had briefly presented the holding in a case that he suggested did not lend itself "to intelligible oral discussion," Justice Blackmun responded with an extensive discussion of his objections to the majority view (*The New York Times,* Nov. 3, 1976).

Institutional practices change continually as a result of particular actors and controversies. For the most part they are imperceptible to the public and the institution endures. When uncovered, their policy significance may be difficult to discern. John Marshall's invention of an opinion for the Court or the expanded discretion in the choice of cases has been among the most significant for the institution as we know it today. Other factors, such as the growing role of clerks and shorter time for oral argument, are less obvious indications that the character of the Supreme Court is being affected by structural shifts in the nature of institutional authority.

CONSTITUTIONAL POLITICS

The picture of Court and Constitution merits restatement. In constitutional cases, tradition is a basis for action, the conceptual ground for an opinion of the Court. Judicial attitude is the dynamic force in constitutional choice, and the "behavior" of judges is the turbulent surface of constitutional politics. Yet a focus limited to attitudes and choice fails to join law and politics as corollary elements in a deliberative process; description of behavior alone fails to address the basis for action in the legal tradition. Deliberation does not simply lead to choice; it creates process from which choices emerge. As group action, institutional choice is political and constitutional.

On the Supreme Court, institutional deliberation supports authoritative action. In the lower courts, even where they are composed of many justices, the institutions can act on the basis of individual findings. Around this institutional practice, ambiguously grounded in the Founders' conception of legal guardianship, actions with a majority become law. While individuals comment on the decision and act independently in some circumstances, these comments are authoritative and constitutionally significant only with reference to the whole Court (*Farber, 1978*).

The collective deliberation on the Court has some affinity to individual thought. The institutional framework of practices and conventions brings the various currents of individual interest together, like the tendencies in any thought process. As we conventionally weigh in the mind or consider individually, the Court does too in its institutional guise. As with individuals, institutional deliberation is limited by what is known and structured by traditions of discourse; and like individual thought, various choices have political implications. There are conventions that connect what we do with what we know. As in the mind, so too with the Court, what goes on "inside" is subject to the meaning we give to action on the outside. From the initial "room to maneuver" that the constitutional tradition leaves for the resolution of any case to the opinion, we can trace this process characteristic of constitutional politics at the Supreme Court.

Room to Maneuver

According to political scientists following in the tradition of C. Herman Pritchett, coalitions, blocs, and attitudes tell us how the Court decides the issues before it. Judicial behavioralists concentrated on political associations. It was this scholarship rather than the gossip and the muckraking that established that the Supreme Court is a political institution. Characteristically, behavioralists looked to political alignments to interpret legal politics (Wasby, 1984: 167). Activity on the Court was described in terms of choices and blocs of actors sharing an attitude (Rohde and Spaeth, 1976), and scholarly attention was drawn to this orientation. The justices have been charted over time to show movement from extreme positions to the center, as with Justice Hugo Black, or remain out in left field from the beginning, like Justice William O. Douglas.

Because of the study of attitudes, politics is generally accepted as an attribute of the Supreme Court. "Page One" headlines get their meaning from the political interpretations that ground decision in the institution. Thus, a reporter for *The New York Times,* for instance, announces: "Nixon's Appointees to High Court Voting Less as a Bloc with Burger" (July 4, 1978). Although there was already conventional knowledge of politics on the bench, realists and behavioralists altered the institution by making politics a characteristic. The way scholars have interpreted the Court is in this respect a facet of the institution. Pressures stimulating institutional change from outside, as with President Roosevelt's attack, or producing it from within, as with rulings on jurisdiction, have become recognized parts of the process of constitutional politics. The remarkable development was the extent to which politics, exchange, and coalitions rather than legal reason became central to how the institution was understood. Politics, by the analysis of scholars such as Pritchett, Schubert, and Goldman, was not the activity of deviant justices but characteristic of the institution.

Yet intentional action can't ultimately be explained. It must be interpreted by drawing on a conceptual basis. The behavior that attitude studies purport to explain acts on a political world already symbolized. Justifications offered after the fact as the basis for choice or the explanation for an opinion are not the conceptual parameters governing judicial choice in an institutional setting. Conventions and understanding, knowledge of "free speech" or "due process" present the options around which justices maneuver. At the level where the Supreme Court operates there is of course considerable "leeway" for politics, but this terrain varies with doctrinal areas (Johnson, 1985: 521).

The introduction of politics into the institutional setting has all but displaced these legal factors and relegated them to the background. Other forms of investigation provide balance and a somewhat greater contribution for the part played by institutional factors in joining law and politics. Small-group analysis has shown not only that the justices have values on which they operate but that the activity of justices in the institution is constituted in terms of a tradition. Walter Murphy's rational choice model was rich in descriptive material revealing the internal workings of the Court. His model emphasized the context in which action takes place and the structure of discretion. By institutional tradition, the Chief Justice presides over the conference and he may choose to express his position last. This prerogative has been the subject of strategic models. The "paradox of voting," for instance, has shown that the way a vote is presented influences the outcome of a decision. The voting studies use a decision matrix where losers move on to second choices. However, the current practice of multiple opinions has changed the nature of choice. Now, it is not only at the conference but in coalescing around draft opinions that the justices choose. While the conference suggests how various justices will line up on the issues, the process of deciding reaches beyond.

In explaining judicial choice during the behavioral period, there have been a number of models attentive to institution and doctrine. "Fact patterns" were an attempt to vigorously assess the empirical in cases (Kort, 1966) and "personal stare decisis" was a related attempt at rigor, but with a focus on factors such as race and sex (Lawlor, 1967). Perhaps the most successful and certainly the most sensitive to institutional factors was "role analysis" (Pritchett, 1953; Becker, 1964). The conception of role was first developed as a compensation for the psychological frame of behaviorism. From its beginnings, the concept of role has been a conduit, through judicial orientations and predispositions, for institutional practices to have a place in decisions.

Work with certiorari decisions by Doris Marie Provine (1980) has contributed significantly to our picture of Supreme Court justices making choices. According to Provine, role perceptions are the "intervening variables between the policy preferences of the justices and their case-selection votes" (1980: 8). She finds much greater significance for institutional factors, such as judicial perception of the proper role of the Court or jurisdictional boundaries, than earlier students of cert (Tanenhaus, 1963).[11] The nature of these "self-imposed limits" (Provine, 1980: 175) is hard to determine precisely but they appear to be increasingly linked to the Court's position at the "end of the line." The justices range across the terrain of American law, shepherding certain areas where tradition is strong (like abortion and criminal procedure) and shifting from others when it appears institutionally advantageous (as they have done in the area of economic due process and privacy).

Legal traditions are to judicial choice what language is to the decision to say something (Brigham, 1978). We can form a sentence in many different ways but what we know structures what we chose to say. Every case brings its conceptions and its phrases. The justices don't "hear" conventional descriptions of action ("He took my dope"); they deliberate over legal situations ("The police did not have a warrant"). The actors have position (police, accused, addict) and the actions are embedded in convention (search and seizure). Although both attitude and particular facts influence the choice of how to decide, choice operates within the limited conceptual space available in an institutional setting. Timothy O'Neill pointed out that, in the *Bakke* case, the group rights claim was absent from equal protection analysis (1980). He showed us that the law constrained thinking about equal protection by restricting it to certain paths. The discourse operating as a limit constitutes the activity, the terrain of constitutional politics.

Reaching an Opinion

The conference epitomizes collegial interaction and starts the process of formulating an opinion, during which the written work comes to depict the conceptual terrain more precisely. Since a majority of the justices is authoritative, the position around which the justices coalesce is the institutional opinion. Gerald Garvey (1971) saw this process as "bricolage," a body of conceptual tools. This practice has been developing for the life of the institution.

After John Marshall's move from seriatim opinions, choice and opinion became linked. The votes in conference might be changed as the opinion was constructed so that the period following the conference, when the justices exchange drafts and "opinion" is reached, becomes the real process of deliberation. In the *Bakke* decision (1978), for instance, the pivotal position of Justice Powell, who cast the deciding vote to strike down the University of California Medical School admissions quota and allow Allen Bakke to be admitted, resulted in a majority *opinion* that could be achieved by joining his vote with others. He created another majority, holding that it was sometimes legal to have special preferences for minorities aimed at remedying proven past discrimination. While the first majority was responsible for the decision of the Court, it was not preordained that in the latter instance Powell would have a group with which to join. Had the other justices in this majority not chosen to write on the special preference issue, Powell's observations would have stood alone. Opinions constructed by the Court thus determine the ultimate significance of any individual position.

Justice Powell, in a revealing institutional comment, characterized "the drafting of an opinion" as "a process, not an event." The vision he presents involves internal editing, in chambers, "spurred by criticism and suggestions from other chambers" (1976: 4). According to Powell, the process differed from a law firm with its emphasis on professional expertise, and was more aptly characterized as political activity involving generalists. "I had thought of the Court, in institutional terms, as a collegial body in which the most characteristic activities would be consultation and cooperative deliberation, aided by a strong supporting staff." He found, however, that most of the time the justices functioned independently, "as nine small, independent law firms" (1976: 1–2). According to Justice White, the justices stay at "arms length," a view confirmed by the late Justice Stewart, who reported that "at times, except for the conference, I hardly know what the others do" (Williams, 1977: 91). Although they work independently, the ideas put forth by individual justices gain meaning by association with a group (Carp and Stidham, 1985: 173).

The traditional picture of opinion assignment reflects the majority that emerges in conference. The more accurate characterization, developed here, is that institutional possibilities, including the opinion itself, are constructed in exchanges following the conference. A "sliding issue scale" (Murphy, 1964: 44) along which individual justices move is the terrain of opinion formation. In Clarence Gideon's celebrated case, the prior holding, *Betts* v. *Brady,* requiring that a lawyer be appointed in some circumstances, was presenting difficulties. The justices had begun to reveal an inclination to provide counsel in all crimes where there was a possibility of a jail term. After overruling *Betts,* the justices continued to expand the right to counsel and assistance at trial. In the 1960s, the power of an equal protection claim was so great that even traveling expenses and money for the subsistence of witnesses were within the reach of constitutional discourse.

The activity during the period between the conference vote and its dissemination has been described by J. Woodford Howard on the basis of the "fluidity of judicial choice." This concept is a key to the proposition that in the institutional setting, the process of decision is based on jockeying for position on a conceptual continuum. Here, the power of the past is weighed against countervailing pressure of the times and the past is "distinguished," "overruled by name," or "ignored". (Pritchett, 1948). In almost all areas where the Roosevelt Court reversed prior decisions, the precedents were derived from doctrinal paths that were less than clear (1948: 58–71). Some cases abandon precedent based on an earlier shift in judicial opinion, as in *Hammer* v. *Dagenhart* (1981), which was overruled by *United States* v. *Darby Lumber Co.* (1941). The range of choice, though fluid, is finite. Yet too often the political view of judging focuses attention on the range and ignores the boundary.

Opinions get crafted for months during which the dialectic of preference and conception is at its height. In *Goldman* v. *United States* (1942), where federal agents used a listening device to obtain a conviction, Justices Stone, Murphy, and Frankfurter wanted to reverse and overrule *Olmstead,* but Justice Jackson was able to exert enough pressure to minimize what might have been an otherwise devastating dissent (Murphy, 1964: 68). The possibility of a concurrence or even a dissent from a colleague, described by Hughes as "an appeal to the brooding spirit of the law, to the intelligence of a future day" (1928: 68) is pressure to accept changes. The pressure is applied using the institution as lever. Justice Frankfurter suggested that dissents confused the issues and created a need to piece things together "in order to make out where the Supreme Court really stands as an institution" (Westin, 1961: 26). The possible impact of dissent on the majority opinion and the status of a decision was evident in *Dred Scott,* where Taney's majority opinion became known by the extreme view of it in Justice McLean's dissent. Justice Harlan's dissent in *Plessy* ultimately became an institutional comment with much more significance than the same opinion would have had if it were announced in the old seriatim fashion.

Institutional practice traditionally limited the information on which the justices may act. The Blackstonian conception of judging defines legitimate information as coming into the institution in legal form or through legal practices. This includes briefs, the record from the courts below, oral argument, and past judgments of the Supreme Court. The limitation was one of "strict" notice of the facts, but this appears to be changing in the modern institution. Where outside information had once been handled rarely and with great circumspection, it has become more common to see judicial notice of material not even offered by counsel. This was true in the initial abortion cases where Justice Blackmun's search of medical literature did so much to forge the opinion (Miller and Barron, 1975: 1218), and it was true in Justice Stevens's opinion in the 1986 case where the opinions of Soliciter General Fried, who presented the case, were found in law review articles he had written years before (*The New York Times,* June 16, 1986). The practice in this area seems to have evolved quite a distance from the purer judicial model on which the Court's present status was constructed.

The reasons distributed from the Court after an opinion is reached were traditionally treated as causes of judicial choice. Now we acknowledge that causes, in the scientific sense, are not compatible with the amount of subjective exchange that goes on within the Court. The political view of judging was elevated the decision itself and weakened the significance of the reasons offered as explanation. Opinion is treated as "simply" a rhetorical device. Yet in the Supreme Court, opinions are the basis for subsequent action. They reveal substance and outcome. As the form a decision takes, opinions are objects of struggle. The rhetorical meaning in a case prescribes action in the doctrinal, as well as the practical, sense. Practically, the Court's finality gives the reasons added weight, and as we will see in the next chapter the authority of the Supreme Court goes well beyond the decision.

7

AUTHORITY AND POLICY

IN THE late 1960s, scholarly study of appellate courts in the United States turned from the decisions themselves and the written opinions handed down by judges and justices to their impact as public policy (Wasby, 1970; Dolbeare and Hammond, 1971; Milner, 1971). This shift was part of a more general reaction against earlier preoccupations with High Court opinions and presumptions about that legal rhetoric capturing the social meaning of law (Pound, 1959; Miller, 1968). Subsequently, "impact" became a major focus for social scientists (Baum, 1985; Johnson and Canon, 1984). This scholarship emphasized the limits of legal authority and associated courts with social life. Impact studies added a new dimension to scholarship on appellate courts, yet the positive frame that characterized the recent past in social science left doctrine and impact separated. Law *in society* was different; it was not law school law, and probably not law in the traditional sense of the term.

From this sensitivity to institutional creativity it is possible to look to matters of legal authority and how the system in the United States is affected by the pronouncements of appellate courts. This is especially appropriate in a research environment that increasingly recognizes that ideology is not some amorphous body of mostly false beliefs, but is rather a material constraint operating on the constitution of the political system.

By attention to compliance with the Court's decisions, a facet of impact, we can assess the reserve authority held by the Supreme Court. David Adamany and Joel Grossman recently summarized and evaluated support for the Supreme Court (1983), and their work provides a basis for arguing that an institutional perspective draws attention not to opinion about the Court but to belief in its place as final arbiter of legal issues and derivatively to its ability to influence the terms of political debate. While the Court is ranked more favorably than Congress or the presidency in "about half" of the surveys done by political scientists (Adamany and Grossman, 1983: 408), these scholars find little evidence that the Supreme Court has a "special place either in the psyche or in the childhood socialization of Americans" or that its decisions "command sweeping generalized approval" (1983: 409). Their conclusion is that the Court has gotten its authority from an ideological minority "that was part of the dominant national party coalition," the conservatives in the 1930s and liberals in the 1960s (1983: 434). In the material that follows we expand the discussion of authority to include both compliance and impact and to develop the institutional frame for conceptualizing the significance of the Supreme Court in the American system.

The focus on compliance will emphasize the transmission of policy through the other authoritative institutions that are the subject of judicial commands. The model for the study of compliance has been that of the trial court order. To the extent that we find this situation in practice the institution is seen as operating on the model of rules with which it is conventionally associated. This facet of the policy phenomenon is central to the relationship between legitimacy and policy since the Court represents the authority of the state within whose mantle judicial decisions are wrapped.

This treatment will clarify the distinction between compliance and impact while associating impact with the process of legitimizing government policy. In a political sense, the impact of the appellate courts is on how they structure political life. The concept has been a catchall category including events loosely attributable to these courts. As an opinion enters the political environment it joins with a configuration of defined interests and values operating around institutions, doctrines, and perceptions of what is possible. The influence of the courts in this sphere is their legitimation function. Here, by interpreting the authoritative concepts governing politics, the courts exert their greatest influence. By refining the language of politics they contribute to the association of what is possible with the authority of the state.

COMPLIANCE AND INSTITUTIONAL AUTHORITY

Compliance, or action in obedience to a decision of the Court, as used here includes cases in which people would not ordinarily have taken the action ordered by the Court. Compliance exists only where people are inclined to act in ways other than the Court mandates. The Supreme Court has limited power to compel obedience to its decisions, and its influence on policy is a reflection on its institutional standing. Where traditionally obedience to law has been associated with fear of sanctions, the substantive acceptability of a command, and its legitimacy, compliance in the strict sense involves only the last of these factors.

Because of this lack of an inherent power to sanction, compliance with Supreme Court decisions depends on those below looking up. Justice Robert Jackson expressed this in the following way. By tradition, the Court can rule however it wants, but "the judicial decree, however broadly worded, actually binds, in most instances, only the parties to the case. As to others, it is merely a weather vane showing which way the judicial wind is blowing." (1955: 24). Trials without counsel or special professional school admissions policies are inappropriate, but it can neither provide counsel nor set up admissions committees to determine who should be admitted to medical school. The Court's rulings are addressed to lower courts, legislatures, and the other institutions of government. Private parties become litigants before the Court because of some action by the state. Judicial action, while affecting individuals in their private capacity, seldom commands them to act. This is its nature as an appellate court and this nature is reinforced by the Supreme Court's preoccupation with questions of constitutional and federal statutory law.

Doctrinal traditions and institutional forms constraining the promulgation of policy also influence how officials respond. The power to decide cases, issue written opinions and special orders, and control what the Court decides comprise the technical checks on judicial policy. Obedience to individual decrees may well be encouraged where judicial decisions approximate commands in the manner of clear, unified statements (Wasby, 1984). In order for compliance to be possible the message must get through. The lower the officialdom and the farther it is from Washington, the less likely this is. In the case of another branch of the federal government, the visibility of the decision will be high, leaving little discretion to ignore a ruling. In the case of the other courts, whether federal or state, the visibility of the decision is lower. Here, favorable action will depend on the adjudication process and the activity of legal professionals. In the case of local government, the visibility of a decision is very slight. Because of this factor and the distance from the seat of power, the greatest discretion exists here.

Compliance thus involves more than what the Court says and is a function of the conditions of authority on which the justices rely. In considering the sources of judicial authority offered by Weber—legal, traditional, and charismatic—Walter Murphy has suggested that the Court's authority is characterized by all three (1964: 12). The Constitution, the tradition of judge-made law, and the cult of the robe combine to provide the Court with a basis for action and the presumption that its decisions will be obeyed. Compliance is a measure of the institution's legitimacy relative to the other branches of government on the one hand and in the context of the relationship between the nation and the states on the other.

Legal Hierarchy

Well before it was evident in cases such as those involving subpoenaed tapes (*United States* v. *Nixon,* 1974) and journalistic notes (*Farber,* 1978), the special relationship between the Supreme Court and other courts had been commented upon. These observations, however, were against a backdrop of a mistaken notion of a strict hierarchy. In 1964, Murphy noted that the lower federal and state courts can be characterized as "confused congeries" of mutual controls rather than a neat hierarchical system. The symbolic responsibilities are evident in the judges' oath to uphold the law. Compliance by the lower court judge thus involves recognition of the substantive ruling and the Court's authority. When the Court is clear as to its ruling, its authority with the lower judiciary is seldom disputed. According to Murphy, the key to increasing lower court conformity is an "unambiguous commitment unambiguously stated."[1] However, in cases sent by the Supreme Court to state courts from 1941 to 1951, there was further litigation in 46 of 175. In almost half of these, the success achieved in the Supreme Court was followed by a loss at the lower level (*Harvard Law Review,* 1954). In another study, surveying the last decade over which Earl Warren presided, 27 percent of those who won in the Supreme Court lost at the local level (Beatty, 1972).

The lower courts are the primary recipients of Supreme Court orders. For the most part, the clarity of the relationship, amounting in some respects to what has been described as a judicial bureaucracy at the federal level and a professional class generally, achieves maximum compliance. A degree of encouragement from third parties is of course built into the institutional mechanism. Not only do attorneys watch for instances where Supreme Court holdings can be used in their favor, but other actors affected by a ruling may employ the authority it holds to their advantage. The pressure is toward at least surface compliance. In all respects, the most important factor affecting compliance with the United States Supreme Court is the knowledge that the High Court has ruled. Outside of isolated issues affecting the national institutions, the lower courts are least likely to be able to avoid such knowledge.

The conflict between the Supreme Court and Federal District Judge John F. Dooling of Brooklyn is an example of this bureaucratic dimension of judicial action. Following a ruling by Judge Dooling holding the 1976 ban on the use of federal funds for abortion unconstitutional, his ruling was overturned as part of a series of holdings by the Supreme Court in June 1977 (*Beal* v. *Doe, Maher* v. *Roe,* and *Poelker* v. *Doe,* 1977). The case was remanded by the justices to the judge for action in accordance with their holdings. Dooling first issued a temporary restraining order on the enforcement of the amendment based on new grounds presented to him in rehearing. However, a week later Dooling lifted his injunction and the Secretary of Health, Education and Welfare immediately banned all abortion funding for the remainder of the year. Because the amendment had been attached to an appropriations bill it lived for only a year at a time. For federal judges, the ultimate sanction is impeachment. For state and local courts, the pressure depends on the institutional and political environment. The context in which these actions occur, however, is that of the legal profession.

A case from the Utah courts, *Stanton* v. *Stanton* (1975), caused the Supreme Court considerable embarrassment in its attempts to gain compliance. After the 1975 decisions requiring that Utah set the same age of majority for both sexes, the state justices refused to conform. They claimed a special insight into the biological facts of life bearing on maturity. In its second remand, the United States Supreme Court held the Utah action "obviously inconsistent" with its earlier ruling. Justice Steven's dissent, indicating a special awareness of the limits of judicial compulsion and the need for a sensitive strategy, suggested that since Utah had declared eighteen to be the majority for females, by force of the federal Constitution, it would also become the majority for males. Stevens, however, is not clear about the mechanism this would involve.

Coequal Branches

The conformity with law to which the liberal state subjects policymakers is consistent with the proposition that the authority to make policy rests on the autonomy of the law. The norm is not ignored publicly without threatening the legitimacy from which government power is derived. This is evident in conflicts between the Supreme Court and the President. Congress, however, does not face the same kind of direct confrontation with the Court, and the sway of Court authority is much more subtle in the discourse on congressional action.

The President. In the four most dramatic occurrences of Court v. President confrontation, there has been a propensity for both institutions to back away from the confrontation, but only once has a president actually capitulated. In these instances, conflicts over policy end up as clashes over institutional authority. The history of these conflicts reveals the evolution of the Court's role in determining the range of state power.

In the first of these clashes, that between Thomas Jefferson and the Court presided over by John Marshall, the position of the Supreme Court had not been established, but the clash refined perceptions of each institution. Jefferson expressed his dislike of "judges as a class" and Marshall in particular (Scigliano, 1971) and claimed that "Nothing in the Constitution has given them the power to decide for the executive." Marshall replied that "It is emphatically the province and duty of the judicial department to say what the law is." The evolution of the institution has given Marshall's pronouncements the ring of truth, leaving Jefferson's position difficult to fathom (Cox, 1976).

Andrew Jackson's well-known encounter with the Court came in *Worcester* v. *Georgia* (1832). In this case, Georgia sought to control missionary activity with the Cherokee Indians while the Court held it was not in the state's power. When Georgia defied the Court's order, the president is supposed to have said, "Well, John Marshall has made his decision, now let him enforce it." Jackson never actually had to enforce the order because no direct command was issued, an indication of the authority of the institution at that time.

Roosevelt's Court packing plan confronted the authority of the modern institution and although much commentary has described a victory for the Court, shortly after the plan was announced the Court began to uphold the president's programs. The plan was initially rationalized as an administrative aid grounded in concern about the judicial backlog and the efficiency of the federal courts. The Senate killed the bill and its action is often cited as showing widespread support for the Court over the President. There clearly was diffuse support for the institution and its demand for autonomy. The institution had matured, but there is also ample evidence that a policy shift on the Court came in time to save it from being transformed.

The dramatic conflict between President Nixon and the Court over access to tape-recorded conversations in the White House speaks to Supreme Court authority when the Court is in a position of political advantage (Cox, 1976). The clash elicited much speculation about how the president would react. The press sought an early statement from President Nixon on the question of compliance. In a statement six month prior to the ruling, Nixon's lawyer, Charles Alan Wright, declared, "This President does not defy the law." The statement was no doubt made with the expectation that the case would not get that far, and it may have been calculated to diffuse pressure to bring the case up. As the decision grew near, the president, through a new lawyer, suggested that a "definitive ruling" would be followed. Observers at the time noted that defiance of even a less than unanimous Court would solidify congressional support for impeachment (Mason, 1974). The president's decision to obey the ruling was a recognition of the Court's authority *and the expectation that it would be supported by congressional action.*

The study of compliance tends to be dichotomous. An order is given or it is not, a decision is obeyed or it is disobeyed. But the Supreme Court sends a variety of messages and it does not always let them lie without some nurturing to encourage compliance. Near the end of the term in June 1986, it was Justice Blackmun's tone that seemed to be sending messages of impatience to the Solicitor General of the United States, Charles Fried. Blackmun, not generally known for flamboyance in delivering his opinions from the bench, announced a reaffirmance *once again* of the Court's decision in *Roe* v. *Wade* (1973). The pointed tone drove the Reagan administration's advocate to defend his decision to file a brief asking the High Court to overturn *Roe* in a press conference after the ruling, but the filings at the beginning of the following term found the administration's rhetoric moderated substantially.

Congress. The Supreme Court's authority as measured by the compliance issue is also evident in disputes with Congress over the Constitution. As with the President, judicial review in the classic case pits coequal branches of government against one another. But in the case of Congress, the compliance issue is much less clear. Unlike its dealings with the President, the Court does not confront a single individual able to act (or refuse) but a corporate body where action is a much more complex thing. This institutional structure minimizes direct confrontation. The relationship between Congress and the Court is such that when the justices overrule legislative judgment, the authority of that judgment is called into question, but not the stature of individuals.

In some cases where overturn might have been possible, such as *Schecter Poultry* v. *United States* (1935), by the time the case was decided by the Supreme Court, the policies declared unconstitutional had something less than the congressional commitment they had received when formulated. The legislative action that followed judicial review of the Campaign Reform Act in *Buckley* v. *Valeo* (1976) was characteristic of instances where a portion of legislation is declared unconstitutional. The Court's action seemed to create a symbolic barrier that Congress found difficult to overcome, but this is not inevitable.

In discussing the ideologies of authority in Chapter 2 we introduced the distinction between judicial doctrine on the Constitution and institutional practice. In the *Chada* case this distinction seems to have developed with the Court announcing a sweeping holding that the legislative veto is unconstitutional and Congress proceeding to write into statute this institutional provision. An institutional claim to authority beyond its capacity does not always lead to the proverbial "constitutional crisis." It may, as it did in the case of the legislative veto, simply result in business as usual and a distinction between judicial doctrine on the Constitution and governmental practices, in this case those of the Congress.

The consequences of judicial invalidation with both the President and Congress are not a foregone conclusion, and they suggest the continuing ambiguity of judicial review as a characteristic of national institutions. A decision by the justices to take on the other national institutions rests its authority on the standing of the institution and the decision. Where the Court has asserted its prerogatives, its legitimacy will be enhanced if the political forces are right. In supporting the expansion of the bureaucracy after World War II, the Supreme Court received the kind of welcome support from those it addressed that could only enhance the institution's authority. Judicial interpretation, limited when pitted against a "popular will," is like compliance in that both depend for their success on the qualities of that will.

The Federal System

Local actions such as those involving police and the response to the Court's school prayer decisions have been the most widely studied compliance issues (Becker and Feeley, 1973; Dolbeare, 1971). After the *Schempp* decision forbidding Bible reading and prayer in the schools, Tennessee left it up to the schools to implement the Court's ruling. Out of 121 districts, 70 still followed the state law on Bible reading. The other fifty-one had made some changes, but in only one case had the schools eliminated Bible reading altogether (Becker and Feeley, 1973). Dolbeare and Hammond, seeking to demonstrate the reasons for noncompliance, came up with such massive circumvention of the Court's decision that they were unable to find significant variables bearing on the decision to comply.

Employees at the Court tell stories reflecting this angle. In one situation following the ruling on school prayer, Justice Black is said to have been chatting with an employee who mentioned that his daughter had to learn ten verses of Corinthians for school that day. The justice objected, saying "But the school can't do that. Don't they know about our decisions?" The Court employee reported that the principal, when advised of the decisions, replied, "Do you think we're going to let our children's education be run by nine old coots in Washington?" (Mathews, 1974: 1). Washington is a good deal more removed from a school superintendent, even if the school district is within commuting distance to the nation's capital, than it is from a president or a governor. The situation of noncompliance is usually less amusing and much less ambiguous when executive officers of the national government are involved.

Local Officials. Power over local officials is greatest where public attention is focused on orders by the Supreme Court. In October 1977, after heated battles at the local level, the Supreme Court decided to take up a New York injunction on the flight of the British-French Concorde supersonic airplane into New York's Kennedy Airport. Governor Hugh Carey then announced: "If the Federal Government orders that plane in, they'd better have the 82d Airborne with it to keep the people from choking up the airport." Although seemingly confident about what the federal government would need troops to carry out, the governor was more restrained in his references to the Supreme Court. He said, "If I make a judgment that this aircraft is injurious to the health and security of the homes in this state, I don't believe the Court can stand against the Governor on that point." Yet Carey's statement was attacked in a heated editorial in *The New York Times,* a newspaper that directs particular scorn on those who would flout "the rule of law." "Hugh Carey has hurled himself across the runways," opinied *The Times,* "much as George Wallace stood in the schoolhouse door at the University of Alabama fourteen years ago."

The view presented by the newspaper was as rife with the metaphors of battle as Carey's own, "he deserves to be run down by the force and logic of law and order" (Oct. 14, 1977). Fear of the Court's logic may not have gotten to the governor, but just four days later he accepted the Court's ruling, saying that he would "uphold the rule of law." The governor's bluster in the face of the Supreme Court was a way to remove himself from a difficult situation by soliciting the support of those who opposed the decision yet avoiding personal responsibility by towing to the law. The power of the High Court was also enough to thwart some of the opposition's fervor. Indeed, the very rhetoric of the struggle, the references to George Wallace and the hyperbole more characteristic of war than ordinary politics demonstrate the institutional symbols that bear on compliance to Supreme Court decisions. The political background to compliance is thus part of the Court's legitimation function.

Local Law Enforcement. The criminal procedure decisions of the 1960s suggest the difficulty of limiting the study of Court authority to compliance. Cases involving police practices depend on more than strict compliance. The police, to whom many of the procedural guarantees of the "due process revolution" were addressed, stand somewhere between the judiciary and other local officials. The limits on judicial sanction are evident in the Court's reliance on actions addressing the validity of convictions. After the *Miranda* decision, the police often conformed to the letter if not the spirit of the law. The criminal procedure cases, like others at the local level, are more interesting for the range of issues raised than as strict compliance situations. Similarly, with studies of reapportionment, juvenile justice, and obscenity (Becker and Feeley, 1973), the predominant concern has been compliance defined in terms of the spirit rather than the letter of the law. From minimal policy change in reapportionment cases to the significance of booksellers' attitudes toward pornography, it becomes clear that compliance is a very small part of the policy consequences of the Supreme Court's decisions.

The political environment is thus crucial to compliance while the degree of controversy in a case, associated with the extent to which it breaks from past practices, will affect the amount of action that follows. This has been evident with both desegregation and abortion. Compliance is influenced by the Court's capacity for institutional support. Within the criminal process, for instance, the exclusionary rule left a conceptual and institutional bind that made it difficult for others than the defense bar to rally in support of the decision. And while the impact of *Miranda* was weaker than might have been anticipated since confessions constitute the primary basis for conviction only part of the time, studies done since the Burger Court began shifting away from the *Miranda* ruling found far less movement away from what the Warren Court had done than the new rulings might have suggested. The explanation, it seemed, was that local courts were adhering to the older, more liberal decisions rather than move with the latest trend in Washington (Gruhl and Spohn, 1981).

IMPACT, IDEOLOGY, AND FORM

This section recasts the study of impact in the framework of interpretive social science in order to examine the substantive contributions made by upper courts to how we understand the social and political world. From this angle on institutional creativity it is possible to look at impact in terms of how the public authority in the United States is affected by appellate court decisions. This is especially appropriate in a research environment that is recognizing that the beliefs constituting that system are not just "values" but rather a part of the culture (Merry, 1985). They operate like knowledge of the material world to constitute the political system.

The Ideological Approach

In contemporary scholarship, legal doctrine often seems abstract. It is understood as rules or commands, exhortations of a symbolic or normative character, rather than something real. Impact, on the other hand, is excessively concrete in its focus on the response to these commands. With the conceptual richness of a toggle switch, either on or off, we understand impact and its relationship to the institution only superficially. In order to be able to see both doctrine and impact as relevant to the very nature of political activity, it is useful to enlist a particular version of ideology. Following clarification of the term, we go to work on impact with an eye to forging an ideological perspective on doctrine *in society* that looks not simply to ideas and norms but is attentive to those basic or "constitutive" practices introduced in the first chapter.[2]

Alan Hunt, in lectures given at Amherst College (1983), called attention to ways in which ideology is misunderstood and misused, limiting its utility for social science. He identified three views that it would be necessary to eliminate from the conception of ideology in order to use it effectively. The first was "Ideology" (with a capital "I") used to refer to systematic and total world views. The very perception of contesting political systems as ideologies in this sense (like Socialism or Liberalism) gives the concept a contingent character substantially different from the constitutive character of the practices developed thus far in the study of the Supreme Court. The second misuse was the reduction of ideology to false beliefs or consciousness. In the realm of the social sciences this is the most pervasive conception because it is linked to the separation of ideas from reality. Social scientists have found it difficult to expose the contingent, historical character of an article of faith without seeming to suggest that it is not "true." Finally, ideology need not necessarily be tied to classes, as Marx would have had it, or even interests more broadly defined (Hunt, 1983: 5–6). This clarification is necessary to establish the utility of a well-worn social scientific tool.

Insight into the constitutive dimensions of ideology comes from establishing a context that can be delimited. The advantage of focusing on appellate doctrine is that as a self-consciously cared for body of ideas, doctrine confines what might otherwise be abstract and diffuse. In addition, the very institutional relations that constitute the communities responsible for interpreting the law have considerable importance for social research. Following Louis Althusser, Roger Cotterrell points out that appellate doctrine has the "materiality and specificity" required for rigorous investigation. This is due to the embodiment of the ideology in the social relations of institutional life (1983: 251). In the Marxist tradition, Cotterrell calls legal doctrine "state law" (1983: 242), distinguishing it from other forms of ideology. Opinions of the Supreme Court are traditional subjects for impact analysis. They are "state law" in the purest form and the focus here.

Doctrine as ideology can be understood through the social and institutional relations that determine its impact. Such relations ought to be the paramount considerations in any study of doctrine but they are particularly important here because the appellate courts have a profound impact on the structure of public discourse (e.g., how defendants are to be treated, whether segregation is constitutional). This essay shifts the focus of impact research by associating doctrine with the beliefs and knowledge that constitute social life.

Impact. Investigation of what happened after an appellate court made a decision was a popular form of inquiry throughout the 1970s. As it flourished, it influenced how we talked about courts and also how we understood them. For example, impact analysis led to a flowering of the verb form in such uses as "The *Miranda* decision impacted the police" or "The *Bakke* decision will impact universities." The conceptions implicit in this language are part of a system framework and they have remained influential long after the popularity of the theoretical orientation that spawned them. We learned that what courts said did not immediately or necessarily have any effect. For the law to matter "other courts or . . . nonjudicial actors" (Johnson and Canon, 1984: 25) had to act. Thus, we learned that reception of appellate court decisions was as political as the process of deciding, which had begun to be viewed from a political perspective with the advent of legal realism and judicial behavioralism years before.

The gap between court orders and public action was central to the impact scholarship associated with compliance. With impact studies generally, the focus may include the significance of the institution and the consequences of action well beyond a response to direct orders. To the extent that courts engage in policy making, the political ramifications of a court's actions go well beyond compliance. In the United States, these ramifications appear to be greatest with decisions of the Supreme Court.

As we have suggested, the narrowest impact studies focused on compliance, the part of impact associated with individual responses to institutional demands. The more general approaches to impact involve action taken or withheld that goes beyond the precise orders associated with compliance. The institution has authoritative significance both prior to and in the absence of a ruling. For example, the initial reaction of the United States Senate in 1976 to the Hyde Amendment (barring the use of federal monies for abortion) was minimal because the Senate could anticipate that the Supreme Court would strike down the law. When the Court approved the congressional action, the situation changed. Inaction had led proabortion senators to avoid the issue in 1976. The confrontation a year later resulted in a three-month stalemate in that house of Congress.

Impact studies took place in the context of a political view of the courts and the law. The approach supported social research and the best of this research lays the foundation for a more comprehensive framework. The scholarly debate over how best to examine the Court's relation to dominant interests (Dahl, 1957; Casper, 1976) has operated on the premise that the institution has a broad effect. Indeed, the Court's influence on the political process has been suggested there.

Jonathan Casper (1976) laid the foundation for the conceptual contribution by criticizing the traditional winners-and-losers approach that had characterized earlier political science work. In the area of obscenity, he speculated that even if a constitutional amendment were to "reject the Supreme Court's policies since 1957 dealing with the freedom to distribute and possess 'obscene' materials," future practice would be influenced by the eighteen years of relative openness. He writes that "the Court, like other political institutions, has and will continue to make important contributions to the 'solutions' that carry the day, become the subject for further debate, and are modified or rejected" (1976: 62–63). Thus, the actions of an institution, even if ultimately repudiated, will have influenced the development of subsequent political struggles.

Until recently, social research on impact has lacked structure. The concept has been used at times as a catchall category, loosely attributing events in society to appellate courts. Impact is simply seen as everything that happens after the decision is announced. It includes such diverse phenomena as improvements in police work as a result of the criminal procedure decisions, the election of segregationist governors following *Brown,* and the *Miranda* warning cards upon which the famous rights are printed. The range is not only from activity clearly related to the Court to the very tangential, but also from the meaningful to that which barely merits attention. Other than the distinction between compliance and impact in a broader sense, there had not been much interest in synthesis and organization. The subject thus lacked both conceptual rigor and significance for an investigation of the role of the Supreme Court in political life.

A recent treatment of impact deserves note as a synthesis from which to consider the ideological dimensions that are the subject of this section. Charles A. Johnson and Bradley C. Canon, in *Judicial Policies* (1984), take judicial impact theory seriously and offer a functional classification of populations affected by judicial decisions. Although Johnson and Canon's approach is limited by its behavioral frame, the attention they call to interpreters, implementers, consumers, and secondary populations is a step toward conceptualization of doctrine as having an impact when it constitutes a political reality. In addition, their analysis is unusually sensitive to the issue of legitimacy. Johnson and Canon use legitimacy to explain "individuals" acceptance of and response to institutional policies as a function of their attitudes toward the institution's authority" (1984: 191). The concept applies to the nature and function of authority and provides a dynamic for the political view of law. Missing from the idea of legitimacy as applied by behavioralists, however, are the processes that allow authority to function.

To understand these processes, it is necessary to go beyond politics and attitudes. The more accurate representation of the behavioral factors, interests, and attitudes is as functions of knowledge. Interests, like those of the business or Hispanic community, and attitudes, like those associated with liberalism, depend on our taking certain things to be true or given—like the marketplace or the language of Spain, the existence of the Supreme Court or the First Amendment. To examine that truth sociologically we can apply the concept of practice developed to deal with institutions.[3]

Constitutive Practices. As an institution representing the last word on the law, the Supreme Court maintains the conceptual and institutional forms through which interests can be expressed and to which they inevitably appeal. We pay attention to this function of Supreme Court opinions, the creation and transformation of constitutive practices, because it is the most important contribution of this institution and the least obvious. As an opinion enters the political environment it joins with a configuration of defined interests and values operating around institutions, doctrines, and perceptions of what is possible. The influence of the courts in this sphere depends on their authority and is evident in their capacity to make policy. Here, by interpreting the authoritative concepts governing politics, the courts exert their greatest influence. By refining the language of politics they associate what is possible with the authority of the state.

The following discussion replaces a positive or political treatment of impact with an ideological view. As examined here, this reconstruction of the framework raises different questions and makes a different contribution. It is not the authority of the institution to compel but rather the institution's capacity to provide new ways of understanding political prospects that channel human action according to dictates coming from the Court. Through the language of politics the appellate courts in general and the Supreme Court in particular contribute most broadly to the authority of the state.

The Court's treatment of issues is clearly episodic in the sense described by critics of the "High Court myth" and legal realists (Horwitz, 1978) and simply a contributory part of a larger cultural process. Yet the decisions and the opinions confine politics within ideological parameters. The general characteristics of law and legal institutions in the rationalization and systematization of political opportunities performed by the state has been evident for a long time (Weber, 1968: 304–305). Courts and the legal rationality they are associated with have also recently been discussed as central to the process by which politics is legitimated (Balbus, 1973). In this tradition, the legitimation of the legal order "is not primarily a function of its ability to live up to its claims or 'redeem its pledges' but rather of the fact that its claims or pledges are valued in the first place" (Balbus, 1977: 581).

To the extent that the symbols with which the justices work become accepted in the polity, the impression left about the Supreme Court is one of permanence. This enforces the institutional claim to being autonomous from the political processes. Because of the effective institutionalization of the Court, minor divergences from strict neutrality are more likely to call for adherence to the norm than contribute to a diminution of legitimacy. Neither the market nor the political system profits by public perception that there is a biased application of the rules, and holders of economic and political power must be bound by the rules in order for them to serve their purposes. Legitimacy, in this sense, is an aspect of "effective authority" (Weber, 1968).

The forms with which the courts in America work constitute a tradition that is not simply a reflection of custom. The constitutional tradition has its own forms to rely on in making its decisions (Brigham, 1978). The Supreme Court fashions tools for the times by constructing and reconstructing constitutional, common, and statutory law for different political and economic conditions. The manner and the extent to which the Court can respond to changing conditions, like the operation of the institution, is rooted in convention. The passing on or dissemination of these conventions is a subtle yet wide-ranging form of impact. Justice Holmes's metaphoric theater on the verge of panic presents the limits on free expression to people who have never heard of *Schenck* v. *United States* or perhaps even "clear and present danger," although the concept and the methaphor are more clearly linked to each other than either is to the case in which it was first announced.

The conceptual tradition available to the justices is infused with ideological constructs that limit the range of judicial choice. Operation within this range is the source of the Court's authority, and the justices contribute to that authority by providing credible symbols. This is a process by which ideology achieves its institutional as well as social significance.

When constitutional discourses are internalized in the thoughts of the political community, some strange developments occur that can be adequately understood only if they are assessed in terms of their conceptual heritage. The *Bakke* case of 1977–1978 is an example of this process. The case would not have emerged without the tradition of legal constructs that the Supreme Court fashioned in its earlier attempts to eliminate discrimination for racial minorities. Although frustrated with the affirmative action programs that the government has mandated, whites are more likely to see their plight in terms of racial discrimination because of the language and discourse that has emerged from the Supreme Court in the last three decades. Public fascination with this case was only partially linked to affirmative action policy. A significant part of the interest in the litigation came from the peculiar use of a doctrine fashioned by the NAACP against affirmative action for minorities and the extent to which the court has disseminated the idea of color blindness into American life. In short, the language of disputes is often traceable to appellate doctrine about which the participants may not even be aware.

That commentary carries the traditions of society and what it is appropriate to do. General and often unself-concious understandings are the ideologies of social life. Attitudes and idiosyncratic factors tell us much about individual choice while the range of possibilities "will depend in important respects on the cumulative relationships between people in social groups" (Felstiner, 1974: 64). Not only is "resort to the supernatural . . . rare in an American suburb" (Felstiner, 1974) but other types of institutional responses are common. Courts teach us what is acceptable in the sphere they cover, contributing to a web of understandings that constitute social life.

Conceiving Things Political

Appropriately, a traditional legal distinction is the basis on which we will develop the nature of ideological impact. This is the distinction, so common in legal circles, between "substance" and "process." Although the distinction itself is an ideological product, it characteristically offers a convenient basis for approaching the subject of ideological impact. We begin the meat of the chapter with attention to the things politics is about, the substance, and then turn to the channels through which the struggles are waged, the processes. In each case, practices traceable to the Supreme Court and indicative of its authority set the parameters for policy.

Substantive Forms. The justices of the Supreme Court have become an "authoritative faculty of political economy." They have played a small but significant role in the system of economic, social, and political relations. In announcing what solutions will be forthcoming from the polity as well as how problems may be discussed, the Court has molded economic and political issues into forms uniting current interests with accepted or at least familiar modes of proceeding (Commons, 1924; Schmidhauser, 1979). The link between ideology and legitimacy is the fact that acceptance of these forms as givens minimizes the destabilizing effect of political interests.

Authority maintained through belief perpetuates itself by recognizing emerging interests and needs and incorporating them in the language of authority. According to Arthur Miller, from 1787 to the Civil War, the Court "cut away the remnants of mercantilism so as to create a national common market," and from the Civil War to 1937 the justices fashioned new legal instruments that were used "to strike down both state and federal legislative measures regulatory of business transactions." In both instances, the Court promulgated what Miller called "juristic theories of politics" that solidified the position of economic interests (Miller, 1968: 26–30). From the Dartmouth College case establishing "a precedent for the immunity of business corporation charters from state control" (Mendelson, 1960) through the interpretation of due process to protect corporations, judicial policy helped guarantee the interests of those forces dominating the economic sphere. In reading the principles of laissez-faire into the Constitution, the Court placed itself apart from other popular institutions relying on the mystique of the law to fashion tools to check public pressures (Paul, 1969).

By the Depression, the mythical nature of the American worker as an independent contractor on a par with his or her employer had become so evident that it was being recognized in the unified policy stands of the national institutions. The Court's retreat, in 1937, from the repudiated ideology of laissez-faire to a more acceptable position was a dramatic reminder that the capacity to legitimize economic conditions depends in part on the stature of the institution. No institution can stand as a source of authority for long in opposition to conditions that offer constraints that materially belie the promulgated interpretations. In turning to individual rights in the 1950s and 1960s, new membership preserved the perception of autonomy by limiting its commentary on contentious economic matters.

Yet even under the new orientation, the Court plays a role in reconceptualizing various disputes that arise in the market. In the mid-1970s, for instance, the Court signaled major changes in the regulation of professions by establishing the right to advertise for routine services, thus bringing lawyers under the purview of the First Amendment. This was accomplished in traditional fashion, by conceptual development. There was room for the Court to allow professional associations to continue to bar advertising. But the ideological contribution has great bearing on what free expression under the Constitution means.

The Court's role as "bricoleur" (Garvey, 1971), or fashioner of the symbolic routes through which policy must be woven, is insufficiently examined. Since the Court fashions its rulings from established traditions, small changes in the inclusiveness of categories or their application can have a tremendous effect on political life (Bobbitt, 1982: 181). In the 1963 case of the *N.L.R.B.* v. *Fruit and Vegetable Packers and Warehouseman, Local 760,* the Court was particularly creative in its interpretation of the contested concept "consumer boycott." The issue was informational picketing at a supermarket in support of a packer's strike. The N.L.R.B. had held that such picketing was prohibited by the National Labor Relations Act. The Court, however, ruled that since the picketers appeared after the stores opened, left before they closed, and simply requested consumers not to purchase the disputed apples, the action was covered by protection for the free expression of ideas. As information, the picketing was acceptable. The range of political action was not simply a compromise between competing interests in some ad hoc fashion. It was a choice influenced by and ultimately contributing to the idea of protected expression.

The changes in terminology in the area of abortion following the Court's 1973 decision have had a marked political impact. The effect of legalization was to alter the legal status of abortion as an act on the fetus. This led to concern for the rights of what some would begin to call, very pointedly, an unborn child. These developments were not precisely a failure of the Court to compel, but the conceptual developments and the degree of humanity attributed to the fetus was a new development on the national political scene. These are direct but "open-textured" developments stemming from judicial opinion.

The concepts handed down by justices can also take on a life of their own. This has been evident with the First Amendment. Recent attacks by the Women's Movement on "violent pornography" have assumed a position vis-à-vis libertarians that was traditionally held by conservative moralists. The political struggle and attention to the debate is a function, at least in part, of the meaning given to freedom of expression by the Court. The response to censorship rests as much on the familiar "pure tolerance" conventionally associated with the First Amendment (Brigham, 1984) as it does on the authority of the Court. Another example of this indirect significance was evident during the struggle to ratify the Equal Rights Amendment. The amendment, in prohibiting discrimination on the basis of sex, was solidly in the tradition of constitutional equality, but that tradition meant that distinctions based on sex would be prohibited, not just those disadvantageous to women. Many women feared the loss of some of the protections they had been receiving in the past such as alimony and exemption from military service (Brigham, 1984).

Clearly, knowledge of the decision itself is not essential for judicial opinion to have an effect on political action. The channels of communication, although predominately professional, can be traced in various aspects of the culture, including television. Attorneys look to the rulings and the media covers court decisions. But for most people the doctrinal aspect of the legitimation function operates without recognition that the Court is responsible. This can be true even where the conceptual frame (and sometimes even the exact words) is taken from judicial opinion. We often judge the freedom of expression in terms of "crowded theaters" and police procedures in terms of what "shocks the conscience" without knowing where the ideas came from.

Institutional Channels. The impact just discussed does not involve obedience to an order of the Court. The impact of the ideas in an opinion, rather than the decision itself, is an aspect of ideological authority traceable to the courts. In this instance, the substantive ideas determine the subject of politics. Another form of legitimation is associated with the institution and its place among the channels of political action that are available. Two facets of these institutional channels stand out. The first is political mobilization. This aspect of impact links politics to the channels thought to be available for action. In some cases it dictates strategies and in others it simply influences perception of when it makes sense to admit defeat. The second facet involves changes in the institution itself.

The 1973 abortion decision, *Roe* v. *Wade,* had a dramatic impact on various groups. It turned the attention of proabortion women's groups from political action, amounting, as it did, to a total victory with relatively little struggle. The effect on those who opposed abortion was to turn comfortable adherents of the status quo into the opposition. Here the dramatic nature of the decision seems to have served as an invigorating tool for movements in the Catholic Church, and it made the "Pro-Life Movement" into a national political force. In the institutional arena constituted by the processes of American law, the new antiabortion animus at the state and local level sought the available avenues, the processes that remained open. Thus, in 1975, Boston obstetrician Kenneth Edelin was indicted for manslaughter in the death of a fetus. The indictment was an attempt by the local prosecutor to circumvent the Court's abortion decision through a loophole in the law with regard to the status of the aborted fetus. The conviction at the local level in this case was struck down on appeal.

In the *Bakke* case, the Court became the focus of struggle as the authoritative institution responsible for having fashioned the symbols of controversy. One of the remarkable events in this controversy was how groups with revolutionary ideologies, like the John Brown Anti-Klan Committee, mobilized around the nation's highest Court. This was evident in the picketing and protest addressed to the institution. Protest before the Supreme Court would seem to be no way to make a revolution but it was an opportunity for mobilization. What the Court decided, since it was well within the traditions of discourse, seems ultimately to have been of less significance than the fact that a struggle over affirmative action was centered on the Supreme Court and the ideology of equality it had fashioned.

The claim to go "all the way to the Supreme Court," often heard early in litigation, has consequences that are another dimension of ideological impact. One consequence of this claim is a consciousness that having reached the Supreme Court one has reached the end of the line. The case of landing rights in the United States for the British-French Concorde Supersonic airplane in the late 1970s is an example of this institutional form of legitimation. When the Long Island protesters learned of the High Court's decision to allow the plane to land in the United States, their enthusiasm for the struggle diminished dramatically and precipitously. Certainly, protest does not necessarily cease when the Court makes a decision. The abortion situation is a case in support of that point.

However, the burden in continuing to struggle is greatest where a group has consciously seen the Court as a last resort or placed it in a position of final authority, however grudgingly. When struggles begin with the intent of thwarting or turning back a Supreme Court decision already made, the psychological impact of disappointment may not exist, certainly not to the same extent. The "Pro-Life" effort that formed after the Court's decision in *Roe* and *Doe* are of the latter sort. The gay and lesbian activism of groups like the Lambda Legal Defense Fund, which sought to end discrimination on the basis of sexual preference and litigated for the repeal of sodomy laws, are in the former category. To them, the shock of the Supreme Court's 1986 decision in *Bowers* v. *Hardwick* was all the harder to take because they had gone to the Court as part of their strategy and had sought to apply the right of constitutional privacy to their sexual relations only to be presented an ominous turn of events. In this instance, the claim to go "all the way to the Supreme Court" had a corollary. Having gone all the way to the Supreme Court, and lost, having presented a claim before the high bench, the impact of the loss was that much the greater.

In some instances, the impact of judicial action is on how the institution itself is constituted. Judicial reform has been a situation in the twentieth century where judicial decisions have led to institutional changes. As Peter Fish noted, the interest in judicial reform expressed by the Chief

Justice of the United States has been a "response to progressive attempts to exert popular control over the judiciary" (1975) that were motivated in the first place by dissatisfaction with decisions. With Taft, institutional reform involved perceived attacks on the legal profession, with Hughes, judicial independence at the national level was the issue, and with Burger, it seems to have been a response to the activism of his predecessors and those in the lower courts who would perpetuate the tradition. Thus, reconstruction of the judicial process may be a counterattack on those who would make substantive changes. According to Fish, Taft's elevation of the status of federal appellate courts and reduction of the Supreme Court's obligatory jurisdiction placed the access of "harassed property owners" to the federal forum behind a "facade" of efficiency (1975: 135). Presently, the plea for increases in the number of judges as well as expansion of alternative forms of dispute resolution (Burger, 1976) are based on belief that busy courts need to become more efficient. The ideology of efficiency is supposed to be apolitical, "the mechanisms of justice, the means to implement the ideals that we accept, are largely neutral concepts on which most can agree" (Burger, 1977: 2). The claims to neutrality and efficiency are becoming as commonplace around the Court as the reliance on judgment once appears to have been (Wolfe, 1986: 5).

The traditional appeals to neutrality and judicial expertise are giving way to a political stance and the consequent potential for a diminution of ideological authority are real. The demise of the doctrine of "political questions" shows the authority of convention in a sphere where judicial convention is most important. As recently as 1946, in *Colegrove* v. *Green,* Felix Frankfurter articulated a strict doctrine of judicial restraint and a distinction between judicial and political activity. Within twenty years, in *Baker* v. *Carr,* the Court was denying that distinction and accepting as within its purview a range of activity including issues traditionally considered political. The result was a shift in how the Court was viewed and ultimately an accommodation between politics and judicial authority based on the principles of legal realism.

Among the many places the convention can be found is the commentary on Supreme Court decisions. In the case of this doctrine, there was a movement to accommodate the new formulations as soon as they came from the Court. Looking at Mason and Beaney's text, *American Constitutional Law,* from the second to the fourth edition, for instance, one sees that the old distinction between questions that a judge can deal with and those he or she cannot handle break down. Listed in the second edition of Mason and Beaney as a political question is "whether officials have 'districted' the state in a proper manner" (1959: 19). In the third edition, following *Baker* v. *Carr* in 1962, the authors observe that "One of the most important fields in which the Court had invoked this self-imposed limitation upon judicial power is legislative apportionment" (1964: 20). Following discussion of the *Baker* decision, the authors conclude that it may rank as one of the "most momentous decisions in our judicial history." By the third edition, with racial discrimination as the justification, we have a picture of a new institutional universe in the area of political questions reaching to legislative apportionment. With this as the fulcrum, Mason and Beaney describe the fashioning of "a new Constitution" and a worthy "vehicle of the nation's life" (1964: 22).

Doctrinally, in cases like *Davis* v. *Bandemer* (1986) the Court has shown that it holds out its authority as final arbiter even where that institutional basis for its authority conflicts with a tradition of confining the assertion of authority to distinctively legal arenas. Here, Justice White ruled that political gerrymandering "which effectively and egregiously limits the representation of a political minority" in state legislatures is unconstitutional. By associating his holding with past districting cases, White sought to minimize the significance of the shift from one of the last realms beyond judicial reach due to a distinctive *legal* quality of judicial power. But the eradication of that distinction is becoming increasingly hard to mask.

Compliance, we have stipulated, is only part of impact. But having investigated the more general phenomenon, we see compliance more clearly as a function of the institutional symbols and substantive ideology promulgated by the courts. Through the symbols it fashions, the Court makes its greatest contribution to the state, not by the threat of sanctions, but by confining the discourse and action of politics along well-worn paths. As Michael Shapiro and Deane Neubauer described the situation, "Climbing to the top of the mountain with singular purpose, one has little opportunity to notice that the "mountain" achieved may hardly be the tallest of the range" (1985: 16). In the long run, this is the greatest significance of the institution for the structure of political authority. (See also Bennett, 1980: 817)

Joseph Vining, in *The Authoritative and the Authoritarian* (1986), offers a provocative and somewhat curious vision of the relationship among law, courts, and authority. He suggests the affinity of theology to the discipline of law based on shared methodology and speculates on a legal system without a Supreme Court at its head. That unusual proposition is the beginning, not the end, of a challenging portrayal of the nature of legal authority, legal hierarchy, and the future of the Supreme Court in an increasingly bureaucratic system of authority in which the Court itself loses its deeply and traditionally personal character. Vining begins with a pedagogical practice, the attraction of Supreme Court texts as a teaching and learning device for American lawyers. He sees that practice threatened by the increasingly bureaucratic nature of the Supreme Court's product, cases that "are very long, much too long to be written by judges struggling with an enormous increase in caseload: they are things of patchwork which seem, on their face, to express the institutional process of their making rather than the thinking, feeling, and reasoning of the author" (1986: 10). Vining's picture is compelling. It was suggested earlier and its affinity with the analysis presented in this chapter is striking.

Along with Vining, we have seen the courts as "among the last of the great voices to be rationalized" (1986: 19), and with Vining we have seen the tide of rationalization. In the system of authority as it is presented here, the import of the law has already begun to depend as much on bureaucracy and hierarchy as on the traditional "habits of *mind*" that gave the courts such stature in the first place. While Vining observes the impact of this change from within the legal profession, we have expanded the inquiry with attention to the authority of the Supreme Court's work in the community at large. The practices have a shared form. They depend on exchange, on knowledge, and they are conditioned by the stature of the parties in the exchange.

The Supreme Court's involvement with a particular case had, until ten years ago, been portrayed as beginning with the oral arguments and ending with the reading of the decision. Like the setting and the ways in which its authority is legitimated, the aftermath of the decision has come to be critical for understanding the institution's role in the formation of public policy. What the Court in Washington, D. C., does must be related to a wider set of responses in order to understand the institution. The Court contributes to policy by influencing substantive concerns and the perception of possible actions. It makes its greatest contribution not by threatening sanctions, but by confining political discourse and political action to paths of its own creation or application. Thus, the Court creates forms for the resolution of disputes and the authority of the state, while its legitimacy depends on the extent to which these institutional decisions become accepted as delineating what is politically possible.

8

BEYOND THE LEGALIST
PARADOX

AMERICANS ARE in a bind when assessing institutions like the Supreme Court. Although we know the Court is political and pay a great deal of attention to policy formation and outcomes, we are not supposed to evaluate the institution simply in terms of its policies. Rather, judicial policy is expected to be evaluated within a legal framework. On the one hand, we are constantly presented with judges as politicians, justices as liberals, conservatives, or moderates. From the president's choice to reports on the decision, politics is in the forefront. Yet the uniquely "judicial" is still significant. We've mentioned the reception of *The Brethren,* which depended on justices of the Supreme Court being something more than "pols," and we've seen the old "cult of the robe" quite comfortably coexisting with the contemporary "cult of the judge." The result is a certain tension and a paradox when it comes to evaluation. This paradox reflects the law and politics poles in the legalist tradition and is present in the way we ordinarily look at the Supreme Court.

The institutional perspective developed throughout the book makes evaluation easier and more compelling. Institutionally, legal ideology in the form of language, doctrine and convention influences the Court's political decisions. And appointment, life tenure, and the finality of the modern Court set its politics on another level. When we see this institution as a set of practices that include politics and law and through which both function in the American system, we gain a perspective for evaluation and a framework for the contradictions. Former Chief Justice Burger

219

may have been unprepared in cases before the Court or more ambitious than judicious in his pursuit of appointment, but his emphasis on judicial administration was very effectively oriented to the Court's contemporary institutional place. Since institutional legitimacy has shifted from legal learning to the Court's position as the final authority in American law, as expressed in the cult of the Court, Burger's efforts were consistent with a new basis for understanding judicial action.

We may be able to transcend the paradox when we are able to see the institution itself as a construct. This is the promise of good scholarship and social research that draws its analytic character from social life rather than academic formula. In this case, the institutional "construction" or workplace is housed behind the Capitol. This structure is the apex of the constitutional system. The institution that today plays such a central role in our system emerged in the twentieth century along with a national legal profession and the administrative state. When we see those interests in the institution and understand how the Court is constructed, we inevitably bring the constitutional system back a little closer toward its republican roots.

TRADITIONAL EVALUATION

The framework of liberal legalism, when it appears in the evaluation perspective imposed on the Supreme Court, distinguishes legal consequences from the political interests. Although inchoate at the Founding, the distinction was not originally the sort of limitation on evaluation that it has become. The provision for judicial independence in the Constitution shows a predisposition not to see the Supreme Court in a policymaking role, initially Court simply provided the new polity with a basis for settling disputes. The functions of the Court have grown and the nature of the institution has changed. Law and politics are united at the Supreme Court and their significance for American government is in how they operate together. The Court has come to make policy from a new institutional foundation, and our ability to assess the significance of that policy, the central issue in an institutional approach to evaluation, has become confused. In this concluding chapter, legal and policy evaluation are examined for their continuing significance while building toward the more critical dimensions of institutional evaluation.

Legal Evaluation

Since courts were not supposed to be policymakers, John Marshall's assertion of judicial power for constitutional interpretation was a credible claim only as it applied to limited judicial prerogatives. "The province and duty of the judicial department," he wrote in *Marbury* v. *Madism*, "is to say what the law is." The traditional Engligh conception of judicial role reinforced this presumption. Today, the institutional position of the Supreme Court as the final authority on the Constitution for the states and for the other branches has given the initial statement new meaning. The Court is the institutional anchor for a constitutional system where policy has become the province of the legal profession and the administrative apparatus as much as for the legislature. We can see this in commentary on the Court's significance from its friends and even from critics like William Kunstler, director of the Center for Constitutional Rights, Elizabeth Holtzman, Brooklyn District Attorney, and former U.S. Attorney General Ramsey Clark. Their commentary at a symposium broadcast over WBAI in New York City, September 26, 1986, focused on the impact of a partisan conservative, William Rehnquist, as Chief Justice and the addition of another conservative, Antonin Scalia, to the Supreme Court. Their conclusion was that "The Constitution is in trouble." This fear reflects a remarkable view of how much power the Court has acquired— two appointments and the Constitution is in jeopardy.

Similarly, review of the Supreme Court's 1985–1986 term assessed what the justices had done in policy terms, by comparison with the policy aspirations of the president. Faced with a push for conservative outcomes from the chief executive, *The New York Times* (Oct. 8, 1986) reported, in large type, that the justices had "rejected" that pressure in the area of abortion, affirmative action, minority voting rights, and rules designed to require medical care for infants with severe disabilities (Taylor, 1986). This angle took the policy issues developed in the executive branch and evaluated the Court by the judicial response. Institutional autonomy was the legal aspect of this evaluation and commentators obviously appreciated judicial resistance to pressure from the executive branch. Yet, the paradox was evident in appreciation of autonomy without a distinctive legal framework.

The path to this authority began with expertise, grew along independent lines, and achieved preeminance through institutional finality. As the Court would like us to remember, it gives no advisory opinions and waits for cases to come up. Many have questioned judicial competence to practice policymaking. On the Court from Story to Frankfurter and off the Court from Gibson through Hand to contemporary critics like Walter Berns, the message has been that the justices are not qualified as policymakers. Berns and other conservative critics made their most strident attacks while the Court was dominated by liberals, and there is considerable evidence in the logic of their position and in their long-standing commitment that they will continue to adhere to this stance despite con-

servative appointments to the Court. Younger partisans are not so likely
to be restrained. Thus a change in the policies produced by the Court will
affect the sources of legal evaluation.

Again paradoxically, some forms of *legal* evaluation draw attention to
political activity on the bench. The attention drawn to such activity is of
course generally not flattering. This point about *The Brethren* has been
established already. The response from the community of authorities defended the institution against what was perceived as an intemperate attack by muckraking authors *and* damaging evidence of petty political (and
personal) interest they so dramatically "placed" on the Supreme Court.
In his response, Anthony Lewis (1980) challenges the credibility of journalists Bob Woodward and Scott Armstrong by drawing on his own "superior" sources. His review focuses on one instance in which Justice
Brennan is reported in *The Brethren* as having changed his vote in *Moore*
v. *Illinois* (1972) to gain favor with a colleague, Justice Blackmun. Lewis
gets a denial from former clerks on this point and builds his case that *The
Brethren* lacks credibility. This, along with a limited number of other
inaccuracies and our *political* knowledge of the sort of commitments and
integrity justices such as Brennan have established (1980: 3) is the best
defense this influential commentator can produce. Another aspect of
Lewis's treatment, the claim that the interesting material in *The Brethren*
is already public knowledge, reveals a defensiveness from the author of
Gideon's Trumpet. The defense of the Court here and in other places
(Mason, 1980) is a rallying around a fundamentally traditional view of the
Court and the justices. In subsequent commentary Lewis has another
vehicle for defending the justices. This is the perception of continuity
between the Burger and the Warren courts with the Burger justices accepting Warren Court doctrines as "the premises of constitutional decision making" (Blasi, 1983: 16). Lewis can take the legal high road and
draw attention to the conservative justices who for fourteen years, at his
writing and in his view, had resisted the policy aspirations for which they
were appointed by Richard Nixon and toward which they might have
been expected to lean under pressure from their ideological kin in the
White House.

Bruce Murphy's study of the relationship between Justice Louis Brandeis and Harvard Law Professor Felix Frankfurter (1982) is more explicit
in its attention to the scope of judicial propriety, but it too digs up considerable dirt in order to affirm the legal aspiration for justices to be above
the political fray. In fact it is again the tone of condemnation and claims of
revelation in Murphy's book that most upset the reviewers who would
portray the relationship between Brandeis and Frankfurter as more ordinary than sinister (Schlesinger, 1982). By exploring the retainer paid to

Frankfurter by Brandeis, which amounted to one-third of his law school salary, and Frankfurter's own work on the other side of the bench, Murphy raises questions about our standards for justices of the Supreme Court. Like *The Brethren* the distinct impression is that our standards for justices should be higher than for other areas of public life and that judicial politics is different from other politics by institutional degrees but not "in kind."

For one thing, the idea that courts don't let the bar present a range of socially relevant information is excessively traditional. The Supreme Court of the United States is not the passive recipient of disputes it was conceived to be. With 5,000 cases to choose from and highly visible opinions, the justices can influence what comes up and what they chose to attend to at a level comparable to the other national institutions. Traditional legal evaluation required criticism in legal terms. Now, as we have seen, much of that is left to the legal profession. The bar evaluates the experience and competence of nominees to the bench; legal academics evaluate judicial tenure. Politics or policy is either submerged, as in the case of the bar, or separated from the law, in the case of most evaluation produced by legal academics.

Thus a facet of legal evaluation with ongoing significance for the meaning of institutional practices is their link to the legal profession, which relies heavily on its place and its access to courts. In this context, lawyers provide support for the institutional authority of the Court.

Since the success of "realism" in law, place in the system of government has been as important as judgment in characterizing judicial power, and there is evidence that this filters down to the population at large. The public doesn't simply judge the decisions in terms of whether they agree with them or not. There is respect for the Supreme Court, relative to the other national institutions (Adamany and Grossman, 1983), but like the power of the legal profession, the power of the Court is an institutional construction no longer captured by traditional legal considerations. The justices have a place at the top, the end of the legal line. As such the Court doesn't have to be venerated. It just needs to be considered final.

Policy Evaluation

The tradition of legal evaluation has lost ground to the political. Surveying commentary from the beginning of the term or the end, the recurrent frame is politics. In the review of the Court's work for the 1985–1986 Term, *The New York Times* commentary operates from the expectation of politics in noting its relative absence in major decisions by the justices. But it is the professional, not the colloquial that goes farthest in policy or political evaluation. From John Agresto and Alexander Bickel on the right

to Mark Tushnet and Roberto Unger on the left, the professional literature is full of essentially political pronouncements on the Supreme Court
and the justices. When the institution is evaluated on these terms, the
judges are held accountable as political actors and the emphasis is on
policy outcome and interests (Shapiro, 1977) rather than on legal form.
Although we may hope for more, political considerations have become
dominant in how Americans view the institution in practice.

The legacy of progressive realism and the cathartic activism of the
1960s combined to thrust political interests onto the Supreme Court. In
the 1930s, the attack on a conservative Supreme Court as a political body
transformed the conventional understanding of the institution. The "old"
claim on judicial expertise with its associated reliance on text and prior
decision began to be ridiculed. Such a thesis about interpretation was no
longer tenable and the picture it presented was lampooned as mechanical.
Judge Jerome Frank, calling attention to the "cult of the robe," described
the "ceremonial costume" as part of a rite that left the justices "ritually
protected . . . from attack by critical reason" (1949: 256). This critique
was a foundation for new cults of judge and Court that now dominate
policy evaluation. The success of the movement for which Frank spoke
led to new protective rituals epitomized by policy evaluation in the context of institutional finality.

The Roosevelt appointees and their observers made the Court a political institution. The Warren Court, with a commitment to racial justice
that was unusual for a national institution, made it even less likely that the
Supreme Court could pass as a group of disinterested jurists. With decisions like *Brown* v. *The Board of Education* resting on social research
rather than legal precedent and justices like William O. Douglas, whose
passion in support of civil liberties made him a very public spokesman for
those causes, the political view of the justices became the most familiar
one. Alexander Bickel, the most important spokesman for the legalist
position after the Second World War, feared that results would overwhelm method as the dominant concern for those who observe the Court
(1970; 7). Bickel's work is dominated by his belief that the Warren justices
were excessively committed to an egalitarian ideal, but he failed to guage
the success of a popular ideal as a basis for institutional authority.

David O'Brien's book *Storm Center,* while less clearly policy-
focused, is even more politically oriented. The book takes for its title the
image of the political maelstrom swirling about the justices. Although its
rich institutional description gives the "calm at the center" a legal quality, the overwhelming impression is of an institution whose *place* is political. From the opening treatment of Norma McCorvey's desire to get an
abortion in Texas to the closing disclaimer that "the Court's influence on

American life cannot be measured precisely, because its policy-making is inextricably bound up with that of other political institutions" (1986: 321), O'Brien's tale is about politics. Characteristically this work, like that of Lief Carter (1985), another political scientist, does not take policy stands in the way the lawyers do. For this tradition it has been enough to point out the indeterminacy of the law and the political character of courts.

The wonder of all this "politics" is that the Supreme Court seems to have gained in stature rather than lost ground because of it. Neither legal nor policy evaluation is capable of accounting for this. Now, more than ever in its history, the institution sits as the final authority on the Constitution in the American polity. This fact of our political culture calls for a frame that incorporates a range of institutional considerations for evaluation of the Supreme Court.

INSTITUTIONAL EVALUATION

We have reason to be suspicious of evaluation schemes dominated by the distinction between law and politics. Legal evaluation privileges the contributions of a professional elite and political evaluation privileges the institutional place the Supreme Court has achieved. The distinction has also become an anachronism that is no longer adequate to evaluate the institution. Power has been reorganized around a political Court and maintains its place and that of the institution through a myth of mechanical jurisprudence that is entirely its own creation. An institutional perspective on the Supreme Court reveals the limits on legalist forms of evaluation, since institutional practices channel interests without being "outside" them.

A problem inherent in traditional assessment of the justices became evident with the retirement of Justice William O. Douglas. Characterized as a sloppy opinion writer and a flamboyant political figure, Douglas was seldom seen as a great justice because his actions were so clearly identified with interests. Professor Bickel, holding out Douglas's statements on legislative reapportionment as epitomizing the result-oriented caste of mind, quoted the justice as saying, "The conception of political equality from the Declaration of Independence, to Lincoln's Gettysburg Address, to the 15th, 16th, and 19th Amendments can mean only one thing—one person, one vote" (1970: 7). Although he was a monumental political figure on the Supreme Court, Justice Douglas suffered when evaluated by the legalists. The prevailing dichotomy between law and politics does not provide an adequate basis for engaging the legalist dimension of the critique.

A component of the institutional smoke screen, "strict construction," masks policy agendas beneath "neutral" institutional claims (Dworkin, 1977). C. Herman Pritchett in *The Roosevelt Court* (1948) described liberal criticism of conservative justices who had substituted their judgment for that of Congress or the state legislatures on economic matters. Political interests gained leverage from an appeal to institutional practice. Once in power they adjusted the practice. The "double standard" advanced by the Roosevelt Court was an accommodation, an adjustment of the tension between law and politics. The result as Pritchett notes is that judicial inquiry into "legislative action varies according to the position which the value threatened by legislation occupies in the Court's scale of deference" (1948: 92). The Court in the mid twentieth century relied on the covering rationale of the *Carolene Products* footnote. The result is a reciprocal relationship between institutional practices and action.

In the end, the paradox of liberal legalism manifested in the evaluative tension just discussed is a way of constructing political reality. It separates what we want from the way things are, the needs from the rules. And as such, it leaves the rules, the institutional setting, in place and largely immune from the emotive responses of the polity. This is the power of institutional finality. Institutions don't have to be loved; contrary to a generation of inquiry into "legitimacy," they just have to be taken as given. These presumptions channel policy. They leave wants up for grabs and treat judicial decisions as "fluid". The implications of judicial choice are quite a bit more stable. Thus, this investigation has sought to make the institution problematic by calling attention to the what holds the government together. The two considerations drawn from the tradition, legal ideology and judicial independence, tell us a great deal about the institution. They are the focus in this section. But in the end, the ability to get beyond the legalist paradox will require an accounting of the institution's success in establishing itself as the final authority for the constitutional system.

Legal Ideology

The justices are associated with the Founding Fathers because both are ideologues who have articulated the meaning of the Constitution and its standards for political action in the culture. The Court is linked to the tradition of American political theory identified with Madison, Hamilton, and Jefferson. Since the end of the nineteenth century, the most comprehensive effort to explain the American polity is generally understood to be the compendium of Supreme Court decisions. While political figures have offered alternative conceptions of the polity in all periods of American political life, the justices, however, do it in the name of law, with attention to the past, and with an eye to the dominant ideological positions that surface in society. This gives their views special significance.

The Supreme Court has acquired a capacity to address "the great open questions that plague America" (McCloskey, 1960: 226), questions about the relation between the nation and the states, between business and the bureaucracy, and between an individual and the government. While the Court's action tells us little about the ordinary character of American law (Horwitz, 1978), its decisions are part of an interactive process. The institutional product, authoritative decision and legal opinion, have both affected public debate and, at least marginally, altered "the great open questions."

We have come to believe that most of the things Americans do and say, particularly in the realm of politics, have been discussed by the justices of the Supreme Court. In civil rights, the justices have developed and monitored the political discourse. The contribution of the Supreme Court to criminal procedure under Earl Warren made those standards a keystone to the legitimacy of the liberal state. Here, the "exclusionary rule" elevated due process standards for the system of criminal justice. Similarly, the Supreme Court, more than any other institution of government, has fostered, developed, and explained the importance of free speech, dissent, and public discourse; with reference to classified documents and government secrecy, with reference to shopping malls as a new form of public property, and in the obscenity cases, where the Court has developed a doctrine that goes beyond the range of material that the public seems likely to consider acceptable.

The work of the justices, like the work of the Founders, operates within a tradition of ideas and is constrained by past practices and traditional conceptions of what is appropriate. In the case of the Court, the practices are confining because of the professional character of this discourse. The Supreme Court's link with lawyers, though not expressly mandated, has become institutionalized and the work of this profession places limits on decisions. Although this discourse is not easily subjected to public evaluation, the forms of professional or "artificial" reason developed by lawyers and used by the Court constrains the range of choices open in the polity and for the justices. That tradition may be a boon to the Court's capacity to preserve fundamental liberties but it also supports those who profit from the established authority in the United States. In either case, the boundaries of interpretation belie the idea that legal ideology is indeterminant.

The formal view of law, the one we now consider naive, assumed that a stable body of doctrine governed the decisions made by judges. The political view proposed that judges make choices on idiosyncratic bases and manipulate doctrinal traditions to serve their political ends. Positivism gave us this distinction and rather than fading along with that view of social science, it is being replicated as a new formalism (Posner, 1985) at one end of the political spectrum on a cynical subjectivism (Kairys, 1982) at the other. Neither of these traditions is ideologically sensitive to an activity that is partially rule-governed and partially discretionary.

The constitutional ideology associated with the Court and professional authorities includes some things and not others. This is the significance of practice and of ideology. In the appellate courts, questions arise so that doctrinal phenomena become linked to institutional practice . Constitutional equality, for instance, extends protection from discrimination to the loss of fundamental rights. The right provides recourse for individuals but groups have had greater difficulty establishing the basis for a claim (O'Neill, 1981; 1985). Similarly protection from material deprivation, like substandard housing or low-quality education, which was the promise of "separate but equal", is missing. Protection from the most deep-seated and oppressive classifications, those based on the conditions in which we live, has disappeared from the Constitution. Perhaps this was the price of the constitutional guarantee of desegregation, an equal protection that excludes material inequality. Whatever its heritage the equal protection announced in modern Supreme Court decisions is a very narrow one.

Law professors have begun to acknowledge the rhetorical and ideological dimensions of their activity. The best of modern scholarship, whether in the law reviews or in political science journals, incorporates elements of both politics and law. But invariably, politics dominates our picture of courts and study of judicial opinion on the Constitution that focuses on the disagreement among justices make the Constitution seem essentially political. Yet it is much more. The Constitution creates a normative system full of substantive judgments and institutional relations (Cover, 1983; Harris, 1982). The legalist paradox is part of that system and a source of professional authority over the Constitution.

We can see the circumscriptions, and, in the language of these matters, we can see the worlds that are lost and the new worlds that are ascending.[1] Legal ideology, the study of these worlds in the sociology of law (Hunt, 1983), is the basis for further institutional investigation. Invariably realism is put forth as a defense by those who would deny the compulsion of legal promises. Such talk, however, must ultimately acknowledge the power, manifest in ideology and an interpretive community, to set the terms and constrain action.[2]

The outcomes in individual cases, the success of Linda Brown or the failure of Demetrio P. Rodriguez, reflect shifting political coalitions. Taken as a whole, the choices and the rationalizations reveal the ideological predispositions of a liberal state. These deserve close scrutiny. The Court's reasons constitute a limitation on the institutional capacity to deal with the issues that arise in political life. An evaluation of the institution must incorporate the doctrinal practices with which the Court is associated. When the justices are limited by these practices in their capacity to deal with the issues of the day in an enlightened fashion, then the institution must be held accountable for this failure. And when the practices provide insight into the political issues that come to the Court, this must also be acknowledged.

Following the Court's success during the Watergate scandal, Archibald Cox argued that the institution depends on the acceptability of decisions relative to popular expectations and interests (1976). Some call this statesmanship, and link it to the way a polity will develop. Here, the Warren Court may well have contributed more to the Court's stature than these justices withdrew from the institutional reserves in pursuing their vision. To the extent that judicial decision represents choices the polity has come to accept, the foresight of the justices serving from the early 1950s to 1970 certainly contributed to the present standing of the institution. Even after a period of retrenchment, the vision that Alexander Bickel called an "idea of progress" remains a part of the institution.

Institutional Finality

The political view that makes it so hard to accept the constraints of legal ideology has changed our perception of the Supreme Court's institutional standing. The claim to independence has little ongoing validity when posed in the traditional frame, whether legal or political. Independence makes more sense when the focus is institutional. Any modern understanding of the Court must take into account the " 'new realism' about the Court's nature" (McCloskey, 1960: 222). Institutional investigation builds on that realism by attention to the forms of legitimation that have emerged. Three "crises of legitimacy"—the discrediting of mechanical jurisprudence, the political struggle over the New Deal, and the role of the judiciary in the welfare state—reflect legal realism (White, 1976: 292–295). Each crisis produced a reaction to the dominant tradition and each proposed a basis for evaluating judicial action. When the Court moved beyond certainty and its policymaking became visible, its institutional standing had to be reconstructed. The new position grounded a claim of authority and political wisdom in the Court's finality. This is particularly clear in the realm of economic regulation where the Roosevelt Court limited constitutional recourse in comparison with civil liberties. Contemporary jurisprudence has been dominated by institutional justifications for the Court's role as guardian of fundamental freedoms. Because of the alleged infallibility of the nation's highest court and the deference paid to it by the other branches of government, the demise of mechanical jurisprudence has cost the Court little of its stature. When Justice Jackson said, in *Brown* v. *Allen* in 1953, that "We are not final because we are infallible, but we are infallible only because we are final," he was cautioning his brethren not to make too much of themselves. He wrote from the tradition popularized by Jerome Frank, as a criticism of the cult of the robe. But an observation presented as institutionally self effacing has come to describe the contemporary character of the institution. Jackson's assumption of a centralized hierarchy was still emerging when he wrote. Now it has transformed the meaning of independence. Generally, the Court's position at the top of a legal hierarchy and the life tenure of the justices allows them to hold out as commentators on majoritarian predispositions. In the modern period, the Court depends on administration and its position at the head of the nation's judiciary rather than a traditional perception of independence.

Some have tried to state a modern way to evaluate the contributions of a Supreme Court. Roger Traynor, who was Chief Justice of the California Supreme Court, suggested replacing "traditional distinctions between branches of government with a theory of governance in which activity by one branch could stimulate activity by another" (White, 1976: 295). He would enlarged the scope for judicial action and expand the audience for decisions. Others have relied on the traditional triadic relationship in a conflict and the desire for a neutral third party (Shapiro, 1981) or umpire (Cox, 1976). This practice gains in significance as the institution increases reliance on its position as final arbiter. We have seen this in the choice of justices and it is certainly a factor when decisions work their way up the legal ladder.

Evaluation must account for the significance of finality. The hope for the Court in the modern state is that the position of the institution not allow it to become an impediment to popular interests. Even without the myth of mechanical jurisprudence, the sphere of judicial activity may be circumscribed. Judges have an institutional vantage point for observing the needs of society. Thus, the setting itself provides a basis for holding any particular judges accountable.

Recent disputes over policymaking by jurisdictional decision and summary judgments suggest that we still expect the institutional position of the Supreme Court to be buttressed by "judgment." In sitting to deliberate and not simply as a group cut off from the political maelstrom, the Court's claim to legitimacy must rise from the ashes of past practice. The shift to a bureaucratic institution has been noted by Justices Brennan and Marshall, who have called attention to the problems inherent in deciding cases without argument and without opinion. The justices' criticism, which comes from outside the traditional forum for announcing the views of the Court, was in a dissent to the majority's refusal to hear a case from Indiana. The dissenters argued that summary dispositions will lead to a situation where "respect for our constitutional decision-making must inevitably be impaired" (*The New York Times,* Nov. 9, 1976: 24). The Court's authority depends on both a perception of rational deliberation and institutional standing. These aspects of the institution are central to the Court's status. However, only the latter seems capable of addressing the modern need to see the Court as a policymaking body.

With the Supreme Court, more than other national institutions, public knowledge about how the Court operates has played off of expectations (Woodward and Armstrong, 1979) and shaped attitudes about the institution (Ulmer, 1973). Institutional candor has revealed Supreme Court practices formerly known only by those who operated within it. However, getting beneath the robes and behind the purple curtain has been less an exercise in delegitimation and more like a new form of legitimation. This transforms the claim of independence into one of institutional finality.

Professor Cox portrayed Richard Nixon's downfall as due to the fact that "the most respected branch of government" was arrayed against him. In 1973, an institutional practice beyond the conception of John Marshall in 1803 had become widely acknowledged. This transformation took place over 170 years in which the Supreme Court emerged as the dominant source of constitutional interpretation. The habit of voluntary compliance to the Court's pronouncements had taken hold as authoritative, at least when there was institutional support like that coming from Congress in 1973. The Supreme Court had become final, the destination one might aspire to go "all the way" to from the street level.

Institutional legitimacy, in supporting unique professional prerogatives, raises some concerns related to its final authority. Having a focus of professional attention at the end of the line may have precluded the development of a real public space (Arendt, 1963). Further, the Court's professional discourse detracts from participation in full consideration of constitutional issues, and the special place for the legal profession in matters before the Supreme Court limits the substance of debate on political issues. The justices are limited by conceptual constraints through which issues have traditionally come to them. Where those traditions are damaging to the conditions under which Americans live, an independent institution, self-conscious of the limits to legal authority, may be able to reconstruct the concepts. However, an institution sitting where the Supreme Court does is served best by restraint. The Court mystifies through its charisma and constrains extended political discourse. By demystifying the Court, recognizing not only how it works, but its place in the system of authority, we broaden the debate and set parameters for legitimate judicial action.

The cult of the Court overrates the judicial function under the Constitution. According to Learned Hand, "a society so riven that the spirit of moderation is gone, no court can save . . . a society where that spirit flourishes, no court need save" (1944). American society has not thrust its problems on the courts. These institutions have taken up formulations proposed by the legal profession reflecting the profession's link to state power. The Court's resolutions will generally be well within the ideological frame which contains national power. The Court is dominated by an ideological tradition, like most American institutions, but when the Supreme Court makes its statements, they stand as authoritative for the entire society. Thus, the demystification of the institution ultimately depends on an accompanying ideological demystification. Recognizing the traditional play of ideological forces in the development of the law is as much a part of the investigation as the foray behind the "purple curtain."

As legal rationality may be understood in ideological terms, ideology may be seen in its institutional manifestations. The practical limits of free speech or equal protection are represented in the work of the Supreme Court, and the limits imposed by institutional practices constrain democratic aspirations. This is a dialectical relation with the constraints affected by the creative development of political rights from a legal foundation. Although originating in the ideological predispositions of a rising middle class in the eighteenth century, the Constitution and the Bill of Rights have become fundamental to modern political life and appreciated as characteristics of a "civilized humanism" (Kaufman, 1968: 52). The promise of constitutional interpretation is that it attempts to keep this humanism alive. Constitutional interpretation dominated by the Supreme Court truncates that promise.

APPENDIX

SUPREME COURT BUDGET REQUESTS*

	1977	1987
Salaries and Expenses	7,571,000	14,631,000
Care of Building and Grounds	800,000	2,455,000
Total	8,371,000	17,086,000

The Care of the Building and grounds account remains individually identified. This appropriation is primarily the responsibility of the Architect of the Capitol.

FISCAL YEAR 1977

	1977 Request	
	Perm. Pos.	Amount
Summary of changes:		
Appropriations 1976 (enacted to date)	274	$6,581,000
Proposed supplemental for pay costs	. . .	93,000
Budget authority, 1976	274	$6,674,000
Adjustments to base and built-in changes:		
1. Annualization of October 1975 pay increases	. . .	+158,000
2. Annualization of 20 positions authorized for fiscal year 1976	. . .	+ 62,000
3. Within-grade step increases	. . .	+ 55,000
4. Increase in cost of employee benefits (Life and Health Insurance)	. . .	+ 49,000
5. Travel and subsistence allowance (P.L. 94-22)	. . .	+ 10,000
6. Increase for rent, communication and utilities	. . .	+ 25,000
7. Increase for printing, supplies and equipment	. . .	+ 88,000
8. Increase for printing and binding Supreme Court Reports	. . .	+176,000
9. Nonrecurring costs authorized in 1976:		
a. Bicentennial Project	. . .	− 50,000
b. Oil portrait and marble bust of former Chief Justice Warren	. . .	− 25,000
c. Extra compensable day in 1976	. . .	− 16,000
Subtotal, adjustments to base and built-in changes	. . .	+532,000

Program Increases:

10. Four Law Clerks and five Secretaries for Justices' Offices .	+ 9	+161,000
11. Ten Police Officers	+10	+135,800
12. Secretary (Office of the Administrative Assistant to the Chief Justice)	+ 1	+ 13,900
13. Secretary to Personnel Officer	+ 1	+ 13,900
14. Two full-time Laborers and 2 part-time Housekeepers	+ 1	+ 33,400
15. Employee professional development project	. . .	+ 2,000
16. Official reception and representation expenses	. . .	+ 5,000
Subtotal, program increases	+23	+365,000
Total increases requested	+23	+897,000
Total appropriation requested, 1977	297	$7,571,000

FISCAL YEAR 1987
(Dollar amounts in thousands)

	1987 Request	
	Perm.	
Summary of changes:	Pos.	*Amount*
Appropriation 1986 (enacted to date)	318	$15,000
Sequestered pursuant to P.L. 99-177	. . .	−601
Budget Authority, 1986	318	$14,399
Adjustments to base and built-in changes:		
1. Other increases in contract rates and charges for services, supplies and equipment	. . .	+132
2. Cost of within-grade salary advancements	. . .	+109
3. Printers for Atex System	. . .	+ 25
4. Integrated Library System	. . .	−100
5. Work Stations for Research Librarians	. . .	− 11
Subtotal, adjustments to base and built-in changes	. . .	+105
Program changes:		
6. Phototypesetter—Data Systems Office	+1	+ 27
7. Supreme Court Observance of the Bicentennial of the Constitution of the United States	. . .	+100
Subtotal, program changes	+1	+127
Total net increases, requested	+1	+232
Total appropriation requested, 1987	319	$14,631

* For the basic statutory authority for these accounts, reference is made to sections "A–F" of the Digest on Appropriations, The Judiciary, on file with the Appropriations Committees of the Congress and the Office of Management and Budget.

NOTES

Introduction

1. The New York State Library building is much bigger.
2. *Constitutional Language: An Interpretation of Judicial Decision* (1978); *Civil Liberties and American Democracy* (1984).

Chapter 1

1. Social scientists have been avoiding the positivist label for a decade now, although the pejorative edge is sharper when quantitative work is criticized from this perspective than when the critique is applied to theoretical discussions.
2. Around 1400, Sir John Fortesque used the work to denote an activity. Machiavelli looked to institutional arrangements much as Montesquieu would some years later. By 1551, the concept was used by Thomas More in his *Utopia* as "an established law, custom, usage, practice, organization or other element in the political or social life of a people."
3. According to Stanley Cavell (1984), an early disseminator of interpretive approaches in the social sciences, the study of convention or "the ordinariness in question spoke of an intimacy with existence, or an intimacy lost . . . something Emerson and Thoreau mean in their devotion to what they call the common, the familiar, the everyday, the low, the near."
4. Weber distinguished between the concept of an institution as used in social research and what appeared in the law as a juristic term of art (Weber, 1954: 158).
5. Thorstein Veblen's *The Theory of the Leisure Class* was identified with institutional economics along with the scholarship of John R. Commons and Wesley C. Mitchell.

235

6. Felix Frankfurter and James Landis (1928) linked the business of the Court with institutional developments and portrayed jurisdictional shifts as affecting the work and status of the institution.

7. See the fuller discussion of Wasby and judicial review scholarship in the next chapter.

8. There are a number of good treatments of this point although it has dropped from general view. See Ellis (1971) and Corwin (1938).

9. The idea comes from Stanley Fish (1980).

10. This was put very nicely in a comment by Martin Shapiro (1967: 209) on equal protection for indigent defendants.

11. An analogous dimension of professional practice placing a premium on knowing "the ropes" rather than formal rules may be emerging as a new ideology of lawyering (Simon, 1978).

12. See Brinkley Messick for his discussion of Arabic legal documents that although they appear similar to American documents do not stand alone as evidence and hence are not "constitutive instruments" (Messick, 1983: 48).

13. Another form of interpretation proposes logical limits on action (Barber, 1984).

14. The implications of the "double standard" for the work done by the Supreme Court are discussed in Chapter 5.

Chapter 2

1. Corwin's treatment is not historically or conceptually careful, but his work deserves continued attention because it shows the relationship between idea and action. His approach is valuable to the contemporary study of political life because it generates questions we have not been asking.

2. Corwin described the legacy of Locke for America as the creation of rights (Corwin, 1928). Modern legal form joined seventeenth-century science to tradition, elevating legal thought to the status of natural reason.

3. This is the Constitution in a "material" sense according to a custom Corwin attributes to the French in which "material" is distinguished from "formal" (Corwin, 1938: 87).

4. This discussion draws on "The Study of Institutions" in the first chapter.

5. Marxists such as Ralph Miliband (1969), Nicos Poulantzas (1975), and others such as C. B. Macpherson (1977) agree that institutions legitimate state authority but they disagree over the extent of institutional autonomy. Macpherson views the state as somewhat above classes. Miliband holds that the task of state power is "safeguarding" bourgeois order (1969: 99) through a relative autonomy that maintains the existing system of domination. Surprisingly, this idea of relative autonomy comes quite close to that of the ideologues of judicial neutrality (Bickel, 1962: 30). Institutional legitimacy can be squandered through inadequate care for the perception that the institution is not simply a political one.

6. "The headquarters of classicism through the 1930s was the United States Supreme Court itself, always the chief source of symbolic leadership for the legal

profession's conceptions of its appropriate role in public affairs. Its place at the apex of the administrative process meant that all decisions taken in the Progressive-purposivist mode had to be rationalized in the language of classical-legal Constitutional analysis." (Gordon, 1985: 53).

7. Without reference to scholars outside the immediate professional community (i.e., O'Neill, 1980; Harris, 1982).

8. In Chapter I, interpretive communities were discussed to emphasize the sociological dimension which is essential to an institutional perspective. Here attention is drawn to the ideological forms which define these communities.

9. Karl Klare's discussion of the constitutive dimension in law built on Douglas Hay and gave us a picture of how legal worlds are posited.

10. This debate was first introduced to me in a seminar conducted by Walter Murphy in the summer of 1985 and a further elaboration of the debate is carried in the new text by Murphy, Flemming, and Harris (1986).

11. Somewhat parenthetically, it ought to be noted that the effort to amend the Constitution through the political process has different implications because the project is explicitly to introduce something that is not there (Houseman, 1979).

Chapter 3

1. A reference exists in the Philadelphia *Public Ledger* of June 12, 1828.

2. For a more penetrating discussion of this issue, see John Gunnell (1976: 6) on social scientific knowledge.

3. These were the middle to upper strata of the "middling classes" whose practice of a learned craft could itself distinguish them from idle landlords (Bledstein, 1976).

4. During Roosevelt's struggle with the Court in the late 1930s, a Gallup Poll found that seven out of ten Americans were opposed to having nonlawyers on the Supreme Court (Krislov, 1965: 2). Lawyer justices is the convention, although on occasion, as at the confirmation hearing for John Paul Stevens, a voice critical of the professional dominance of the institution was raised.

5. G. Harrold Carswell, who failed to be confirmed, turned out to have had a not altogether orthodox sex life. He was arrested in a compromising situation at a bar association convention not long after the nomination fight.

6. A letter to the editor by Professor Christopher Pyle of Mount Holyoke College that was printed in *The New York Times* on September 9, 1986, drew attention to Rehnquist's deciding vote in *Laird* v. *Tatum* in 1972. Pyle describes the former Justice Department official as custodian of the records in the case he later decided.

7. Auerbach pointed out the consistency of this sort of jurisprudence with the "end-of-ideology politics of the Cold War" described by Thurman Arnold as "the new professional 'theology'/" or establishment counterattack on the Supreme Court's protection of individual rights.

8. "The statesmanlike judge will adapt the Constitution to changing social realities without altering the meaning of the document" (Jacobsohn, 1977: 17).

Chapter 4

1. The twentieth century has seen a steady decline in population per lawyer from a high of 863 in 1920 to 572 in 1970 (Grossman and Sarat, 1975). The proportion of lawyers in the United States relative to the rest of the world (one lawyer serves 1,600 persons in Italy, 2,000 in the United Kingdom, 3,000 in West Germany, and 13,000 in Japan) is even more startling.

2. Some of this state sensitivity about lawmaking power is reflected in a federal statute providing that the only state court decisions reviewable in the Supreme Court are "final judgments or decrees rendered by the highest court of a state in which a decision could be had." The doctrine is called *abstention* and it was evident in the case of *Roe* v. *Wade* with regard to a doctor who sought to join in the abortion appeal but who was still going through the legal process in Texas and was thus precluded by the abstention doctrine from joining the case.

3. Increasingly apparent to those who care for the Court, the shrine needs attention. With the encouragement of Chief Justice Burger, the late Justice Tom Clark, and the daughter of the late Chief Justice Hughes, the Supreme Court Historical Society was formed in 1974. The society publishes a yearbook and provides an opportunity to celebrate at annual meetings where "white tie" is optional. In addition, exhibits of Court history maintained by the curator add an institutional capacity to communicate.

4. The ATEXT system used at the Court and by large publishers permits the exchange of drafts and editorial work at a level characteristic of profit-making institutions.

5. The law school class from which that group was drawn was approximately 40 percent female.

6. To be admitted to the Supreme Court Bar an applicant must first have been admitted to a state bar and then he or she must have the support of a member of the bar of the Supreme Court. Until recently the induction of new members into the Supreme Court Bar was a ceremonial function supervised by the justices, but after Warren Burger became Chief Justice, the Court has allowed admission to its bar by mail, an efficiency questioned by some traditionalists (Keefe, 1975: 1511).

Chapter 5

1. For some this is the best-established limit on how the Court can be used (Gunther, 1975: 1532).

2. Table III, adapted from Frankfurter and Landis, provides for a central term within each of the periods being discussed and an additional year to bring the table up to date in the modern period.

3. These were the "miscellany of common law and statutory questions" disposed of today by a denial of certiorari, a summary affirmance, or reversal without opinion (Burger, 1977: 4).

4. Although interpretation and related approaches are making inroads into the study of law (Klare, 1979; Brigham, 1978), they are too often simply "critical"

(i.e., a mode of attack grounded in the social and historical relativism of all culture) (Unger, 1976). My approach is tied to attempts to interpret cultures (Geertz, 1973) and shows how conventions constitute the social world.

5. McCloskey noted this in his "exhumation and reburial" of economic due process. He wrote of the double standard, "It seems to have been a kind of reflex, arising out of indignation against the excesses of the Old Court, and resting on the vague, uncritical idea that 'personal rights' are 'O.K.' but economic rights are 'Not O.K.'/" (1962: 54). For an exhumation of "the old laissez-faire court" that cautions against reburial, see M. C. Porter (1977).

6. Martin Shapiro's *Law, Politics and the Supreme Court* (1964) put forth the thesis that the Court made economic policy in the area of statutory interpretation and Shapiro urged attention to that docket. Glendon Schubert, in *The Judicial Mind,* described his confrontation with the double standard by noting that prior to 1937, the issues that grouped under economic liberalism "would have been considered to involve the decision of 'constitutional questions.'/" After the switch these issues were treated as statutory questions (1965).

7. This position was affirmed recently in *United States* v. *50 Acres of Land* (1984), which held that the Fifth Amendment does not require that the United States pay a public condemnee compensation measured by the cost of acquiring a substitute facility, even where the condemnee has a duty to acquire such a facility. Here, the market value was all the property owner could legitimately expect.

8. "[I]t is precisely because a whole generation of political scientists continued to be brain-washed by the legalists, that they continue to interpret the policy-making of the United States Supreme Court almost exclusively in terms of civil-liberties decisions" (Schubert, 1965).

Chapter 6

1. Only where some aspects of the institution are beyond question, where there is confidence in their social meaning, can other aspects be questioned short of radical transformation (Will, 1974: 297).

2. This satire on constitutional practices was reprinted in a publication of the American Bar Association entitled *Update* in August 1978, in *The Chicago Tribune* in May 1978, and in Wasby (1984). It was also cleared for broadcast by the Pacifica Radio Foundation in January 1982.

3. Johnson (1985) identifies a renaissance in the study of judicial opinion by social scientists, and his own work quantifies citation practices allowing him to observe the use of prior cases in Supreme Court opinions from 1946 to 1974.

4. This later setting is where the justices may be observed "talking law." Thus, it reveals a world depicted by language and used by the justices to interpret events. With oral argument we can tie the tradition of discourse to behavior. In written communication the link to human action is much less clear, especially if we are concerned about particular action by individuals.

5. The independence of legal grammar from ordinary grammar happens also to be evident in this passage.

6. The exceptions are the *in forma pauperis* petitions that are less likely to have been subjected to legal filtering and hence more likely to be treated as legal nonsense. The evaluation of these claims is cursory. Justice Douglas even characterized most prisoner petitions as "surpassing credulity" (Lewis, 1964: 34).

7. "This right of privacy, whether it be founded in the Fourteenth Amendment's concept of personal liberty . . . or . . . in the Ninth Amendment's reservation of rights to the people, is broad enough to encompass a woman's decision whether or not to terminate her pregnancy" (*Roe,* 1973: 153).

8. The oral argument in *Bakke* was extended an hour from the norm because of the importance of the case. A record ninety newspaper and broadcast reporters attested to its importance.

9. People who study the Supreme Court have become aware that tapes of the arguments dating back to 1955 are available three years after the hearing. This should provoke research into this facet of the Court's activity (Cortner, 1977).

10. Mike Libby, a clerk for the 1983 term, speaking before a group of political scientists in August 1984, reported that Chief Justice Burger had assigned 90 percent of the cases for the preceding term.

11. Provine also finds a similarity between case selection and voting on the merits. Votes to review tend to be votes to reverse, at least half the time (1980: 109).

Chapter 7

1. The problem with such statements is that they conflict with the equally important goal of unanimity. To get a number of judges together, as in the Nixon Tapes case, the Court may have to be satisfied with the narrowest possible statement.

2. A foundation has been laid by study of the inner workings of the institution such as Walter Murphy's (1964) investigation of strategic behavior and the journalism of Linda Mathews, Nina Totenberg, and Bob Woodward and Scott Armstrong. All link ideas and physical structure in a way that suggests a route to ideological practice.

3. An application of this frame through the closely related "rhetorical" tradition of discourse analysis was undertaken by Adelaide H. Villmoare (1981) in a paper on law and order themes evident in electoral rhetoric from 1964 to 1973.

Chapter 8

1. Somewhat parenthetically, it ought to be noted that the effort to amend the Constitution through the political process has different implications because the project is explicitly to introduce something that is not there (Houseman, 1979).

2. A surface limitation of my approach has been that the orientation comes from political science. It has been an effort to give definition to the unstructured

world of "discretion." From another perspective, that of the law schools, one might move in the other direction, away from structure, as CLS has been doing. (The lesson here is that my work begins to recognize that the possibilities are more open than the approach has suggested when the language book is viewed as the story of constraints. This paper is meant to bring together the sources of constitutional thought (the interpretive community) and present a fuller view of constitutional thought.

REFERENCES

While it is traditional to cite cases as authority separate from the scholarly bibliography, the nature of this investigation requires more than that cases just be listed as documentary sources. Here, those materials that are "official" (i.e., integral to the institutions) are listed as documents. These include the commentary of sitting justices and officers of the Supreme Court in addition to materials produced by or for the institution.

Book and Articles

ABEL, RICHARD. 1974. "A Comparative Theory of Dispute Institutions in Society," 8 *Law and Society Review* 217.

ABRAHAM, HENRY J. 1977. *The Judiciary: The Supreme Court in the Government Process*. 4th ed. Boston: Allyn and Bacon.

———. 1983. *Freedom and the Court*. New York: Oxford University Press.

———. 1985. *Justices and Presidents*. 2nd ed. New York: Oxford University Press.

ADAMANY, DAVID, AND JOEL GROSSMAN. 1983. "Support for the Supreme Court as a National Policy Maker," 5 *Law and Policy* 405–437.

AGRESTO, JOHN. 1984. *The Supreme Court and Constitutional Democracy*. Ithaca: Cornell University Press.

ARENDT, HANNAH. 1963. *On Revolution*. New York: Viking.

ATKINSON, DAVID N. 1975. "Minor Supreme Court Justices: Their Characteristics and Importance," 3 *Florida State University Law Review* 348.

AUERBACH, JEROLD S. 1976. *Unequal Justice: Lawyers and Social Change in Modern America*. London: Oxford University Press.

AUSTIN, JOHN. 1885. *Lectures on Jurisprudence*. 5th ed. London: No pub.

BAKER, C. EDWIN. 1984. "Thoughts on Property and Its Relation to Constitutionally Protected Liberty and Autonomy." Unpublished.

243

BALBUS, ISAAC D. 1973. *The Dialectics of Legal Repression*. New York: Russell Sage Foundation.

———. 1977. "Commodity Form and Legal Form: An Essay on the 'Relative Autonomy' of the Law," 12 *Law and Society Review* 571.

BARBER, SOTIRIOS. 1984. *On What the Constitution Means*. Baltimore: Johns Hopkins University Press.

BARKER, ERNEST. 1962. *The Politics of Aristotle*. New York: Oxford University Press.

BAUM, LAWRENCE. 1985. *The Supreme Court*. 2nd ed. Washington, D.C.: CQ Press.

BAUM, LAWRENCE, ET AL. 1978. "Transformations in Appellate Activity: A Look at the Business of Three United States Courts of Appeals, 1895–1975." American Political Science Association Paper.

BEARD, CHARLES A. 1912. *The Supreme Court and the Constitution. 1962 ed. Englewood Cliffs, N.J.: Prentice-Hall.*

BEATTY, JERRY K. 1972. "State Court Evasion of United States Supreme Court Mandates During the Last Decade of the Warren Court," 6 *Valparaiso University Law Review* 260–285.

BECKER, THEODORE. 1964. *Political Behavioralism and Moern Jurisprudence*. Chicago: Rand McNally.

BECKER, THEODORE, AND MALCOLM FEELEY. 1973. *The Impact of Supreme Court Decisions*. Oxford: Oxford University Press.

BELZ, HERMAN. 1978. "Comments on the Living Constitution." Convocation for Project '87, Philadelphia.

———. 1985. "Constitutionalism and Bureaucracy in the 1980's," 47 *DEA News* 16.

BENNETT, W. LANCE. 1980. "The Paradox of Public Discourse: A Framework for the Analysis of Political Accounts," 42 *Journal of Politics* 792.

BENTLEY, ARTHUR F. 1908. *The Process of Government*. 1949 ed. Evanston, Ill.: Principia Press.

BERKSON, LARRY C. 1978. *The Supreme Court and Its Publics: The Communication of Policy Decisions*. Lexington, Mass.: Lexington Books.

BICKEL, ALEXANDER. 1962. *The Least Dangerous Branch*. Indianapolis: Bobbs-Merrill.

———. 1970. *The Supreme Court and the Idea of Progress*. New York: Harper and Row.

BLACK, CHARLES L. 1969. *Structure and Relationship in Constitutional Law*. Baton Rouge: Louisiana State University Press.

———. 1970. "A Note on Senatorial Consideration of Supreme Court Nominees," 79 *Yale Law Journal* 65.

BLACKSTONE, SIR WILLIAM. 1771. *Commentaries on the Laws of England*. Philadelphia: J.B. Lippincott, 1900.

BLASI, VINCENT, ED. 1983. *The Burger Court: The Counter-Revolution That Wasn't. New Haven: Yale University Press.*

BLAUSTEIN, ALBERT, AND ROY MERSKY. 1972. "Rating Supreme Court Justices," 58 *American Bar Association Journal* 1183–1186.

BLEDSTEIN, BURTON J.. 1976. *The Culture of Professionalism*. New York: Norton.

BLOOMFIELD, MAXWELL. 1981. "The Supreme Court in American Popular Culture," 4 *Journal of American Culture* 4.

BOBBITT, PHILIP. 1982. *Constitutional Fate: Theory of the Constitution*. New York: Oxford University Press.

BOURDIEU, PIERRE. 1977. *Outline of a Theory of Practice*. London: Cambridge University Press.

BRADLEY, PHILLIPS. 1937. "Constitution, the Court, and the People," in Julia E. Johnsen, ed., *Reorganization of the Supreme Court*. New York: H. W. Wilson.

BREITEL, CHARLES D. 1968. "Counsel on Appeal," in Arthur A. Charpentier, ed., *Lectures on Appellate Advocacy*. New York: McGraw-Hill.

BREST, PAUL, AND SANFORD LEVINSON. 1983. *The Processes of Constitutional Decisionmaking: Cases and Materials*. 2nd ed. Boston: Little, Brown.

BRIGHAM, JOHN. 1978. *Constitutional Language: An Interpretation of Judicial Decision*. Westport, Conn.: Greenwood Press.

———. 1983. "Do the Justices Make Sense?" 16 *Polity* 242–262.

———. 1984. *Civil Liberties and American Democracy*. Washington, D.C.: Congressional Quarterly Press.

———. 1986. "The Economy and the Court: The 'Double Standard' as Institutional Practice," *Research in Law and Policy Studies*. Greenwich, Conn.: JAI Press.

BRISBIN, RICHARD A., JR. 1976. "The Supreme Court and the Power of the Legal Profession." Prepared for delivery at the Annual Meeting of the American Political Science Association.

BRYCE, JAMES. 1891. *The American Commonwealth*. London: Macmillan.

CAEMMERER, H. PAUL. 1970. *The Life of Pierre Charles L'Enfant*. New York: Da Capo Press.

CAIN, MAUREEN, AND KALMAN KULCSAR. 1981/82. "Thinking Disputes: An Essay on the Origins of the Dispute Industry," 16 *Law and Society Review* 375.

CARDOZO, BENJAMIN N. 1921. *The Nature of the Judicial Process*. New Haven: Yale University Press.

CARLSON, HAMPTON. 1892. *The Supreme Court of the United States*. Philadelphia: A.R. Keller.

CARP, ROBERT A., AND RONALD STIDHAM. 1985. *The Federal Courts*. Washington, D.C.: CQ Press.

CARTER, LIEF. 1985. *Contemporary Constitutional Lawmaking: The Supreme Court and the Art of Politics*. New York: Pergamon Press.

CASPER, GERHARD, AND RICHARD POSNER. 1974. "A Study of the Supreme Court's Caseload," 3 *Journal of Legal Studies* 346.

———. 1976. *The Workload of the Supreme Court*. Chicago: American Bar Foundation.

CASPER, JONATHAN. 1976. "The Supreme Court and National Policy Making," 70 *American Political Science Review* 50–63.

CAVANAUGH, RALPH, AND AUSTIN SARAT. 1980. "Thinking About Courts: Toward and Beyond a Jurisprudence of Judicial Competence," 14 *Law and Society Review* 371.

CAVELL, STANLEY. 1984. *Themes Out of School*. San Francisco: North Point Press.

CHAYES, ABRAM. 1976. "The Role of the Judge in Public Law Litigation," 89 *Harvard Law Review* 1281–1316.

CHOPER, JESSE. 1980. *Judicial Review in the National Political Process*. Chicago: University of Chicago Press.

CLARK, DAVID S. 1981. "Adjudication to Administration: A Statistical Analysis of Federal District Courts in the Twentieth Century," 55 *Southern California Law Review* 65.

CLAYTON, JAMES E. 1964. *The Making of Justice: The Supreme Court in Action*. New York: Dutton.

COMMONS, JOHN R. 1924. *The Legal Foundations of Capitalism*. Madison: University of Wisconsin Press.

COOLEY, THOMAS. 1888. *Treatise on Torts*. 2nd ed. Chicago: Callaghan and Co.

CORTNER, RICHARD. 1977. "Tapes of Oral Argument," 15 *DEA News*.

CORWIN, EDWARD S. 1928. *The "Higher Law" Backgrounds of American Constitutional Law*. Ithaca: Cornell University Press.

———. 1934. *The Twilight of the Supreme Court: A History of Our Constitutional Theory*. New Haven: Yale University Press.

———. 1938. *Court Over Constitution: A Study of Judicial Review as an Instrument of Popular Government*. Princeton: Princeton University Press.

COTTERRELL, ROGER. 1983. "The Sociological Concept of Law," 10 *Journal of Law and Society* 241.

COVER, ROBERT. 1983. "Foreward: Nomos and Narrative," 97 *Harvard Law Review* 4–70.

COX, ARCHIBALD. 1976. *The Role of the Supreme Court in American Government*. London: Oxford University Press.

COX, JOSEPH. 1890. "Sketches of the Supreme Court of the United States," in *United States Supreme Court: Its Organization and Judges to 1835*. Cincinnati: Ohio Bar Association.

CROSSKEY, W. W. 1953. *Politics and the Constitution in the History of the United States*. Chicago: University of Chicago Press.

CURTIS, CHARLES P. 1947. *Lions Under the Throne*. Boston: Little, Brown.

DAHL, ROBERT. 1957. "Decision-Making in a Democracy: The Supreme Court as a National Policy-Maker," 6 *Journal of Public Law* 279–295.

DALTON, THOMAS CARLYLE. 1985. *The State Politics of Judicial and Congressional Reform: Legitimizing Criminal Justice Policies*. Westport: Greenwood Press.

DANELSKI, DAVID. 1968. "The Influence of the Chief Justice," in Sheldon Goldman and Thomas Jahnige, eds., *The Federal Judicial System: Readings in Process and Behavior*. New York: Holt, Rinehart and Winston.

DENNIS, EVERETTE E. 1974. "Another Look at Press Coverage of the Supreme Court," 20 *Villanova Law Review* 765–799.

DOLBEARE, KENNETH M. 1967. "The Public Views the Supreme Court," in H. Jacob, ed., *Law, Politics and the Federal Courts*. Boston: Little, Brown.
———. 1973. "The Supreme Court and the States," in Theodore Becker and Malcolm Feeley, eds., *The Impact of Supreme Court Decisions*. 2nd ed. London: Oxford University Press.
DOLBEARE, KENNETH M., AND PHILLIP HAMMOND. 1971. *The School Prayer Decisions from Court Policy to Local Practice*. Chicago: University of Chicago Press.
DORFMAN, JOSEPH, ET AL. 1964. *Institutional Economics: Veblen, Commons, and Mitchell Reconsidered*. Berkeley: University of California Press.
DUDLEY, ROBERT L., AND CRAIG R. DUCAT. 1985. "Recent Voting Patterns on the Burger Court in Economic Cases." Prepared for delivery at the 1985 Annual Meeting of the Western Political Science Association.
DWORKIN, RONALD. 1977. *Taking Rights Seriously*. Cambridge: Harvard University Press.
———. 1982. "Law as Interpretation," 60 *Texas Law Review* 527.
EASTERBROOK, FRANK. 1984. "The Supreme Court, 1983 Term, Forward: The Court and the Economic System," 98 *Harvard Law Review* 4.
ELLIOTT, RICHARD N. 1931. "New Home for Highest Court," 1 *Federal Bar Association Journal* 12.
ELLIS, RICHARD E. 1971. *The Jeffersonian Crisis: Courts and Politics in the Young Republic*. New York: Oxford University Press.
ELY, JOHN HART. 1973. "The Wages of Crying Wolf: A Comment on *Roe v. Wade*," 82 *Yale Law Journal* 920.
———. 1980. *Democracy and Distrust*. Cambridge: Harvard University Press.
ESTREICHER, SAMUEL, AND JOHN SEXTON. 1985. "Supreme Court Project," 14 *New York University Law Review* 1.
ETHRIDGE, MARCUS E. 1985. "A Political-Institutional Interpretation of Legislative Oversight Mechanisms and Behavior," 17 *Polity* 340–360.
EWING, CORTEZ A. M. 1938. *The Judges of the Supreme Court. 1789–1937: A Study of Their Qualifications*. Miami: University of Miami Press.
FAIRMAN, CHARLES. 1938. "The Retirement of Federal Judges," 51 *Harvard Law Review* 397–443.
———. 1939. *Mr. Justice Miller and the Supreme Court, 1862–1890*. Cambridge: Harvard University Press.
FARRAND, MAX. 1913. *The Framing of the Constitution of the United States*. New Haven: Yale University Press.
FEELEY, MALCOLM. 1979. *The Process Is the Punishment*. New York: Russell Sage.
FEIBLEMAN, JAMES K. 1968. *The Institutions of Society*. New York: Humanities Press.
FELSTINER, WILLIAM. 1974. "Influence of Social Organization on Dispute Processing," 9 *Law and Society Review* 63.
FISH, PETER. 1973. *The Politics of Federal Judicial Administration*. Princeton: Princeton University Press.

————. 1975. "William Howard Taft and Charles Evans Hughes: Conservative Politicians as Chief Judicial Reformers," *The Supreme Court Review* 123–145.

FISH, STANLEY. 1980. *Is There a Text in This Class?* Cambridge: Harvard University Press.

FISHER, GEORGE SYDNEY. 1897. *The Evolution of the Constitution of the United States*. Philadelphia: J.B. Lippincott.

FISHER, LOUIS. 1985. "Constitutional Interpretation by Members of Congress," 63 *North Carolina Law Review* 707–747.

FISS, OWEN. 1982. "Objectivity and Interpretation," 34 *Stanford Law Review* 739–763.

FLATHMAN, RICHARD. 1976. *The Practice of Rights*. New York: Cambridge University Press.

FOSTER, JAMES C. 1976. "Lawyers and the American Political Tradition: Rules, Rights and Rhetoric." Paper presented to the American Political Science Association.

FRANK, JEROME. 1949. *Courts on Trial*. Princeton: Princeton University Press.

FRANK, JOHN P. 1968. *Marble Palace*. New York: Knopf.

FRANKFURTER, FELIX. 1947. "Reflections on Reading Statutes," in Westin (1961).

FRANKFURTER, FELIX, AND JAMES LANDIS. 1928. *The Business of the Supreme Court*. New York: Macmillan.

FRARY, I. T. 1940. *They Built the Capital*. Richmond: Garratt and Massie.

FREEDMAN, MAX. 1956. "Worst Reported Institution," 10 *Nieman Reports* 2.

FREEMAN, ALAN. 1978. "Legitimizing Racial Discrimination Through Antidiscrimination Law," 62 *Minnesota Law Review* 1.

FREUND, PAUL. 1962. *The Supreme Court of the United States*. Cleveland: Meredian Books.

FREUND, PAUL, ET AL. 1972. *Report of the Study Group on the Caseload of the Supreme Court*. Washington, D.C.: Administrative Office of the United States Courts.

FRIEDMAN, LAWRENCE M. 1973. *A History of American Law*. New York: Simon and Schuster.

————. 1985. *Total Justice*. New York: Russell Sage.

FRIENDLY, FRED W. 1978. "Bakke, Unmuddy," *The New York Times,* June 15.

FRIENDLY, FRED, AND MARTHA ELLIOTT. 1984. *The Constitution: That Delicate Balance*. New York: Random House.

FUNSTON, RICHARD. 1975. "The Double Standard of Constitutional Protection in the Era of the Welfare State," 90 *Political Science Quarterly* 261–292.

GARLAND, A. H. 1898. *Experience in the United States Supreme Court*. Manuscript in the University of Chicago Library.

GARVEY, GERALD. 1971. *Constitutional Bricolage*. Princeton, N.J.: Princeton University Press.

GAWALT, GERALD W., ed. 1985. *The New High Priests: Lawyers in Post-Civil War America*. Westport, Conn.: Greenwood Press.

GEERTZ, CLIFFORD. 1964. Ideology as a Cultural System," in David Apter, ed., *Ideology and Discontent*. New York: The Free Press.
——. 1973. *The Interpretation of Cultures*. New York: Basic Books.
GENG, VERONICA. 1978. "Supreme Court Roundup," *The New Yorker,* May 15.
GOEBEL, JULIUS. 1971. *History of the Supreme Court of the United States: Antecedents and Beginnings to 1801*. New York: Macmillan.
GOLDMAN, SHELDON. 1985. *The Federal Courts as a Political System*. 3rd ed. New York: Harper and Row.
GOLDSTEIN, JUDITH. 1986. "The Political Economy of Trade: Institutions of Protection," 80 *American Political Science Review* 161–184.
GOODRICH, PETER. 1984. "Rhetoric as Jurisprudence," 4 *Oxford Journal of Legal Studies* 88.
——. 1986. *Reading the Law*. Oxford: Basil Blackwell.
GORDON, ROBERT. 1985. "The Elite Bar in the 19th Century." The Holmes Lectures, Harvard Law School, Feb. 1985.
GRAFSTEIN, ROBERT. 1981. "Legitimacy of Political Institutions," 14 *Polity* 51–69.
GREENHOUSE, LINDA. 1983. "Does the Workload Justify a New Appellate Court?" *The New York Times,* July 20.
——. 1985. "Court Voids Limit on PAC's Spending," *The New York Times,* March 19.
GREY, DAVID L. 1968. *The Supreme Court and the News Media*. Evanston: Northwestern University Press.
GROSSMAN, JOEL. 1965. *Lawyers and Judges: The ABA and the Politics of Judicial Selection*. New York: Wiley.
GROSSMAN, JOEL, AND AUSTIN SARAT. 1975. "Litigation in the Federal Courts," 9 *Law and Society Review* 322.
GRUHL, JOHN, AND CASSIA SPOHN. 1981. "The Supreme Court's Post-Miranda Rulings," 3 *Law and Policy Quarterly* 29–54.
GUNNELL, JOHN G. 1976. "Social Scientific Knowledge and Policy Decisions: A Critique of the Intellectualistic Model."
GUNTHER, GERALD. 1985. *Cases and Materials in Constitutional Law*. 11th ed. Mineola, N.Y.: The Foundation Press.
GUSFIELD, JOSEPH R. 1981. *The Culture of Public Problems: Drinking-Driving and the Symbolic Order*. Chicago: University of Chicago Press.
HAINES, CHARLES GROVE. 1944. *The Role of the Supreme Court in American Government and Politics, 1789–1835*. Berkeley: University of California Press.
HALL, JEROME. 1963. *Comparative Law and Social Policy*. Baton Rouge: Louisiana State University Press.
HAMILTON, ALEXANDER, ET AL. 1788. *The Federalist Papers,* Clinton Rossiter, ed. New York: New American Library, 1961.
HAMILTON, WALTON. 1938. "The Path of Due Process of Law," in Conyers Read, ed., *The Constitution Reconsidered*. New York: Columbia University Press.

HAND, LEARNED. 1944. *The Spirit of Liberty: Papers and Addresses.* New York: Vintage Books.

HANDLIN, OSCAR, AND MARY HANDLIN. 1966. *Popular Sources of Authority.* Cambridge: Harvard University Press.

HARLAN, JOHN M. 1955. "What Part Does the Oral Argument Play in the Conduct of an Appeal?" 41 *Cornell Law Quarterly* 6.

HARRINGTON, CHRISTINE. 1985. *Shadow Justice: The Ideology and Institutionalization of Alternatives to Court.* Westport, Conn.: Greenwood Press.

HARRIS, RICHARD. 1971. *Decision.* New York: E.P. Dutton.

HARRIS, WILLIAM. 1982. "Binding Word and Polity," 76 *American Political Science Review* 34.

HART, HENRY. 1953. "The Power of Congress to Limit the Jurisdiction of the Federal Courts: An Exercise in Dialectic," 66 *Harvard Law Review* 1362.

———. 1959. "The Time Chart of the Justices," 73 *Harvard Law Review* 84–101.

HARTZ, LOUIS. 1955. *The Liberal Tradition in America.* New York: Harcourt, Brace.

HAURIOU, MAURICE. 1925. "La Théorie de L'Institution et de la Fondation," *La Cité Moderne et les Transformations du Droit.* Paris: Blond et Gay.

HEUMANN, MILTON. 1978. *Plea Bargaining: The Experience of Prosecutors, Judges, and Defense Attorneys.* Chicago: University of Chicago Press.

HEYDEBRAND, WOLF. 1976. "The Technocratic Administration of Justice." Paper presented to the American Political Science Association.

HEYDEBRAND, WOLF, AND CARROLL SERON. 1987. "Administration versus Adjudication: The Political and Historical Contradictions of the Federal District Court System." Unpublished manuscript.

HODDER-WILLIAMS, RICHARD. 1980. *The Politics of the US Supreme Court.* London: Allen and Unwin.

HOROWITZ, DONALD. 1977. *The Courts and Social Policy.* Washington, D.C.: Brookings Institution.

HORWITZ, MORTON. 1978. *The Transformation of American Law: 1780–1860.* Cambridge: Harvard University Press.

HOUSEMAN, GERALD L. 1979. *The Right of Mobility.* Port Washington, N.Y.: Kennikat Press.

HOWARD, J. WOODFORD. 1968. *Mr. Justice Murphy.* Princeton: Princeton University Press.

———. 1981. *Courts of Appeals in the Federal Judicial System: A Study of the 2nd, 5th, and DC Circuits.* Princeton: Princeton University Press.

HRUSKA, ROMAN. 1975. *Preliminary Report.* Washington, D.C.: Commission on Revision of the Federal Court Appellate System.

HUGHES, CHARLES EVANS. 1928. *The Supreme Court of the United States.* New York: Columbia University Press.

HUNT, ALAN. 1983. "The Ideology of Law: Advances and Problems in Recent Applications of the Concept of Ideology to the Analysis of Law." George Lurcy Lecture, Amherst College, Amherst, Mass., Sept.

HURST, JAMES WILLARD. 1950. *The Growth of American Law: The Law Makers.* Boston: Little, Brown.

———. 1980–1981. "The Functions of Courts in the United States: 1950–1980," 15 *Law and Society Review* 401–472.

HUSSERL, EDMUND. 1965. *Phenomenology and the Crisis of Philosophy*. New York: Harper and Row.

IRONS, PETER. 1983. *Justice at War*. New York: Oxford University Press.

JACOB, HERBERT. 1969. *Debtors in Court*. Chicago: Rand McNally.

———. 1978. *Justice in America*. 2nd ed. Boston: Little, Brown.

———. 1983. "Courts as Organizations," in Keith Boyum and Lynn Mather, eds., *Empirical Theories About Courts*. New York: Longman.

JACOBS, CLYDE D. 1954. *Law Writers and the Courts: The Influence of Thomas M. Cooley, Christopher G. Tiedeman, and John F. Fillon upon American Constitutional Law*. Berkeley: University of California Press.

JACOBSOHN, GARY J. 1977. *Pragmatism, Statesmanship, and the Supreme Court*. Ithaca: Cornell University Press.

———. 1986. *The Supreme Court and the Decline of Constitutional Aspiration*. Totowa, N.J.: Rowman and Littlefield.

JAWORSKI, LEON. 1974. *The Sovereignty of the Law: Selections from Blackstone's Commentaries*. London: Macmillan.

JENKINS, JOHN A. 1983. "A Candid Talk with Justice Blackmun," *The New York Times Magazine*, Feb. 20.

JOHNSEN, JULIA E. 1937. *Reorganization of the Supreme Court*. New York: Wilson.

JOHNSON, CHARLES A. 1985. "Citations to Authority in Supreme Court Opinions," 7 *Law and Policy* 509.

JOHNSON, CHARLES A., AND BRADLEY C. CANON. 1984. *Judicial Policies: Implementation and Impact*. Washington, D.C.: CQ Press.

KAHN, RONALD C. 1984. "Process and Rights Principles in Modern Constitutional Theory," 37 *Stanford Law Review* 253–269.

KAIRYS, DAVID. 1982. *The Politics of Law*. New York: Pantheon.

KAUFMAN, ARNOLD. 1968. *The Radical Liberal*. New York: Atherton Press.

KEEFE, A. J. 1975. "Inside the Supreme Court," 61 *ABA Journal* 1509–1512.

KLARE, KARL. 1978. "Judicial Deradicalization of the Wagner Act and the Origins of Modern Legal Consciousness, 1937–1941," 62 *Minnesota Law Review* 265.

———. 1979. "Law-Making as Praxis," 40 *Telos* 122.

KLUGER, RICHARD. 1975. *Simple Justice*. New York: Random House, Vintage Paperback, 1977.

KOESTLER, A. 1959. *The Sleepwalkers*. New York: Macmillan.

KORT, FRED. 1966. "Quantitative Analysis of Fact-Patterns in Cases and Their Impact on Judicial Decisions," 79 *Harvard Law Review* 1595–1603.

KRESS, PAUL F. 1970. *Social Science and the Idea of Progress: The Ambiguous Legacy of Arthur F. Bentley*. Urbana: University of Illinois Press.

KRISLOV, SAMUEL. 1965. *The Supreme Court in the Political Process*. New York: Macmillan.

KUHN, THOMAS. 1960. *The Structure of Scientific Revolutions*. Chicago: University of Chicago Press.

LASKI, HAROLD. 1919. *Authority in the Modern State*. New Haven: Yale University Press.

———. 1935. *The State in Theory and Practice*. New York: Viking.

LASSER, WILLIAM. 1985. "The Myth of *Lochner v. New York.*" Presented at the Midwest Political Science Association meeting, Chicago.

LAWLOR, REED. 1967. "Personal Stare Decisis," 41 *Southern California Law Review* 73–118.

LERNER, MAX. 1937. "Constitutionalism and Court as Symbols," 46 *Yale Law Journal* 1290.

LEVI, E. H. 1949. *An Introduction to Legal Reasoning*. Chicago: University of Chicago Press.

LEVINSON, SANFORD. 1979. "The Constitution in American Civil Religion," in Philip B. Kurland and Gerhard Casper, eds., *The Supreme Court Review, 1979*: 123–151.

———. 1986. "Could Meese Be Right This Time?" *The Nation,* December 20.

LEWIS, ANTHONY. 1964. *Gideon's Trumpet*. New York: Random House.

———. 1980. "Supreme Court Confidential," *The New York Review of Books* 27: 3–8.

LLEWELLYN, KARL. 1934. "The Constitution as an Institution," 34 *Columbia Law Review* 1–40.

LOWI, THEODORE J. 1969. *The End of Liberalism*, 1st ed. New York: Norton.

———. 1979. *The End of Liberalism*, 2nd ed. New York: Norton.

MACPHERSON, C. B. 1977. *Property: Mainstream and Critical Positions*. Toronto: University of Toronto Press.

MAIN, JACKSON TURNER. 1961. *The Anti-Federalists: Critics of the Constitution, 1781–1788*. Chicago: Quadrangle Books.

MALINOWSKI, BRONISLAW. 1944. *Freedom and Civilization*. New York: Roy Publishers.

MARCH, JAMES G., AND JOHAN P. OLSEN. 1984. "The New Institutionalism: Organizational Factors in Political Life," 78 *American Political Science Review* 734–749.

MASON, ALPHEUS T. 1956. *Harlan Fiske Stone: Pillar of the Law*. New York: Viking.

———. 1958. *The Supreme Court from Taft to Warren*. Baton Rouge: Louisiana State University Press.

———. 1974. "The Nixon Tapes: Now the High Court Will Rule," *Los Angeles Times,* June 9.

———. 1980. "Eavesdropping on Justice: A Review Essay," 95 *Political Science Quarterly* 295.

MASON, ALPHEUS T., AND WILLIAM M. BEANEY. 1959, 1964, 1968. *American Constitutional Law*. Englewood Cliffs, N.J.: Prentice-Hall.

MATHER, LYNN M. 1979. *Plea Bargaining or Trial? The Process of Criminal Case Disposition*. Lexington, Mass.: Lexington Books.

MATHEWS, LINDA. 1974. "Supreme Court: World Inside the 'Marble Temple'," *Los Angeles Times,* Feb. 2.

McCLOSKEY, ROBERT. 1960. *The American Supreme Court*. Chicago: University of Chicago Press.

———. 1962. "Economic Due Process and the Supreme Court: An Exhumation and Reburial," in Philip B. Kurland, ed., *The Supreme Court Review*. Chicago: University of Chicago Press.

McDOWELL, GARY L. 1982. *Equity and the Constitution: The Supreme Court, Equitable Relief, and Public Policy*. Chicago: University of Chicago Press.

McELWAIN, EDWIN. 1949. "The Business of the Supreme Court Under Chief Justice Hughes," 63 *Harvard Law Review*.

McEWEN, CRAIG A., AND RICHARD J. MAIMAN. 1984. "In Search of Legitimacy: Empirical and Conceptual Response to Professor Hyde." Presented at the Law and Society Association Meeting, Boston, Mass.

McILWAIN, CHARLES H. 1940. *Constitutionalism: Ancient and Modern*. Ithaca: Cornell University Press.

McLAUGHLAN, WILLIAM P. 1972. "Research Note: Ideology and Conflict in Supreme Court Opinion Assignment, 1946–1962," 15 *Western Political Quarterly* 16–27.

———. 1982. "Spectral Analysis of United States Supreme Court Caseload, 1880–1979." Paper presented at the Annual Meeting of the APSA, Denver.

MEESE, EDWIN. 1986. "The Law of the Constitution." Speech delivered at Tulane University, October 21.

MELONE, ALBERT P. 1980. "A Political Scientist Writes in Defense of *The Brethren*," 64: *Judicature* 140.

MENDELSON, WALLACE. 1960. *Capitalist Democracy and the Supreme Court*. New York: Appleton-Century Crofts.

———. 1961. "The Politics of Judicial Supremacy," 4 *Journal of Law and Economics* 175–185.

MERRY, SALLY, AND SUSAN SILBEY. 1984. "What Do Plaintiffs Want? Reexamining the Concept of Disputes." Paper presented at the Law and Society Association Annual Meeting, Denver.

———. 1985. "Concepts of Law and Justice Among Working-Class Americans: Ideology as Culture," 9 *Legal Studies Forum* 59–71.

MESSICK, BRINKLEY. 1983. "Legal Documents and the Concept of 'restricted literacy' in a Traditional Society," 42 *Int'l. J. Soc. Lang.* 41–52.

MICHELMAN, FRANK. 1981. "Property as a Constitutional Right," 38 *Washington and Lee Law Review* 1098.

MIKVA, ABNER J. 1983. "How Well Does Congress Support and Defend the Constitution?" 61 *North Carolina Law Review* 587–611.

MILIBAND, RALPH. *The State in Capitalist Society*. New York: Basic Books.

MILLER, ARTHUR SELWYN. 1965. "On the Choice of Major Premises in Supreme Court Opinions," 14 *Journal of Public Law*.

———. 1968. *The Supreme Court and American Capitalism*. New York: The Free Press.

———. 1982. *Toward Increased Judicial Activism: The Political Role of the Supreme Court*. Westport, Conn.: Greenwood Press.

MILLER, ARTHUR S., AND JEROME A. BARRON. 1975. "The Supreme Court, the Adversary System, and the Flow of Information to the Justices: A Preliminary Inquiry," 61 *Virginia Law Review* 1187–1245.

MILNER, NEAL. 1971. "Comparative Analysis of Patterns of Compliance with Supreme Court Decisions: Miranda and the Police in Four Communities," 5 *Law and Society Review* 126.

MORGAN, DONALD. 1954. *Justice William Johnson: The First Dissenter.* Columbia: University of South Carolina Press.

MORTON, F. L. 1985. "Racial Injustice: The Origins of an Imperial Judiciary," A.P.S.A. Paper, New Orleans.

MUIR, WILLIAM K. 1967. *Law and Attitude Change.* Chicago: University of Chicago Press.

MURPHY, BRUCE ALLEN. 1982. *The Brandeis/Frankfurter Connection.* New York: Oxford University Press.

MURPHY, PAUL. 1986. "Review of *The Supreme Court and Constitutional Democracy,*" 4 *Law and History Review* 206–209.

MURPHY, WALTER. 1964. *Elements of Judicial Strategy.* Chicago: University of Chicago Press.

———. 1979. *The Vicar of Christ.* New York: Macmillan.

MURPHY, WALTER, JAMES E. FLEMING, AND WILLIAM F. HARRIS. 1986. *American Constitutional Interpretation.* Mineola, N.Y.: The Foundation Press.

MYERS, GUSTAVUS. 1925. *History of the Supreme Court of the United States.* Chicago: Charles H. Kerr.

NAGEL, STUART. 1962. "Political Parties and Judicial Review in American History," 2 *Journal of Public Law* 328–340.

———. 1973. "Court-Curbing Periods in American History," in Becker and Feeley, 1973.

NEUBAUER, DEANE, AND MICHAEL SHAPIRO. 1985. "The New Politics of Mediation: Disclosing Silences." Presented at Int. Pol. Science Assn., Paris.

O'BRIEN, DAVID. 1985. " 'The Imperial Judiciary': Of Paper Tigers and Socio-Legal Indicators," 2 *Journal of Law and Politics* 1–56.

———. 1986. *Storm Center.* New York: Norton.

O'CONNOR, KAREN, AND LEE EPSTEIN. 1981–1982. "Amicus Curiae Participation in U.S. Supreme Court Litigation," 16 *Law and Society Review* 311–321.

O'NEILL, TIMOTHY. 1981. "The Language of Equality," 75 *American Political Science Review* 626.

———. 1985. *Bakke and the Politics of Equality.* Middleton: Wesleyan University Press.

PAUL, ARNOLD. 1969. *Conservative Crisis and the Rule of Law.* New York: Peter Smith.

PAULSON, MONRAD G., ed. 1959. *Legal Institutions Today and Tomorrow.* New York: Columbia University Press.

PELTASON, JACK. 1955. *Federal Courts in the Political Process.* New York: Random House.

PENNOCK, J. ROLAND, AND JOHN CHAPMAN, EDS. 1979. *Nomos XX: Constitutionalism.* New York: New York University Press.
PERRY, H. W. 1985. "Agenda-Setting in the United States Supreme Court," Midwest Political Science Association, Chicago.
PERRY, MICHAEL. 1982. *The Constitution, The Courts, and Human Rights: An Inquiry into the Legitimacy of Constitutional Policymaking by the Judiciary.* New Haven: Yale University Press.
———. 1984. Paper presented to the American Political Science Association.
POLSBY, NELSON. 1968. "The Institutionalization of the US House of Representatives," 62 *American Political Science Review* 145.
PORTER, M. C. 1977. "That Commerce Shall Be Free: A New Look at the Old Laissez-Faire Court," *The Supreme Court Review* 135–159.
POSNER, RICHARD A. 1985. *The Federal Courts: Crisis and Reform.* Cambridge: Harvard University Press.
POULANTZAS, NICOS. 1975. *Political Power and Social Classes,* tr. by T. O'Hagan. London: Humanities Press.
POUND, ROSCOE. 1921. *The Spirit of the Common Law.* Boston: Little, Brown.
———. 1953. *The Lawyer from Antiquity to Modern Times with Particular Attention to the Development of Bar Associations in the United States.* New York: West.
———. 1959. *Jurisprudence.* St. Paul: West.
PREST, Q. E. 1972. *The Inns of Court: 1590–1640.* New Jersey: Rowman and Littlefield.
PRITCHETT. C. HERMAN. 1945. "Dissent on the Supreme Court, 1943–44," 39 *American Political Science Review* 19.
———. 1948. *The Roosevelt Court.* Chicago: University of Chicago Press.
———. 1953. *Civil Liberties and the Vinson Court.* Chicago: University of Chicago Press.
———. 1961. *Congress Versus the Supreme Court.* Minneapolis: University of Minnesota Press.
———. 1967. "The Development of Judicial Research," in Joel Grossman, ed., *The Frontiers of Judicial Research.* New York: Wiley.
———. 1984. *Constitutional Law of the Federal System.* Englewood Cliffs, N.J.: Prentice-Hall. (Replaces *The American Constitution,* 1977.)
PROVINE, DORIS MARIE. 1980. *Case Selection in the United States Supreme Court.* Chicago: University of Chicago Press.
RADIN, MAX. 1982. "Property and Personhood," 34 *Stanford Law Review* 957.
RAWLS, JOHN. 1955. "Two Concepts of Rules," 64 *Philosophical Review* 3.
———. 1971. *A Theory of Justice.* Cambridge: Harvard University Press.
READ, CONYERS. 1938. *The Constitution Reconsidered.* New York: Columbia University Press.
REHNQUIST, WILLIAM. 1957–1958. "Who Writes Decisions of the Supreme Court?" *U.S. News and World Report* 12:13 and 2:21.
REICH, CHARLES A. 1964. "The New Property," 73 *Yale Law Journal* 733–787.
RENNER, KARL. 1949. "The Institutions of Private Law and Their Social Function," in V. Aubert, ed., *Sociology of Law.* London: Penguin Books.

ROCHE, JOHN P. 1961. *Courts and Rights: The American Judiciary in Action*. 2nd ed. New York: Random House.

ROHDE, DAVID W. 1972. "Policy Goals, Strategic Choices, and Majority Opinion Assignments in the United States Supreme Court," 16 *Midwest Journal of Political Science* 662.

ROHDE, DAVID, AND HAROLD SPAETH. 1976. *Supreme Court Decision Making*. San Francisco: Freeman.

ROSEN, PAUL L. 1972. *The Supreme Court and Social Science*. Urbana: University of Illinois Press.

SARAT, AUSTIN. 1976. "Alternatives in Dispute Processing: Litigation in a Small Claims Court," 10 *Law and Society Review* 339.

SCHATTSCHNEIDER, E. E. 1960. *The Semi-Sovereign People*. New York: Holt, Rinehart and Winston.

SCHAUER, FRED. 1983. "Refining the Law Making Function of the Supreme Court," 17 *University of Michigan Journal of Law* 1–24.

SCHEINGOLD, STUART. 1974. *The Politics of Rights*. New Haven: Yale University Press.

SCHLESINGER, ARTHUR J. 1982. "An Ideological Retainer," *The New York Times Book Review*. March 21.

SCHMIDHAUSER, JOHN. 1960. *The Supreme Court: Its Politics, Personalities, and Procedures*. New York: Holt, Rinehart and Winston.

———. 1976. "The Corporate Law Firm and the Convergence of Law and Politics." Presented at the Annual Meeting of the American Political Science Association.

———. 1979. *Judges and Justices: The Federal Appellate Judiciary*. Boston: Little, Brown.

SCHMIDHAUSER, JOHN, AND LARRY BERG. 1972. *The Supreme Court and Congress*. New York: The Free Press.

SCHUBERT, GLENDON. 1965. *The Judicial Mind: Attitudes and Ideology of Supreme Court Justices 1946–1963*. Evanston: Northwestern University Press.

———. 1967. "Academic Ideology and the Study of Adjudication," 61 *American Political Science Review* 106–29.

———. 1974. *The Judicial Mind Revisited: Psychometric Analysis of Supreme Court Ideology*. New York: Oxford University Press.

SCIGLIANO, ROBERT. 1971. *The Supreme Court and the Presidency*. New York: The Free Press.

SELZNICK, PHILIP. 1957. *Leadership in Administration: A Sociological Interpretation*. Evanston: Peterson and Company.

SEMONCHE, JOHN E. 1978. *Charting the Future: The Supreme Court Responds to a Changing Society, 1890–1920*. Westport, Conn.: Greenwood Press.

SERON, CARROLL, AND WOLF HEYDEBRAND. 1983. "The Effects of Social Change on Civil Litigation," Law and Society Meetings, Boston, Mass.

SHAPIRO, MARTIN. 1964. *Law and Politics in the Supreme Court*. New York: The Free Press.

———. 1967. *The Supreme Court and Constitutional Rights*. Chicago: Scott, Foresman.

———. 1977. "The Craftsmanship of the Burger Court." Paper presented at the Annual Meeting of the American Political Science Association.

———. 1981. *Courts: A Comparative and Political Analysis*. Chicago: The University of Chicago Press.

SHKLAR, JUDITH. 1964. *Legalism*. Cambridge: Harvard University Press.

SILBEY, SUSAN S. 1980–1981. "Case Processing: Consumer Protection in an Attorney General's Office," 15 *Law and Society Review* 849–910.

SIMON, WILLIAM. 1978. "The Ideology of Advocacy: Procedural Justice and Professional Ethics," 29 *Wisconsin Law Review*.

SKEFOS, CATHERINE HETOS. 1976. "The Supreme Court Gets a Home," *Supreme Court Historical Society Yearbook* 25–37.

SKOWRONEK, STEPHEN. 1982. *Building A New American State: The Expansion of National Administrative Capacities, 1877–1920*. Cambridge: Cambridge University Press.

SNOWISS, SYLVIA. 1981. "From Fundamental Law to the Supreme Law of the Land." Paper delivered at the Annual Meeting of the American Political Science Association.

SPAETH, HAROLD J. 1985. "Influence Relationships Within the Supreme Court: A Comparison of the Warren and Burger Courts," 38 *Western Political Quarterly* 70–83.

STEAMER, ROBERT. 1986. *Chief Justice: Leadership and the Supreme Court*. Columbia: University of South Carolina Press.

STERN, ROBERT L., AND EUGENE GRESSMAN. 1978. *Supreme Court Practice*. 5th ed. Washington, D.C.: BNA Books.

STONE, JULIUS. 1968. *Legal System and Lawyer's Reasoning*. Stanford: Stanford University Press.

STUMPF, HARRY P. 1965. "Congressional Response to Supreme Court Rulings: The Interaction of Law and Politics," 14 *Journal of Public Law* 382.

SWISHER, CARL B. 1930. *Stephen J. Field: Craftsman of the Law*. Washington, D.C.: Brookings Institution.

TANENHAUS, JOSEPH, ET AL. 1963. "The Supreme Court's Certiorari Jurisdiction: Cue Theory," pp. 111–132, in Glendon Schubert, ed., *Judicial Decision-Making*. New York: Free Press.

TATE, C. NEAL. 1981. "Personal Attribute Models of the Voting Behavior of United States Supreme Court Justices: Liberalism in Civil Liberties and Economic Decision, 1946–1978." 75 *American Political Science Review* 355–368.

TATE, NEAL, AND ROGER HANDBERG. 1986. "The Decision Making of the United States Supreme Court, 1916–1985: A Three-Level Perspective." Paper Presented to the Annual Meeting of the APSA, Washington, D.C.

TAYLOR, CHARLES. 1971. "Interpretation and the Sciences of Man," 25 *Review of Metaphysics* 3.

TAYLOR, RICHARD W. 1957. *Life, Language, Law: Essays in Honor of Arthur F. Bentley*. Yellow Springs, Ohio: Antioch Press.

TAYLOR, STUART, JR. 1986. "High Court's 1985–86 Term: Mixed Results for the President," *The New York Times*, July 11.

THAYER, JAMES BRADLEY. 1893. "The Origins and Scope of the American Doctrine of Constitutional Law," 7 *Harvard Law Review* 129.

————. 1895. *Cases on Constitutional Law*. Cambridge: Charles W. Sever.

TOCQUEVILLE, ALEXIS DE. 1873. *Democracy in America,* vols. I and II. New York, Doubleday, 1969.

TOTENBERG, NINA. 1975. "Behind the Marble, Beneath the Robes," *The New York Times Magazine,* March 16.

TRIBE, LAURENCE. 1978. "The Puzzling Persistence of Process-Based Constitutional Theories," 89 *Yale Law Journal* 1063.

————. 1985. *Constitutional Choices*. Cambridge: Harvard University Press.

TRUBEK, DAVID. 1983. "Where the Action Is: Critical Legal Studies and Empiricism," 36 *Stanford Law Review* 575.

TWISS, BENJAMIN. 1942. *Lawyers and the Constitution*. Princeton: Princeton University Press.

ULMER, S. S.. 1970. "The Use of Power in the Supreme Court: The Opinion Assignments of Earl Warren, 1953–1960," 19 *Journal of Public Law* 49–67.

————. 1973. "Bricolage and Assorted Thoughts on Working in the Papers of Supreme Court Justices," 35 *The Journal of Politics* 286–310.

————. 1984. "The Supreme Court's Certiovari Decisions: Conflict as a Predictive Variable," 78 *American Political Science Review* 901–911.

————. 1986. "The Sectional Impact of Judicial Review: Another Look." Paper Presented to the Annual Meeting of the APSA, Washington, D.C.

UNGER, ROBERTO. 1983. "The Critical Legal Studies Movement," 96 *Harvard Law Review* 561.

VAN ALSTYNE, WILLIAM. 1968. "The Demise of the Right-Privilege Distinction in Constitutional Law," 91 *Harvard Law Review* 1439.

VEBLEN, THORSTEIN. 1899. *The Theory of the Leisure Class*. New York: Macmillan.

VILLMOARE, ADELAIDE H. 1981. "The Political Rhetoric of Law and Order: Ideological Modes of Legitimation," 8 *Social Praxis* 79–84.

VINING, JOSEPH. 1986. *The Authoritative and the Authoritarian*. Chicago: University of Chicago Press.

VOSE, CLEMENT. 1959. *Caucasions Only: The Supreme Court, The NAACP, and the Restrictive Covenant Cases. Berkeley: University of California Press*.

WARREN, CHARLES. 1911. *A History of the American Bar*. Reprinted 1966. New York: H. Fertig.

————. 1925. *The Supreme Court in United States History*. 2nd ed., 1937. Boston: Little, Brown.

WARREN, SAMUEL D., AND LOUIS D. BRANDEIS. 1890. "The Right to Privacy," 4 *Harvard Law Review* 193.

WASBY, STEPHEN L. 1970. *The Impact of the United States Supreme Court*. Homewood, Ill.: Dorsey Press.

————. 1982. "The Functions and Importance of Appellate Oral Argument: Some Views of Lawyers and Federal Judges," 65 *Judicature* 340.

————. 1984. *The Supreme Court in the Federal Judicial System*. 2nd ed. New York: Holt, Rinehart and Winston.

WEBER, MAX. 1954. *On Law in Economy and Society,* Max Rheinstein, ed. New York: Simon and Schuster.

———. 1958. *From Max Weber,* Hans Gerth and C. Wright Mills, eds. New York: Oxford University Press.

———. 1968. *Selected Papers on Charisma and Institution Building,* S. N. Eisenstadt, ed. Chicago: University of Chicago Press.

WECHSLER, HERBERT. 1959. "Toward Neutral Principles of Constitutional Law," 73 *Harvard Law Review* 1.

WESTEN, PETER. 1973. "Threat to the Supreme Court," *The New York Review of Books,* Feb. 22.

WESTIN, ALAN. 1959. "When the Public Judges the Court," *The New York Times Magazine,* May 31, pp. 16–41.

———. 1961. *The Supreme Court: Views From the Inside.* New York: Norton.

WHEELER, RUSSELL. 1973. "Extra Judicial Activities of the Early Supreme Court," *The Supreme Court Review* 123–158.

WHITE, G. EDWARD. 1976. *The American Judicial Tradition.* London: Oxford University Press.

WHITE, JAMES. 1973. *The Legal Imagination.* Boston: Little, Brown.

———. 1982. "Law as Language: Reading Law and Reading Literature," 60 *Texas Law Review* 415.

WICKER, TOM. 1976. "Closing the Courts," *The New York Times,* Dec. 3.

WILKINSON, J. HARVIE. 1974. *Serving Justice.* New York: Charter House.

WILL, FREDERICK L.. 1974. *Induction and Justification.* Ithaca: Cornell University Press.

WILLIAMS, RICHARD L. 1977. "Supreme Court of the United States: The Staff That Keeps It Operating," 7 *Smithsonian* Oct.-Nov.

WINCH, PETER. 1958. *The Idea of a Social Science.* London: Routledge and Kegan Paul.

WOLFE, CHRISTOPHER. 1986. *The Rise of Modern Judicial Review.* New York: Basil Books.

WOLIN, SHELDON S. 1960. *Politics and Vision.* Boston: Little, Brown.

WOOD, GORDON. 1969. *The Creation of the American Republic, 1776–1787.* Chapel Hill: University of North Carolina Press.

WOODWARD, BOB, AND SCOTT ARMSTRONG. 1979. *The Brethren.* New York: Random House.

YNGVESSON, BARBARA, AND PATRICIA HENNESSEY. 1975. "Small Claims, Complex Disputes: A Review of the Small Claims Literature," 9 *Law and Society Review* 219.

YOUNG, JAMES STERLING. 1966. *The Washington Community.* New York: Harcourt, Brace.

Cases

Allgeyer v. *Louisiana,* 165 US 578 (1897)

Amalgamated Food Employees v. *Logan Valley Plaza,* 391 US 308 (1968)

Arkansas Electric Coop v. *Arkansas Public Service Comm.*, 461 US 375 (1983)
Baker v. *Carr*, 369 US 186 (1962)
Bank of America v. *United States*, 103 US 2266 (1983)
Barron v. *Baltimore*, 7 Pet. 243 (1833)
Beal v. *Doe*, 432 US 438 (1977)
Betts v. *Brady*, 316 US 455 (1942)
Board of Regents v. *Roth*, 408 US 564 (1971)
Bolling v. *Sharpe*, 347 US 497 (1954)
Bowers v. *Hardwick*, 54 LW 4919 (1986)
Brown v. *The Board of Education*, 347 US 483 (1954)
Brown v. *Allen*, 344 US 443 (1953)
Brown v. *Hotel and Restaurant Employees*, 104 SCt 3179 (1984)
Buckley v. *Valeo*, 424 US 1 (1976)
Cafeteria and Restaurant Workers v. *McElroy*, 367 US 886 (1961)
Clark v. *Kimmitt*, No. 76–1105 (1976)
Colegrove v. *Green*, 328 US 549 (1946)
Cooper v. *Aaron*, 358 US 1 (1958)
Day-Brite Lighting v. *Missouri*, 342 US 421 (1952)
Dean Witter Reynolds Inc. v. *Byrd*, 105 SCt 1238 (1985)
District of Columbia v. *Carter*, 409 US 418 (1973)
Doe v. *Bolton*, 410 US 179 (1973)
Doe v. *McMillan*, 412 US 306 (1973)
Dred Scott v. *Sandford*, 19 How. 393 (1857)
Durham v. *United States*, 214 F.2d 862 (1943)
Farber, In re 78 NJ 259 (1978)
Fidelity and Deposit Co. of Maryland v. *Arenz*, 290 US 66 (1933)
Flemming v. *Nestor*, 363 US 603 (1960)
Fletcher v. *Peck*, 6 Cranch 87 (1810)
Garcia v. *San Antonio Metropolitan Transit Authority*, 105 SCt 1005 (1985)
Georgia v. *Brailsford*, 2 Dall. 402 (1792)
Gibbons v. *Ogden*, 9 Wheat. 1 (1824)
Gideon v. *Wainright*, 372 US 335 (1963)
Goldberg v. *Kelly*, 397 US 254 (1970)
Goldman v. *United States*, 316 US 129 (1942)
Goss v. *Lopez*, 419 US 565 (1975)
Griswold v. *Connecticut*, 381 US 479 (1965)
Hammer v. *Dagenhart*, 247 US 251 (1918)
Harper v. *Virginia State Board of Elections*, 383 US 663 (1966)
Hawaii Housing Authority et al. v. *Midkiff*, 467 US 229 (1984)
Herb's Welding Inc. v. *Gray*, 105 SCt 1421 (1985)
Hicks v. *Miranda*, 422 US 332 (1975)
Hurtado v. *California*, 110 US 516 (1884)
Immigration and Naturalization Service v. *Chadha*, 462 US 919 (1983)
Jones v. *Hildebrandt*, 432 US 183 (1977)
Korematsu v. *United States*, 323 US 214 (1944)
Laird v. *Tatum*, 408 US 1 (1972)

Linkletter v. *Walker*, 381 US 618 (1965)
Lochner v. *New York*, 198 US 45 (1905)
Logan v. *Zimmerman Brush Co.*, 450 US 909 (1982)
Logan Valley Plaza [see *Amalgamated Food Employees*]
Loretto v. *Teleprompter Manhattan CATV*, 104 SCt 3164 (1982)
Lynch v. *Household Finance Corp.*, 405 US 538 (1972)
Maher v. *Roe*, 432 US 464 (1977)
Mapp v. *Ohio*, 367 US 643 (1961)
Marbury v. *Madison*, 1 Cranch 137 (1803)
Martin v. *Hunter's Lessee*, 1 Wheat. 304 (1816)
Mathews v. *Eldridge*, 424 US 319 (1976)
McAuliffe v. *Mayor of New Bedford*, 155 Mass. 216 (1892)
McCardle, Ex parte, 7 Wall. 506 (1869)
McCulloch v. *Maryland*, 4 Wheat 316 (1819)
Memphis Light, Gas and Water v. *Craft*, 436 US 1 (1978)
Milligan, Ex parte, 4 Wall. 2 (1866)
Milliken v. *Bradley*, 418 US 717 (1974)
Mills Music, Inc. v. *Marie Snyder*, 105 SCt 638 (1985)
Minersville School Dist. v. *Gobitis* 310 US 586 (1940)
Miranda v. *Arizona*, 384 US 436 (1966)
Moose Lodge No. 107 v. *Irvis*, 407 US 163 (1972)
Motor Vehicle Manufacturers Assn. v. *State Farm Mutual*, 463 US 29 (1983)
Muller v. *Oregon*, 208 US 412 (1908)
Munn v. *Illinois*, 94 US 113 (1877)
NLRB v. *Fruit and Vegetable Packers and Warehouseman, Local 760*, 377 US 58
    (1963)
NLRB v. *Bildisco and Bildisco*, 465 US 513 (1984)
National League of Cities v. *Usery*, 426 US 833 (1976)
O'Brien v. *Brown* 409 U.S. 1 (1972)
Olmstead v. *United States*, 277 US 438 (1928)
Olsen v. *Nebraska*, 313 US 236 (1941)
Pacific Railroad Removal Cases, 115 US 1 (1885)
Patterson v. *Colorado*, 205 US 454 (1907)
Penn Central Transportation Co. v. *New York*, 438 US 104 (1978)
People v. *Anderson*, 493 P.2d 880 (1972)
Pierre v. *Louisiana*, 306 US 354 (1939)
Plessy v. *Ferguson*, 163 US 537 (1896)
Poelker v. *Doe* 432 US 519 (1977)
Preiser v. *Rodriquez*, 411 US 475 (1973)
Public Utilities Commission of D.C. v. *Pollak*, 343 US 451 (1951)
Rakas v. *Illinois*, 439 US 128 (1978)
Rathbun v. *United States*, 295 US 602 (1935)
Regents of the University of California v. *Bakke*, 438 US 265 (1978)
Roe v. *Wade*, 410 US 113 (1973)
Ross v. *Moffitt*, 417 US 600 (1974)
Ruckelshaus v. *Monsanto Co.*, 463 US 1315 (1984)

Schecter Poultry v. *United States*, 295 US 495 (1935)
Schenck v. *United States*, 249 US 47 (1919)
Shapiro v. *Thompson*, 394 US 618 (1969)
Stanton v. *Stanton*, 421 US 7 (1975)
Supreme Court of New Hampshire v. *Piper*, 105 SCt 1272 (1985)
Tidewater Oil Co. v. *United States*, 171 US 210 (1972)
Time, Inc. v. *Firestone*, 424 US 448 (1976)
Truax v. *Corrigan*, 257 US 312 (1922)
Twining v. *New Jersey*, 211 US 78 (1908)
United States v. *50 Acres of Land*, 53 LW 4001 (1984)
United States v. *Barnett*, 376 US 681 (1964)
United States v. *Carolene Products Co.*, 304 US 144 (1938)
United States v. *Darby Lumber Co.*, 312 US 100 (1941)
United States v. *E.C. Knight Co.*, 156 US 1 (1895)
United States v. *Nixon*, 418 US 683 (1974)
United States v. *Willow River Power Co.*, 324 US 499 (1945)
Warth v. *Seldin*, 422 US 490 (1975)
West Coast Hotel Co. v. *Parrish*, 300 US 379 (1937)
West Virginia State Board of Education v. *Barnette*, 319 US 624 (1943)
Wheaton v. *Peters*, 33 US 591 (1834)
White v. *Massachusetts Council of Construction Employers*, 460 US 204 (1983)
Williamson v. *Lee Optical*, 348 US 483 (1955)
Wilson v. *Garcia*, 105 SCt 1938 (1985)
Witherspoon v. *Illinois*, 391 US 510 (1969)
Wolf v. *Colorado*, 338 US 25 (1949)
Worcester v. *Georgia*, 6 Pet. 515 (1832)

Documents

BRENNAN, WILLIAM. 1963. "Inside View of the High Court," *The New York Times Magazine*, October 6.
BURGER, WARREN. 1976. "Agenda for 2000 A.D.—A Need for Systematic Anticipation," 70 *Federal Rules Decisions* 83.
———— (1977) "Report to the ABA," Seattle, 2:3.
CANNON, MARK W. 1974. "An Administrator's View of the Supreme Court," *Federal Bar News*, April: 109–113.
———— AND O'BRIEN, DAVID M. 1985. *Views from the Bench*. New Jersey: Chatham House.
Constitution of the United States. Washington, D.C.: U.S. Government Printing Office.
DUNNE, GERALD T. 1976. "The Early Court Reporters," *Yearbook of the Supreme Court Historical Society*, vol. 61.
FRANKFURTER, FELIX. 1947. "Reflections on Reading Statutes," in Westin (1961).
HARRELL, MARY ANN. 1975. *Equal Justice Under Law: The Supreme Court in American Life*. Washington, D.C. Federal Bar Association.

JACKSON, ROBERT H. 1955. *The Supreme Court in the American System of Government*. Cambridge: Harvard University Press.

POWELL, LEWIS. 1976. "Report on the Court," 8 *ABA Labor Law Section* 11.

REHNQUIST, WILLIAM. 1977. "Sunshine in the Third Branch." Remarks presented to Washburn University School of Law, Topeka, Kansas, 1:27.

The Supreme Court of the United States (NA). Washington, D.C.: Supreme Court.

SPRINCE, JOAN. 1976. "The Librarian," 13 *The Docket Sheet* 5. Washington, D.C.: Public Information Office of the Supreme Court.

STORY, JOSEPH. 1873. *Commentaries on the Constitution of the United States*. Boston: Little, Brown.

INDEX